TARGETING FRAUD

Uncovering and Deterring Fraud in Financial Institutions

Benton E. Gup

A BankLine Publication

PROBUS PUBLISHING

Chicago, Illinois
Cambridge, England

A BankLine Publication

ISBN 1-55738-740-0

Printed in the United States of America

BB

1 2 3 4 5 6 7 8 9 0

TAQ/BJS

To Jean, Lincoln, Andy, Carol, and Jeremy

Table of Contents

Appendix C METROPOLITAN BANK—LOAN POLICY 239

Index 249

About the Author 259

Preface

This book is about frauds and insider abuse at financial institutions and how to deter them. Fraud and insider abuse are major problems. They have caused or contributed to the failures of hundreds of financial institutions, and resulted in billions of dollars of losses to institutions, their shareholders, and to tax payers. This book examines numerous cases of fraud and insider abuse. The good news is that by recognizing how they are committed, it may be possible to deter them. The bad news is that by the time they are recognized in your organization, it may be too late—you have been stung. Nevertheless, *some* can be deterred and others detected before they do irreparable harm. I underscored the word *some* because it is not possible to deter all frauds at financial institutions.

This book was written for directors and officers of financial institutions, as well as for accountants, lawyers, and others who are committed to deterring fraud and insider abuse. It suggests various policies and practices that have been used in the fight against crime. Unfortunately, some schemes are so large that they span many continents, and no single financial institution can thwart them. In fact, it is easy to unwittingly become involved in frauds by not taking the proper precautions. For example, we will examine how some financial institutions have committed fraud by *not* "knowing their customers," or by being "willfully blind," to certain transactions. Such frauds are punishable by forfeiture of assets, fines, and lengthy jail terms.

We will also see how jurisdictional disputes between bank regulators and law enforcement agencies result in many frauds going unpunished. Moreover, U.S. attorneys decline to prosecute a very large percentage of the financial institution frauds. Even if they are prosecuted, the jury may find for the defendant. If the defendant is found guilty, the verdict may be overturned in appeal. The bottom line is that it is easier to prevent frauds than it is to uncover and successfully prosecute them.

In one sense, nothing in this book is new. All of the information came from publicly available articles, books, documents, and interviews—sources that are believed to be reliable. What is new is that all of the information from these diverse sources is here brought together into one convenient source.

Because many names of individuals and institutions are mentioned, great care was taken to cite the principal sources of information used about them. Some of the individuals mentioned are being tried for alleged crimes as this book is being written, and they may be found innocent. Some are appealing their convictions, and their convictions may be overturned. Others will be brought to trial at later dates. In any case, I have tried to do a thorough and careful job of research and reporting the information that was available to me. As both an academic scholar and, in writing this book, an investigative reporter, I know that the potential for error exists. Therefore, I want to take this opportunity to apologize in advance for any that may be found. They were not intentional.

Benton E. Gup

Introduction

Financial institutions fraud is fascinating, outrageous, and illegal. Many crooks who commit frauds and insider abuses at financial institutions live in luxury—they have large yachts, personal jets, huge homes, tax-free income, and more. Crime pays, at least until they get caught. Then the criminals have to pay, but so do the institutions, shareholders, and taxpayers who got stuck with their losses. We can take preventative measures to prevent those losses by deterring them and detecting them in their incipient stages of development. These are the two themes of this book—detection and prevention.

This book builds on the solid foundation of *Bank Fraud: Exposing the Hidden Threat to Financial Institutions,* published in 1990. Since then, the types of frauds being committed has changed because of changes in our underlying economy. Then, the major frauds involved real estate that was associated with the boom and bust of the savings and loan industry. Today, the major financial institutions frauds are international in scope. Foreign banks and foreign crime groups have become widespread and recognized for their illegal activities. They were here before, but it took time for them to surface and to achieve the degree of notoriety that they have. One of the lessons of this book is that it takes long periods of time for frauds to be uncovered, stopped, and prosecuted. It is not unusual for three or four years to lapse between discovery and prosecution. Therefore, many of the crimes covered in the following chapters occurred some time ago, and the wheels of justice may grind on for years.

The book is divided into 12 chapters. The first two chapters provide background information about frauds and insider abuse, including the major types of crimes and the difficulties in prosecuting them. Chapters 3 to 5 focus on frauds with international connections that affect U.S. financial institutions. Chapter 6 deals with detection of frauds, as well as with "profiles" of crooks, and "red flags" used to uncover their activities. Chapters 7 and 8 examine crimes by "outsiders"—those people who are not officers, directors, or employees of the organizations. Chapter 9 is about credit card and telemarketing frauds. Chapter 10 covers crimes by insiders. The last two chapters explain how directors can help to deter frauds and the roles played by auditors and examiners. Appendix A lists the "red flags" used by bank examiners to aid in the detection of fraud and insider abuse. Appendices B and C are sample loan policies.

Writing this book and *Bank Fraud* would not have been possible without the help of many people who provided me with information, ideas, suggestions, and materials. This is the place to thank all of them. Special thanks is due to the library staff of the University of Alabama, who provided many of the government documents used in preparation of this book. Others include (in alphabetical order): Anthony Adamski, Jr.. Pat Allen, Skip Baird, Sara Whalen Barry, Philip F. Bartholomew, Pete Brewton, Dan Brigham, Dennis Brosan, Pamela H. Bucy, Christopher A. "Kip" Byrne, John J. Byrne, Janet Campbell, Kenneth Cline, Lyn Cone, William J. Crawford, Frank Donaldson, Donald Drummand, Harold W. Eavenson, Will G. Fisher, Richard Fishkin, Carey Gillam, Maurizio Godorecci, Tim Gruber, Susan G. James, Mark Holder, James Horner, Tim James, George F. Klersey, Jr., Ralph Kolinski, Sue Lindsay, Charles A. McNelis, Stephen R. McSpadden, Bruce Maffeo, J.Virgil Mattingly, Jr., Gregory Meacham, Bill Newman, William M. Noonan, Lawrence T. Oden, Jack Allen Owens, Jr., Ricardo R. Pesquera, Kurt T. Peters, Richard Ringer, Robert Serino, Charles A. Sittason, Sara L. Strait, Zack Thompson, Jack D. Walker, Michael Violano, Joseph T. Wells, Steven R. Woods, and Charles A. Worsham.

1 INSIDER ABUSE AND CRIMINAL MISCONDUCT AT FINANCIAL INSTITUTIONS

Bad Guys Used to Wear Black and Some Still Do

Bank robbers in old cowboy movies were portrayed as tall, dark strangers who wore black outfits and carried large revolvers. They rode lean horses into frontier towns and sacked the local banks. Modern bank robbers are more likely to be well-dressed insiders (officers, directors, and principal stockholders). Instead of carrying guns and stealing thousands of dollars in coin and currency, they develop complex schemes and steal millions of dollars. In one large heist, insiders and others looted more than $100 million in about a one-year period from Empire Savings of Mesquite, Texas.[1] Insiders of the Bank of Credit and Commerce International looted *billions* of dollars. Outsiders still rob banks. They too develop schemes that net millions of dollars. Sometimes they just use banks to carry out their illegal activities. Money laundering is one example of how institutions can be "used" to facilitate frauds.

Most bank crimes do not yield such abundant sums, but they are nevertheless substantial. The Justice Department estimated that between October 1, 1988 and June 30, 1992, major financial institutions offenses that they prosecuted accounted for losses of $11.5 billion. Because of such losses, The Financial Institutions Reform, Recovery, and Enforcement Act (FIRREA) contained provisions to support government efforts to deal with financial institutions fraud. Additional legislation was also introduced in 1992 (HR 3388) and in 1993 (HR 574), but the Financial Fraud Detection and Disclosure Act but was not enacted.

For convenience, the term *bank* is used to describe these institutions unless we are referring to a specific type of institution or to a specific one by name. When there is a known or suspected financial criminal activity, other than robberies or burglaries which are reported directly to appropriate law enforcement agencies, many banks are required to file a Criminal Referral Form with their primary regulators. National banks, for example, file with the Comptroller of the Currency.[2] However, not all state chartered banks have a similar requirement.

Many crimes go unreported because banks do not want adverse publicity, and the loss is written off as a bad loan. Even if crimes are reported, the FBI may not complete the investigation. In regions where the FBI's case load is extremely heavy, they may not have the manpower to deal with all the cases for which they have responsibility. In addition, national banks are not required to report "mysterious disappearances or unexplained shortages" of $5,000 or less. Finally, the rules for state chartered institutions reporting financial crimes vary from state to state; so there is no way to estimate the full extent of fraud.

The epidemic of insider fraud and abuse contributed to the sharp increase in the failures of commercial banks and savings and loan associations in the late 1980s and early 1990s. In 1982 there were 10 failed commercial banks. The following year, 48 failed. Every year thereafter the number increased, reaching 221 failed commercial banks in 1988. Subsequently, the number of failures declined. Only 42 banks failed in 1993.

Estimates of the extent of fraud and insider abuse involved in failures varies widely. During the 1980–1988 period, estimates range from 33 to 50 percent of the failures of commercial banks and from 25 to 75 percent or more of the failures of savings and loan associations.[3] More recently, senior FDIC officials "found indications of suspected wrongdoing ... in 90 percent of failed banks," (1990-1991).[4] In 1992, the Resolution Trust Corporation (RTC) estimated that criminal misconduct by insiders contributed to the failure of 33 percent of the RTC controlled thrifts.[5]

The extent of fraud and the degree to which it contributed to failures varied from case to case. In some cases it played a minor role, while in others it was the cause of failure. The growth of criminal misconduct and bank failures go hand in hand and has always been a major contributing factor in bank failures.[6] Estimates of fraud being the proximate cause of failure range from 3 to 10 percent. The primary causes of the thrift failures were economic forces, regulatory forbearance, and incentives for the thrifts to take risks.[7] It is important to keep in mind that fraud contributes to unsafe and unsound banking practices, even when the banks do not fail.

Heads I Win, Tails the Insurance Funds Lose

Let's examine the reasons for the 1980's epidemic of fraud, insider abuse, and bank failures. Then we will examine the differences in the 1990s.

We must first go back in time, before 1973, when the Organization of Petroleum Exporting Countries (OPEC) demanded and received higher prices for crude oil. For the years prior to 1973, the average price of imported crude oil was $1.80 per barrel. Then OPEC forced prices higher. In 1974 the price per barrel was $12.52, and by 1981 it reached $35. During the period of rising energy prices and the subsequent inflation, many banks made two assumptions concerning their lending policies. They assumed that inflation was here to stay, and that oil prices would continue to rise. They were wrong. Nevertheless, the influx of petrodollars from OPEC countries and the wealth generated from oil and gas production in the United States fueled a boom in real estate construction and speculation, especially in those states that produced oil and gas.

During the early 1980s, when energy prices and inflation rates were high, some banks adopted risky lending policies and speculated in loans for acquisition, development, and construction of real estate projects. Market rates of interest soared—the Treasury bill rate increased from about 7 percent in 1980 to over 16 percent in 1981. Some banks that borrowed short-term funds at high rates of interest and loaned them for long periods at lower rates of interest did not survive the negative spreads—costs exceeding returns—and they failed.

A study by the Federal Home Loan Bank Board put the blame for the failures on a rigid institutional design of fixed-rate mortgage loans and variable rate deposits that set the stage for failures of thrifts.[8] To forestall failures and to promote growth in the housing industry, Congress enacted the Depository Institutions Deregulation and Monetary Control Act (1980) and the Garn-St. Germain Depository Institutions Act of 1982 permitting deregulation of banks. The acts gave federally insured thrifts greater flexibility in deciding how to acquire and invest their funds. The Monetary Control Act provided for the gradual elimination of Regulation Q, which set interest rate ceilings on deposits. As a result, this opened the door for banks to pay higher rates on deposits.

Garn-St. Germain also provided for thrift institutions to broaden their investment powers and have up to 20 percent of their assets in consumer loans, commercial paper, and corporate debt securities. Garn-St. Germain further liberalized the powers by allowing S&Ls to engage in commercial lending. It also permitted the interstate acquisition of failing institutions. Some state laws were changed to encourage the growth of thrifts. In California, the Nolan Bill liberalized state law to "allow state chartered thrifts authority to do anything and everything they wanted to do—no holds barred—using federally-insured deposits," said Edwin Gray, former Chairman of the Federal Home Loan Bank Board.[9]

To facilitate the survival and growth of S&Ls, the minimum regulatory capital on savings and loans (S&Ls) was reduced from 5 percent to 3 percent (from 1981-1983). This, according to Gray, caused a perverse incentive to grow excessively and gamble the store. There were great opportunities to make a killing on the upside, with little or no downside risk because of deposit insurance. The presence of deposit insurance provided little incentive for depositors to be concerned about the financial condition of the banks that held their fully insured funds deposits, or how they invested those funds. Deposit insurance shielded institutions from the financial markets that would have signaled whether they were making unsound investments. Market investors in uninsured loans to banks would have required progressively higher returns on loans to banks taking on increasingly risky loans and investments.

Deposit insurance provided little incentive for management to worry about risk when they had little or no equity capital to lose. One role of equity capital—the owner's investment—is to absorb losses. When there is no equity capital, there is nothing for the owners to lose when losses occur. Someone else—the insurance funds and the public—had to absorb the losses.

A related issue was the differences between regulatory accounting principles (RAP), promulgated by the Federal Home Loan Bank Board, and generally accepted accounting principles (GAAP). According to a congressional report, "Regulatory and statutory accounting gimmicks included permitting thrifts to defer losses from the sale of assets with below market yields; permitting the use of income capital certificates, authorized by Congress, in place of real capital; letting qualifying mutual capital certificates to be included as RAP capital; allowing FSLIC insured members to exclude from liabilities in computing net worth, certain contra-accounts, including loans in process, unearned discounts, and deferred fees and credits."[10] In 1984, the RAP method overstated the GAAP net worth by $9 billion. At the end of 1988, the difference was $14.9 billion. This difference masked the true extent of the thrift's problems and enabled weak institutions to continue to operate when they should have been closed.

In addition, because banks are not required to evaluate their loan portfolios at market value, some banks that appeared to be solvent (have a positive equity capital or net worth) were actually insolvent. As their capital declined or became negative, there were even greater incentives for the owners to speculate and engage in risky loans. The attitude of the day was, "Heads I win, tails the insurance funds lose."

Recognizing this profit opportunity with little or no risk, some real estate developers bought control of banks and S&Ls. Said one FSLIC official, "For the unscrupulous developer, owning a thrift was a dream come true—a virtual printing press to provide money to develop his real estate."[11] Such S&Ls adopted a strategy of rapid expansion. In fact, S&Ls were encouraged by the Federal Home Loan Bank Board to grow faster to enhance their earnings to relieve their financial distress. To do this, they turned to "brokered deposits" as a source of funds. These are insured certificates of deposit that were sold to investors through brokerage houses such as Merrill Lynch and others. The CDs carried high rates of interest to attract investors. To pay for the high-cost deposits, S&Ls invested in increasingly risky projects that promised high returns. The more brokered deposits they sold, the more they invested in risky projects, and the faster they grew.

From December 1982 through December 1986, the assets of 40 risky Texas S&Ls grew 299 percent, compared to 99 percent for other Texas thrifts and 55 percent average growth in the United States.

The Thin Line Between Abuse and Fraud

Insider abuse frequently leads to criminal misconduct. Insider abuse is a technical term which "refers to a wide range of misconduct by officers, directors, and insiders of financial institutions committed with the intent to enrich themselves without regard for the safety and soundness of the institutions they control, in violation of civil banking laws and regulations and perhaps also in violation of criminal banking laws. The term 'criminal misconduct' refers strictly to criminal acts committed by such insiders against the institutions they control."[12] Thus, insider abuse does not necessarily involve criminal misconduct. However, it is frequently a thin line where abuse ends and criminal misconduct or fraud begins. Equally important, insider abuse and fraud lead to "unsafe or unsound" banking practices such as extending credit that is inadequately secured, failing to maintain internal controls, and paying excessive cash dividends.[13]

Self-Dealing

Self-dealing is a common form of insider abuse. It refers to insiders putting their self-interest above those of the bank. One form of self-dealing is when an insider uses his or her authority to grant loans to oneself, or a related business, at preferential terms or by using lower credit standards, with the intent of making profit in that business. By way of illustration, banking regulators sued the National Bank of Georgia, Calhoun First National Bank, and T. Bertram (Bert) Lance, an insider, for engaging in certain unsafe and unsound banking practices that violated federal securities laws. Bert Lance was the former Carter Administration budget director who resigned that post because of his banking practices.[14] The complaint alleged that credit (loans and overdrafts) was extended to Lance, his relatives, and his friends on preferential terms and without regard to their creditworthiness. The extension of the credits caused liquidity problems at Calhoun bank. To solve the problems, Calhoun bank transferred troubled loans to other banks, but Calhoun bank concealed the transfers by making misleading entries on their books. The loans were not reflected as liabilities on Calhoun's financial statements, and no adjustment was made to the provision for loan losses for some of the transactions. The result was that earnings and assets were overstated, and the bank failed to disclose its true financial state to banking regulators and investors. The National Bank of Georgia also extended credit to Lance, his relatives, and his friends on preferential terms so they could pay on the loans and overdrafts at Calhoun bank. The National Bank of Georgia also failed to properly reserve for loan losses.[15]

A related form of self-dealing is when directors and principal shareholders become dependent on fees and income from providing outside dealings with the bank (i.e., legal services) to such an extent that their interests come ahead of the bank's interest. Other types of insider abuse include:

- Paying high cash dividends when the bank is insolvent.

- Payment of personal trips to Europe or elsewhere.

- Putting friends and relatives on the bank's payroll.

- Directing the bank's business to friends and relatives.

- Unwarranted fringe benefits to insiders.

- Kickbacks from customers in return for granting loans or low interest rates on loans.

To further illustrate insider abuse, consider the case of Manhattan Beach Savings and Loan Association, Manhattan Beach, California, that was owned by Peter Sajovich.[16] About one year before Manhattan Beach was closed, Sajovich "contributed" to it a company which he owned that was called National Home Equity Corporation (NHEC). The contribution was made on the condition that Manhattan Beach would recapitalize NHEC with an infusion of $4.5 million in cash, which was more equity capital than the S&L had. The day before he made the contribution to the S&L, Sajovich received a check for $3 million from NHEC. Of that amount, $2.515 million was a "dividend" representing the entire net worth, and the remaining $485,000 was a noninterest-bearing loan, resulting in NHEC having a negative net worth. NHEC went bankrupt. Manhattan Beach Savings and Loan failed.

In recent years there has been an increased amount of fraud and abuse involving outsiders—borrowers, brokers, dealers, and just plain crooks. Consider the case of Consolidated Savings Bank, Irvine, California. Consolidated made a $9 million loan to a corporation owned by a convicted felon, Charles J. Bazarian, who, no doubt, promised them large returns; and they were greedy enough to believe him. The loan was made without any loan application or financial information. There was, however, a one-page opinion from appraisers as to the value of the property being used as security for the loan. Not one payment was made on the loan and it appears to be a substantial or total loss.[17] Bazarian was also connected with the failure of Florida Center Bank. His role in this failure is discussed in Chapter 7.

Butterfield Savings and Loan Association, Santa Ana, California, is an example of faulty appraisal practices and lack of proper internal controls by the S&L. Butterfield was in financial difficulty when their capital declined sharply. The holding company, which owned Butterfield, issued new stock and contributed the proceeds to Butterfield. Butterfield used the funds to purchase 40 parcels of real estate at a cost in excess of $80 million. Management wanted to record as high of a purchase price as possible to inflate the book net worth figures and to relieve the pressure from regulators. The appraisals were made at grossly inflated figures. One parcel purchased for development was a swamp and another was a forest preserve.

A 1989 U.S. Government Accounting Office study of 26 failed thrifts found that they all changed from traditional home lenders to higher-risk lending activities.[18] Indications of fraud and insider abuse were evident in all of them. Most of the criminal misconduct involved officers and directors. The study also found the following violations of laws and regulations:

- Seventeen had inaccurate appraisals for real estate projects.

- Twenty-three exceeded the legal limits of loans available to one borrower.

- Twenty-one conducted business with prohibited persons or entities affiliated with the thrifts.

- Twenty-four did not adequately assess the borrower's financial condition.

Bank Failures

The end of the speculative bubble came in the early 1980s as the Federal Reserve put the brakes on the economy to slow the rate of inflation, and oil prices plummeted from $35 per barrel to $10 per barrel. As cash flow dwindled from oil and gas production, a domino effect began in the economy that resulted in deflation—falling prices. The agricultural export boom came to a halt when the price of farm land declined, especially in the Midwest. The prices of residential and commercial real estate declined in cities, such as Houston, Texas, where there was overcapacity due to speculation. Many loans that were linked to energy and real estate went into default. Some home mortgage loans were jokingly called "jingle loans" because a substantial number of borrowers abandoned their properties and sent their jingling keys to the lenders instead of sending monthly payments to amortize mortgage loans.

Falling energy prices contributed to the international "debt crisis" where both developed and lesser developed countries were unable or unwilling to honor their debts. Mexico, one of the major trading partners of the United States, devalued their peso and took other actions which had a negative impact on the economies of Texas, California, and other states.

Most of the commercial banks that failed between 1985-1987 came from oil-producing states [Texas (88), Oklahoma (60), Colorado (26), Louisiana (22)] and from farm belt states [Kansas (35), Iowa (27), Nebraska (25), Minnesota (21)].[19]

Many S&L failures occurred in these same states. One factor contributing to the S&L failures was a lack of supervision. In 1983, the Federal Home Loan Bank of Little Rock, Arkansas moved to Dallas, Texas. Thirty-seven of the bank's 48 employees quit rather than moved. Only 2 of the 11 employees who moved were examiners, and their responsibility covered 480 S&Ls.[20]

Most of the states where the largest number of failures occurred had laws that restricted branch banking. Ninety percent of the banks that failed in 1987 were in such states.[21] As a result of the banking structure, states such as Texas had a large number of small unit banks. At the end of 1987, Texas had 1,766 banks of which 1,081 had total assets of less than $50 million.[22] Five-hundred-sixty-one banks had assets of less than $25 million. The large number of small banks is important because small banks cannot afford large write-offs as well as large banks can. A bank with $25 million in assets may have about $1.5–$2.0 million in capital (six to eight percent). As mentioned previously, a significant portion of the criminal referrals resulted in losses over $1 million. Large losses wipe out the capital of small banks. In addition, small unit banks have less opportunity to diversify geographically, and they have fewer opportunities to achieve economies of scale through branching. Their resources for qualified management and directors are stretched. For example, 10 unit banks require 10 boards of directors, while one bank with 10 branches requires only one board. Thus, restrictions on branch banking contributed indirectly to the failures by fostering a large number of small unit banks rather than large banks with many branches.

The largest concentration of criminal referrals made to regulators was in small banks, those with assets of $50 million or less. Small banks were easier targets than large banks for crooks who wanted to manipulate them for their own purposes. One reason for the concentration of criminal referrals in small banks is that they are easier and less costly to acquire than large banks. A 1964 Congressional study revealed that 56 percent of all banks had fewer than 50 stockholders, and 75 percent had less than 10,000 shares.[23] Although that study is dated, the figures probably have not changed very much.

Leading the Lambs to Slaughter

Greed is the motive for bank crimes. Greed is a double-edged sword. Those who commit bank crimes are greedy, and many of the so-called victims are greedy. Dishonest loan and deposit brokers showed eager and willing lenders how to make a financial killing on large deals that sounded too good to be true. To paraphrase what one crook is reported to have said, "It was like leading lambs to slaughter." The lenders, wanting to reap huge financial gains, overlooked obvious flaws in underwriting such loans. They got suckered into such deals because they were greedy and careless. They didn't do their homework. They ignored the basic principals of making sound loans—the five "Cs" of credit (character, capacity, capital, collateral, and conditions).

The following case illustrates the point. The Comptroller of the Currency (OCC) published a "Banking Issuance" concerning annuity contracts from American Teachers Life Insurance Company, Humble, Texas, and General Mercantile Finance Corporation, Houston, Texas. At the same time they published an "OCC Advisory" which stated that an insurance company sold single premium insurance annuities (e.g., $100,000) to individuals for a small downpayment. The remainder of the cost of the annuity was financed by a promissory note with the finance company. The buyers were told that interest on the note would cost them, say, $6,000 per year, but that the annuity would pay $7,000 at the end of the year, resulting in a nice profit for them. Most of the individuals lacked the financial resources to make the note payments without the annuity income. A finance company packaged the promissory notes and sold them at discounts to banks, or used them as collateral for bank loans. The banks did their credit checks on the individuals who signed the notes and paid the finance company. However, they failed to check out the insurance company that issued the annuities. The banks assumed that the Texas Board of Insurance Guarantee Fund would back the insurance policies. However, the guarantee fund does not back fraudulent deals. The annuities were worthless or grossly overvalued, so those individuals who bought them were conned. The banks that held the notes may suffer a loss.[24] The OCC was careful not to include the firms named in the Banking Issuance in its advisory. Nevertheless, the implication was clear that the firms were those involved in the annuities fraud. The banks that bought the promissory notes did not do their homework.

Not all lenders or banks were greedy. Moreover, not all frauds involved loans. Sometimes the banks just got hoodwinked and they were truly victims.

Those who were inclined to commit crimes were given the opportunity and the means on a silver platter. High energy prices fueled a speculative boom in real estate and land values. Federal and state laws fostering deregulation opened the door for speculative investments and brokered deposits that weak institutions used to their advantage. Some lawmakers and regulators claimed that industry lobbying groups deceived them and "sucked them into a political black hole."[25] Restrictive state laws on branch banking nurtured a large number of small banks that were ripe for picking. In Texas, for example, control of state-chartered thrifts could be effectuated by buying their stock in the marketplace with no regulatory controls. Regulators imposed low capital requirements and had lax standards. Bank directors, officers, and shareholders frequently choose to ignore or remain ignorant of what was going on with respect to the safety and soundness of their banks. Finally, depositors had no incentive to know it.

The largest bank crime wave in our history was uncovered when the speculative bubble in real estate burst and banks began to fail in large numbers. The problem was exacerbated by the Tax Reform Act of 1986 which made real estate investments less attractive. Had economic activity not declined, many of the crimes involving real estate would have been covered up by economic prosperity and inflation.

Unfortunately, crimes involving real estate are only part of the crime wave. There are many ways to steal from banks. Bank crimes have not stopped and will not end. People will always rob and steal from banks because that's where the money is. But there are things we can do to prevent some bank crimes. First, however, we must learn more about various types of crimes, examine case studies, and then explore ways to prevent some of them, such as to institute proper controls. However, the best controls in the world will not prevent crime from occurring if the controls are not used.

Crimes in the 1990s—A Global Perspective

Because of the policies and conditions described, most of the problems involved were in real estate. Fraud in real estate continues to be a problem, but not to the extent that it was in the 1980s. For example, in April 1994, the Deutsch Bank (Berlin) blamed a real estate developer for a $29.5 million loss.[26] The developer borrowed funds to build a 20,000 square foot shopping center that was expected to generate $19.5 million in monthly rent. Instead the developer built 9,000 square feet that generated about $4 million in monthly rent.

The major change in the crimes today is the involvement of international banks and international crime organizations. In the following chapters we will examine in detail the Bank for Commerce and Credit International (BCCI) (Chapter 3) and the Banca Nazionale Del Lavoro (BNL) (Chapter 4). BCCI was a bank whose policy was to find ways to get around laws and commit frauds and other crimes. BNL is a bank owned by the Italian government. BNL's agency in Atlanta, Georgia, committed the largest bank fraud in history. BNL is particularly interesting because the illegal actions were condoned by the parent bank. Moreover, the case involved political figures in the U.S. and Italian governments, the CIA, Iraq, and other countries.

Money laundering (Chapter 5) is another aspect of international frauds involving financial institutions. It is most often connected with the sale of illegal drugs. It should be of no surprise that money laundering usually involves Latin American and Oriental crime groups converting their ill-gotten gains into "clean" funds that they can use.

Oriental crime organization play a major role in credit card frauds (Chapter 9). And last, but by no means least, West African crime gangs (Chapter 8) engage in large numbers of small scale frauds involving financial institutions and businesses. Together, all of these factors play a key role in keeping fraud at the forefront of security issues that both bankers and regulators must resolve.

Endnotes

1. Dennis Cauchon, "S&L Fraud Trial Opens in $136M Vanishing Act," *USA Today,* February 22, 1989, B1. Empire Savings and Loan is examined in Chapter 6.

2. Comptroller of the Currency, "Criminal Referral Form (Short Form) 1557-0069." Under 12 C.F.R. #21.11, National banks are required to file within 30 days following the detection of a loss or suspected violation of all known or suspected crimes/losses involving financial transactions. A long form is used when executive officers, directors, or principal shareholders are involved (12 C.F.R. #215.2). Also see 12 C.F.R. #21.5(c), 17 C.F.R. #240.17f-1.

3. Federal Deposit Insurance Corporation, *1987 Annual Report,* Washington, D.C., FDIC, 1988, pp. xiii, 6; FDIC News Release, "Interagency Cooperation Controls Fraud and Insider Abuse, But More Action Is Needed, FDIC Chairman Says," PR-2-3-87, November 11, 1987; U.S. House, *Combating Fraud, Abuse, and Misconduct in the Nation's Financial Institutions: Current Federal Efforts Are Inadequate,* 72nd Report by the Committee on Government Operations, House Report 100-1088, 100 Cong., 2nd Sess., October 13, 1988, pp. 10- 11; U.S. House, *Federal Response to Criminal Misconduct and Insider Abuse in the Nation's Financial Institutions,* 57th Report by the Committee on Government Operations, House Report 98-1137, 98th Cong., 2nd Sess., October 4, 1984, p. 7; U.S. House, *Financial Institutions Reform, Recovery and Enforcement Act of 1989,* Report of the Committee on Banking, Finance and Urban Affairs, Report 101-54, Part 1, 101st Cong., 1st Sess., May 16, 1989, 300.

4. U.S. General Accounting Office, "Bank and Thrift Failures: The Government Could Do More to Pursue Fraud and Wrongdoing," GAO/T-GGD-93-1, January 28, 1993, Testimony of Harlod A. Valentine.

5. U.S. General Accounting Office, "Bank and Thrift Criminal Fraud: The Federal Commitment Could Be Broadened," GAO/GGD-93-48, January 1993.

6. Bank failures in earlier periods were analyzed by Joseph F. Sinkey, Jr., *Problem and Failed Institutions in the Commercial Banking Industry,* Greenwich, CN:

JAI Press, Inc., 1979. Also see Irvine H. Sprague, *Bailout: An Insider's Account of Bank Failures and Rescues,* New York: Basic Books, Inc., 1986; George J. Benston, *An Analysis of the Causes of Savings and Loan Failures,* Monograph 1985–4, New York: Salomon Brothers Center for the Study of Financial Institutions, New York University, 1985; Richard L. Peterson and William L. Scott, "Major Causes of Bank Failure," appears in *Proceedings, Bank Structure and Competition,* Federal Reserve Bank of Chicago, May 1–3, 1985, 166–183; Gregory R. Gajewski, *Bank Risk, Regulator Behavior, and Bank Closure in the Mid-1980s: A Two-Step Logit Model,* unpublished Dissertation, George Washington University, 1988, Chapter 2.

7. U.S. Congress, Congressional Budget Office, *The Economic Effects of the Savings and Loan Crisis,* January 1992, 12. Also see James R. Barth, *The Great Savings and Loan Debacle;* American Enterprise Institute Press, 1991; and Lawrence J. White, *The S&L Debacle: Public Policy Lessons for Bank and Thrift Regulations,* New York, Oxford University Press, 1991.

8. James R. Barth, Philip F. Bartholomew, and Carol J. Labich, *Moral Hazard and the Thrift Crisis: An Analysis of the 1988 Resolutions,* Research Paper #160, Federal Home Loan Bank Board, May 1989, 13.

9. Edwin J. Grey, "Statement of Edwin J. Grey, Past Chairman, Federal Home Loan Bank Board, before the Committee on Banking, Housing and Urban Affairs, Senate," August 3, 1988. Also see Council of Economic Advisors, *Economic Report of the President,* Washington, D.C.: Government Printing Office, 1989, pp. 200–205, for a discussion of the impact of regulation and deposit insurance.

10. U.S. House, *Financial Institutions Reform, Recovery and Enforcement Act of 1989,* ibid., 298. For details on how RAP differs from GAAP, see U.S. General Accounting Office, "Bank Regulation, Information on Independent Public Accountant Audits of Financial Institutions," GAO/GGD-86-44FS, April 1986.

11. William K. Black and William L. Robertson, Director ORPOS, before the Subcommittee on Financial Institutions, Supervison, Regulation, and Insurance of the Committee on Banking, Finance, and Urban Affairs, House of Representatives, 100th Cong., June 9, 1987.

12. U.S. House Report 98-1137, p. 2, n. 5; U.S. House Report 100–1088, p. 7–9; U.S. House, *Fraud and Abuse by Insiders, Borrowers, and Appraisers in the California Thrift Industry,* Hearing before the Commerce, Consumer, and Monetary Affairs Subcommittee of the Committee on Government Operations, 100th Cong., 1st Sess., June 13, 1987, testimony of William K. Black, Federal Home Loan Bank Board, pp. 188–191; the Comptroller of the Currency has a different definition of insider abuse and fraud which may be found in *Bank Failure: An Evaluation of the Factors Contributing to the Currency,* June 1988, 45–46.

13. Additional examples of "Unsafe or Unsound" practices are listed in the *FDICs Manual of Examination Policies*. They are also shown in U.S. House, *Federal Response to Criminal Misconduct and Insider Abuse in the Nation's Financial Institutions, Part 2*, Hearings before the Commerce, Consumer, and Monetary Affairs Subcommittee of the Committee on Goverment Operations, 98th Cong., 2d Sess., May 2 and 3, 1984, 1384.

14. Bert Lance is also mentioned in Chapter 6 in connection with UAB Knoxville and Jake Butcher's financing the World's Fair.

15. *Hearings, Part 2*, ibid., 1573–1574.

16. *Fraud and Abuse by Insiders*, ibid., 188–189.

17. *Combating Fraud*, House Report 100–1088, ibid., 185–186.

18. U.S. General Accounting Office, *Thrift Failures: Costly Failures Resulted from Regulatory Violations and Unsafe Practices*, GAO/AFMD-89-62, June 1989, 3.

19. Most insolvent savings and loan associations were located in Texas, California, Illinois, Louisiana, Florida, and Oklahoma. For details, see U.S. General Accounting Office, *Thrift Industry: Forbearance for Troubled Institutions 1982–1986*, GAO/GGD-87-78BR, May 1987, 20; also, U.S. Government Accounting Office, *Thrift Failures*, ibid., 92–93.

20. Rick Atkinson and David Maraniss, "Only Ambition Limited S&L Growth," *The Washington Post*, June 12, 1989, Al.

21. U.S. General Accounting Office, *Bank Failures: Independent Audits Needed to Strengthen Internal Control and Bank Management*, GAO/AFMD-89-25, 33.

22. The number of banks by size for each state can be found in *FDIC, Statistics on Banking, 1987*.

23. U.S. House, *The Market for Bank Stock, Subcommittee on Domestic Finance, Committee on Banking and Currency*, 88th Cong., 2d Sess., 1964, 1.

24. Comptroller of the Currency, "OCC Advisory," "OCC Banking Issuance," 1989.

25. Jackson Brooks and Paulette Thomas, "As S&L Crisis Grows, U.S. League Loses Lobbying Clout," *The Wall Street Journal*, March 7, 1989, A1, A18.

26. Ferdinand Protzman, "Deutsch Bank Blames Developer," *The New York Times*, April 26, 1994, C2.

2 TYPES OF CRIMES

There is a saying that one cannot see the forest through the trees. So it is with bank fraud, because it is a covert activity; and unless one knows what to look for, only those who are involved may be aware that it is occurring. Frauds may go on for years before they are detected, if ever. Certain types of frauds, however, are more prevalent and preventable than others. This chapter examines the most prevalent types of fraud and explains why they are difficult to detect and even more difficult to prosecute.

Relatively Small Frauds

There are many types of criminal misconduct involving banks. Table 2.1 lists the principal federal criminal statutes involving banks and some of the crimes. Rather than dealing with each type of violation, bank frauds—the general term used to describe the crimes covered—is divided into two broad categories: those that involve large dollar amounts and may or may not contribute to bank failures (major frauds) and those that involve relatively small dollar amounts (relatively small frauds). According to the U.S. Department of Justice, major frauds involve $100,000 or more.[1] In addition, major frauds may involve the owners (including shareholders), directors, or officers, and multiple institutions. Thus, by the Department of Justice definition, $10 million is a large fraud. However, we will examine frauds as much as $4 *billion* (Chapters 3 and 4). Given that perspective, a $10 million fraud is relatively small.

As explained in the previous chapter, a $2 million loss from fraud has a different impact on large and small size banks. It may have little or no effect on the capital of a large bank, but it may eradicate the capital of a small bank, causing it to fail. For example, a $50 million bank may have only $4 million in total capital. Finally, although a bank failed and fraud was present in some degree, the fraud may not have been the proximate cause of the failure. In fact, most of the bank failures are due to loan losses, not to fraud.

Frauds can be committed by trusted employees in any department of a bank. For example, computer related crimes are hard to detect because there are no witnesses or hard-copy records. The crimes may be as simple as crediting a small fraction of interest payments to the perpetrator's account, or they may be complex schemes. By way of illustration, a senior computer operator on a bank's night shift of the main computer facility used information from recently closed demand deposit accounts (DDAs) to open fictitious new ones. He had access to the correct passwords and per-

---

Table 2.1

Selected Federal Criminal Statutes Involving Banks

- *18 USC, Section 215:* kickbacks and bribes prohibition; making it unlawful for any officer, director, employee, agent, et al. (insiders) of a financial institution to solicit, accept, or give anything of value in connection with a transaction or the business of the institution.
- *18 USC, 656; 961(c):* theft, embezzlement, or misapplication of bank funds willfully by an insider with the intent to injure or defraud the bank.
- *18 USC, 1344:* financial institution fraud; scheme or artifice to defraud a federally insured institution to take money, funds, credits, assets, securities, or other property by misrepresentation.
- *18 USC, 1001:* general false statements statute: knowingly and willfully falsifying or concealing a material fact or making a false statement, etc.
- *18 USC, 1005:* false entries in bank documents including material omissions, with the intent to injure or defraud the commercial bank regulatory agencies' examiners or other individuals or companies.
- *18 USC, 1014:* false oral or written statements, such as a loan application, an agreement with the financial institution, or another document made knowingly for the purpose of influencing federally insured institutions.
- *18 USC, 1341 and 1343:* mail and wire fraud, respectively, a scheme or artifice to defraud that makes use of either the U.S. mail or electrical transmission.
- *18 USC, 2, 371:* the general federal aiding and abetting statute and general federal conspiracy statute, often applicable when two or more persons are involved in the commission of an offense.

Other Laws Affecting Financial Institutions' Fraud

- Money Laundering Control Act, Annunzio-Wylie-Anti-Money Laundering Act
- Racketeer Influenced Corrupt Organizations (RICO)

Source: U.S. House, *Combating Fraud, Abuse, and Misconduct in the Nation's Financial Institutions: Current Federal Efforts Are Inadequate,* 72, Report by the Committee on Government Operations, House Report 100-1088, October 13, 1988, 193; Financial Institutions Reform, Recovery and Enforcement Act of 1989. For 18 USC 215, 656, 657, 1005, 1006, 1007, 1014, 1341, 1343, 1344, and other sections, not all of which were discussed previously. The act amends the civil penalties, criminal penalties, and it contains other revisions including civil and criminal forfeiture of assets.

sonal identification numbers (PIN) to do it. He credited various amounts of funds to the new accounts by debiting one of the bank's "suspense accounts." Funds were credited to the suspense accounts from inactive savings accounts and high balance DDAs. He withdrew funds from the new accounts using counter checks and the accounts' PIN numbers. He also used the home banking telephone service to instruct the bank to pay for various goods and services he purchased. Over the seven months he operated the scheme, the number of accounts and amount of funds in each increased. His undoing occurred in a major gambling resort when he met a bank auditor whom he knew. The bell captain addressed the perpetrator by the wrong name, and the auditor became suspicious and investigated. The loss in this scheme was about $200,000.[2]

The following cases illustrate frauds and abuses by insiders. Consider the case of an assistant supervisor of an automatic teller machine (ATM) department who had 27 years of service and who was a gambler. Over the years he won large sums, but he lost even more. Unfortunately, he was unable to pay off his gambling debts, so he gambled more in the hopes of winning. When he was deep in hock to the bookies, they allowed him to satisfy his gambling debts by providing them with security information about his bank's ATM system. Shortly thereafter, thefts occurred at the ATMs, and he knew that his information had contributed to them. He became depressed, and his work and home life suffered. His wife, who was concerned about his health and his role in the thefts, reported him to bank authorities. The total loss to the bank was an estimated $135,000.[3]

The next case concerns an 11-year veteran employee who worked as a customer representative. Part of her job was to sell savings bonds and traveler's checks to bank customers. She created false records to make it appear as if the $175,000 she received over a period of time had been sent on to American Express. She kept the money and used part of it to pay for her mother's medical expenses. However, the total amount stolen far exceeded the medical expenses. Gradually the paperwork involved in the "cover up" became so time-consuming that she was unable to find time to do her job. She turned herself into her attorney and then contacted federal authorities.[4]

Finally, there is the case of F. Ray Harvard, a vice president in the trust department of a large bank. He had 18 years of service. It is alleged that over the period of a decade, Harvard misapplied trust funds by withdrawing large sums from certain accounts entrusted to him. To cover the withdrawals, he sent inaccurate and deceptive financial statements to the account holders. He also told them that selected investments had increased in value to a greater extent than they had. Harvard used some of the funds to speculate in the stock market and lost more than $1 million.

The day after returning from a two-week vacation, Harvard followed his usual routine and left for work in the morning, but he never arrived at the bank.[5] Following an extensive search, his body was discovered near a hunting club of which he was a member. He committed suicide. His death occurred after stock prices declined sharply in August 1987, but before "Black Monday" when the stock market "crashed." Perhaps the falling stock prices forced him to the realization that his crimes were going to be exposed. We will never know.

The previous frauds were committed by insiders. Check kiting, however, is a type of fraud perpetrated by outsiders. Check kiting is a scheme to create false bank balances without sufficient funds to cover them. It involves two or more accounts at different banks. The perpetrator writes a check for an amount sufficient to overdraw the account on which it was written. For example, there is $100 in the account and a check is written for $1,000. The overdraft is covered by depositing a similar check drawn on another bank and depositing it before the first check has been returned for payment. The result of the continuous interchange of worthless checks is that artificial balances are created in the accounts of the banks involved in the scheme.

Two conditions must exist for a check kiting scheme to be successful. First, there must be a period of several days in the collection process before the depository bank can present the check to the drawee bank. Second, the banks must be willing to pay checks drawn against uncollected funds—items in the process of collection.

The "Expedited Funds Availability Act" (12 USC. 4001) gave the Board of Governors of the Federal Reserve System the authority to regulate the availability of funds deposited in depository institutions. Federal Reserve Regulation CC calls for next business day availability for wire transfers, government checks, certified checks, and cashier's checks, and longer periods for other types of deposits. In many cases it takes more than one day to determine if a certified or another type of check is good. It remains to be seen what impact Regulation CC will have on check kiting. Other effects of Regulation CC will be examined in Chapter 8.

Major Frauds

The largest frauds examined in this book involve international banks: the Bank of Commerce and Credit International (Chapter 3) and Banca Nazionale Del Lavoro (Chapter 4). In addition, money laundering (Chapter 5) involves large dollar amounts and hundreds of domestic and foreign banks.

The greatest dollar losses from fraud come from large commercial and real estate transactions, and they frequently involve insider participation. The five most common types of schemes that result in major frauds, according to the Federal Bureau of Investigation (FBI), are summarized here, and are examined in detail in later chapters.[6]

1. *Nominee loans.* These are loans obtained by one person on behalf of another, undisclosed person. The nominee, or "straw borrower," may have no involvement in the loan transaction other than to obtain the funds, and pass them on to someone else who does not want their identity known.

2. *Double pledging of collateral.* The same collateral is used at two or more financial institutions to obtain loans. The lenders are not aware that the collateral is pledged on another loan. The combined amount of the loans exceeds the value of the collateral.

3. *Reciprocal loan arrangements.* These are loans made between insiders in different financial institutions who lend funds to each other. A variant of this device is to sell loans to other institutions with the agreement to buy loans from that institution. The purpose of such agreements is to conceal the loans or sales from bank examiners.

4. *Land flips.* This refers to the transfer of land between related parties in order to fraudulently inflate the value of the underlying property. The land with the inflated values is used as collateral for loans. The amount of the loans frequently exceed the actual value of the underlying property.

5. *Linked financing.* Large amounts of funds are deposited in a financial institution, using brokered deposits or some other means, with the understanding that the institution will make a loan conditioned on the deposit. The loans may be used to finance land flips or other types of deals.

Some of these schemes, such as linked financing and land flips, are not necessarily illegal in and of themselves. However, they usually occur in connection with willful misapplication of funds, making false statements, willfully overvaluing property, and other illegal activities that were outlined in Table 2.1. Although these types of transactions are presented separately, they often occur in combination. For example, large-scale fraud involving real estate requires two misrepresentations. The first essential misrepresentation is that the value of the property is inflated. The second misrepresentation concerns the creditworthiness of borrowers. The crooks misrepresent their creditworthiness, the buyers they control, and the value of the properties with false income tax returns and false financial statements.

Property values are inflated by using a "double escrow" or a "straw buyer." In a double escrow, the same property is sold simultaneously to two separate parties controlled by the perpetrator. The first transaction is from a legitimate seller at a fair market price to a buyer who is controlled by the perpetrator. The second sale is from the first buyer to a second, both of whom are controlled by the perpetrator. The second sale is made at two or three times the fair market price. In some cases the value is inflated as much as twenty-fold by using improper appraisals.[7] This type of operation is used in connection with a land flip.

If a straw buyer is used, the straw buyer buys the property from the legitimate seller at the fair market price. Then the property is sold again, but at a higher price to a buyer who will qualify for a loan on the property at an inflated value.

To obtain inflated appraised property values, the perpetrators hire real estate appraisers from distant locations who want to increase their fee income, or who may be crooks too. The appraisers, who are not familiar with the property, are provided with false information about the comparable worth of properties in the area. To illustrate this process, one bank loaned over $54 million on an office complex and relied on a borrower ordered appraisal. The appraisal did not consider that more than half of the rentable space was leased at rates that were 50 percent below the current market prices, or that occupancy levels were low in nearby comparable properties due to overbuilding.[8] The result of such actions is faulty and inflated appraised values.

Then "loan packages," including financial statements, appraisals, and other information, are presented to prospective buyers by "loan brokers" or others pretending to be independent and objective third parties. The buyers of the overvalued real estate are individuals, limited partnerships, or financial institutions who rely on the honesty and thoroughness of the independent and objective third parties.[9] Rarely do the buyers do their own credit analysis or appraisals, especially if the property is at a distant location. Their failure to do so puts them at substantial risk if and when the deals fail.

In some cases the perpetrators sell funds (brokered deposits) to the financial institutions and link the sale of funds to real estate deals of the type described previously. There are an infinite number of ways to commit frauds.

Obstacles to Prosecuting Major Frauds

According to Gregory C. Jones, First Assistant U.S. Attorney for the Northern District of Illinois (Chicago), major frauds "are sophisticated crimes that by their very nature are designed to disguise and conceal the financial relationships that exist between the offenders."[10]

Even when a fraud is discovered, banks may choose not to report it, or federal authorities may decline to prosecute, which makes it attractive for perpetrators to try it if they know beforehand that there is little risk in being caught. For example, a member of the board of directors of a bank was suspected of kiting $373,000. The United States Attorney declined to prosecute because restitution was being made. That means the theft was converted into a loan and there was no loss to the bank.[11]

Why did the bank let the director get away with it? Part of the answer is given by Robert Serino, deputy chief counsel of the operations section of the Comptroller of the Currency. In a discussion about banker's ethics he said that individual bankers should not do anything that they wouldn't want to appear on the front page of the morning paper.[12] This is the so-called embarrassment test that applies to individuals. Unfortunately, many bankers interpret this to mean that they should not expose criminal activities in their banks because it might tarnish the bank's image; especially if the top management of their bank is involved.

Another problem is that some bankers interpret the Right to Financial Privacy Act in such a way that prevents them from providing details about suspected crimes. The act deals with the disclosure of financial information about their customers, which includes all borrowers and savers (except corporations). However, the act was liberalized (in the Anti-Drug Abuse Act of 1986, Title 12, USC. 3403c), to facilitate criminal investigations. Nevertheless, some bankers are reluctant to provide law enforcement officials with information about the crime for fear of being sued. For these and other reasons, some banks wait long periods before reporting the crimes. In California, a loan officer altered loan documents and received kickbacks from a loan broker in 1981 and 1982. The crime was not reported until 1985.[13] It may take the FBI 20 to 24 months to investigate complex financial crimes. Therefore, the long delays between the commission of a crime and the time when it may be brought to trial may invoke the five-year statute of limitations on certain crimes, insuring that they will not be prosecuted.

A corollary of the untarnished image is that banks are unwilling to share with other banks information about former employees or customers who are suspected or convicted of criminal misconduct. Similarly, regulators and law enforcement agencies have not shared such information. The result is that crooks can operate their scams in one bank after another with virtual impunity. This is the financial counterpart of the "Typhoid Mary" syndrome.

Bank regulators may also drag their heels when it comes to making timely criminal referrals to the FBI. This is demonstrated by the Ramona Savings and Loan failure. Donald P. Mangano, Sr., and John L. Molinaro acquired Ramona Savings and Loan Association (Orange, California) and transformed it from a traditional S&L which served the local population to a real estate development company. In one transaction, Ramona sold 173 units of Cherokee Village condominium (Palm Springs, California) to associates of Molinaro for $29.4 million. Ramona had lent the buyers the funds to pay for the transaction, secured by first and second trust deeds on the units. However, no payments were required on the first note for three years and none on the second note for five years. In fact, the buyers were really strawmen who had no responsibility or control over the units.

This and similar transactions gave the appearance of profitability to Ramona. Ramona concurrently entered into an agreement with the buyers to operate Cherokee Village as a hotel and to pay all the expenses for three years. The accounting adjustments changed Ramona's apparent profit on the deal from $6.9 million to $0. Michael Sage, the auditor for Ramona, issued a fraudulent financial statement that the S&L had a net worth of $8.3 million, when it was actually a negative $19.6 million, which allowed it to pay a $2 million cash dividend to John Molinaro. Sage, who was Molinaro's and Mangano's personal tax accountant, was paid two checks of $75,000 and $45,000 for his tax services. Sage had a background in engineering before switching to accounting in 1975. According to California Savings and Loan Commissioner, William J. Crawford, Sage cashed the checks and exchanged them for $100 bills.

Supervisory letters covering Reports of Examination criticizing Ramona's aggressive growth strategy, funded with large CDs, and requesting information about contracts signed with Mangano & Sons, were sent to the S&L in 1984 and 1985. In August 1986, a Supervisory Directive imposed restrictions on Ramona's growth. It was insolvent and it went into receivership the following month.

In October 1986, the District Accountant for the Federal Home Loan Bank of San Francisco wrote a memo detailing the allegations and possible violations and recommended that a formal investigation be implemented. But neither the FHLBSF, nor FSLIC, nor the fee counsel notified the FBI. Instead, the fee counsel told the District Accountant to "buzz off" until he had made a complete analysis, and that he wanted to work out a settlement agreement with the principals. The referral was not made and Sage fled the area. Then, instead of notifying the FBI, the FHLBSF and Federal Savings and Loan Insurance Corporation (FSLIC) hired a private detective to find him, which he did not do. As of June 1987 the matter had still not been referred to the FBI. In mid-July 1987, Molinaro tried to flee the country and was arrested by a Customs Agent at the airport on a false passport charge. He was brought to trial in mid-1989. Sage is believed to be in Mexico. Commissioner Crawford also heard rumors that Sage was in Australia, or even in the United States with a changed identity. Sage is facing several criminal indictments if and when he returns.[14]

Calling the FBI to make a criminal referral is not necessarily a simple task. California Savings and Loan Commissioner William J. Crawford wanted to refer an incident concerning North American Savings and Loan Association to the FBI. He made 17 calls over 8 days to Orange County and Los Angeles County FBI offices, the Federal Home Loan Bank of San Francisco, and a U.S. Senator trying to initiate an FBI investigation.[15] One difficulty was that the FBI had more cases than it could handle at that time.

The Los Angeles office had 32 agents and 450 bank fraud cases. Another was that Crawford's calls did not reach the right people in the FBI until almost his last call. However, Crawford said that once the FBI got on the case it did an excellent job.

Bankers and others can avoid problems like those experienced by Commissioner Crawford by establishing a working relationship with their local FBI agents. Alternatively, if they want to report a crime, they should contact the Bank Fraud Supervisor in their local FBI office. This procedure avoids the Complaint Clerk and the paperwork that follows before it gets to the Bank Fraud Supervisor.

The fact that the FBI has been alerted to a crime does not mean that the crime will investigated. As of July 31, 1991, the FBI had 9,659 active financial institutions fraud investigations pending. Because of manpower limitations, the FBI prioritizes investigations according to the amount of the loss, the number of victims, the nature of the crime, the position of the insiders involved, and other factors. In Los Angeles, for example, losses below $100,000 that have no prosecutive merit are not investigated. Losses between $100,000 and $250,000 are opened and investigated. Losses above that amount are given the highest priority.[16] The amount of loss necessary to trigger an investigation varies in other areas from $5,000 to $100,000.

The FBI is more likely to prosecute insiders in banks that fail than in those that remain open for business. It is easier to convince a jury that harm has been done when a bank has failed than when it remains open. In one case senior bank officials were involved in kickbacks, falsifying loan applications and bank records, double mortgaging of property, granting loans in excess of the legal lending limits, embezzlement, and false statements to the government. Nevertheless, the U.S. Attorney "did not feel that extensive investigation revealed any prosecutable violations."[17] Some other reasons given for declining to prosecute cases include lack of gain by the insider, no loss to the bank, a loss too small to warrant prosecution, lack of criminal intent, weak evidence, and the availability of civil remedies. Data from the executive office for U.S. Attorney's indicated that for fiscal 1991, the declination rate was 51 percent. Most of the cases declined were not major alleged frauds.

Theodore J. McDonald, Jr., former Assistant U.S. Attorney, Southern District of Illinois, may have hit the nail on the head when he said that the prospect of the FBI having to expend funds and manpower for several years to analyze financial statements to catch two or three sophisticated bank manipulators is not as appealing to them as the public relations gained from standing next to 500 bales of marijuana, a briefcase full of money, and a speed boat on the beaches of Florida.[18]

It is not surprising that two-thirds of insiders who are suspected of criminal misconduct in institutions that did not fail escape from criminal and civil sanctions. Nor is it surprising that many known major frauds are not prosecuted. Beverly Hills Savings and Loan is one such case. There were four sets of allegations of criminal misconduct associated with the failure of Beverly Hills, and the estimated loss to FSLIC was about $800 million. The FBI had manpower to investigate the $400 million Stout-Newberry Apartment loan. The FBI told FSLIC that they wanted criminal referrals on other parts of the transaction. However, FSLIC's fee counsel, who was busy dealing with civil cases, did not believe it appropriate to look for criminal misconduct.[19] Since then the policy has changed and fee counsel have been informed that it is their obligation to make criminal referrals. Nevertheless, from the Federal Home Loan Bank Board's point of view, seeking civil money damages through litigation to help prop up the beleaguered FSLIC insurance fund may be a higher priority than seeking criminal prosecutions. Unfortunately, the success rate of collecting of civil money penalties has not been good.[20] The Federal Deposit Insurance Corporation has collected 21 percent of the civil money penalties assessed from open banks and 2 percent from failed banks.

Even when the FBI "gets its man," the story is far from being over. For example, bank frauds may be tried under Title 18, U.S. Code 656, and other sections of the Code.[21] Section 656 of the U.S. Code applies to insiders of federally connected banks who willfully misapply funds for their own use or that of a third party. Assistant U.S. Attorney Gregory C. Jones (mentioned on page 20) goes on to say that:

> *Insider offenses are difficult to prosecute because the government bears the burden of proving beyond a reasonable doubt that the loan officer acted with the specific intent to injure and defraud the financial institution. It is not good enough to prove that the loan officer demonstrated bad judgment, stupidity, or complete incompetence. To prove what knowledge a bank official had or with what intent he acted when he approved a loan several years before can be a burdensome if not impossible task. By the time a criminal investigation is initiated, financial records necessary to prove the offense may have already been removed or destroyed. It is not uncommon in these cases to find that entire bank files are missing. In addition, relevant witnesses may be difficult to locate and even when located may have little recollection of events that occurred years before.*
>
> *One way of establishing fraudulent intent is to show that the loan officer received a concealed financial benefit for approving the loan. To prove this, however, may require a time-consuming analysis of a loan officer's personal finances as well as tracing of the loan proceeds to determine how they were disbursed and by whom they were ultimately received. If kickbacks were paid in cash or through nominees, it may be impossible to prove a criminal offense without the cooperation of another participant in the scheme. To obtain the coop-*

eration of others involved in a scheme, it may be necessary to enter into a plea agreement with them or give them immunity. All of these investigative avenues take time and there is no assurance that even if they are explored that they will be fruitful. Many individuals refuse to cooperate with the government even if offered immunity. Many defendants recognize that if none of them cooperate with the government it may be impossible for the government to convict any of them. Unfortunately, therefore, despite a thorough investigation, the government may be unable to come up with sufficient evidence to prove the crime.[22]

Bringing a bank fraud case to trial is analogous to directing a movie and presenting the facts in a dramatic fashion. The complex plot, consisting of 90 counts of fraud, must be condensed into a few counts that the jury will be able to understand. Therefore, the prosecutors seek "sexy examples" of frauds that will keep the judge and jury awake. They are more interested in frauds involving topless dancers than those involving mundane real estate loans. The prosecutors go for frauds that are clear cut, such as misapplication of funds and making false statements, rather than those involving business judgments, which may have been wrong but not illegal. The prosecutors may find securities violations and tax frauds associated with the bank frauds. They may decide they have a strong case using securities violations than under the banking laws. Finally, they have to convince the jury beyond a reasonable doubt that someone is guilty as charged.

The defense, which helps select 12 people least likely to understand the complex transactions, does its best to obfuscate the crime. Part of this includes convincing the jury that the accused, who is a pillar of the community, is of such fine character that he would never do anything wrong. It was his own bank, his own castle, and he should be able to do what he wants with his funds.

Defendants use influential character witnesses to dispel the notion that they are crooks. The fraud case against Thomas M. Gaubert, a Texas real estate developer, S&L owner, and Democratic fundraiser, was lost after both a federal judge and the Texas State Treasurer testified on his behalf. These testimonials of his good standing and other evidence were considered by the jury that acquitted him. In another case, television personality Art Linkletter helped convince a federal judge to go easy on his son-in-law who pleaded guilty to kickbacks on real estate loans. Linkletter's testimony helped to get the sentence reduced from seven years to six months.[23] However, such pleas from notables are no guarantee of being acquitted. Lady Bird Johnson, Walter Cronkite, and Liz Carpenter asked for leniency for former United Bank (Texas) chairman Ruben Johnson. According to Lady Bird, he was "a worthy citizen who practiced love and mercy." Walter Cronkite said that "Locking him away would deprive the community of one who contributes much to it."[24] The judge and jury disagreed and Ruben Johnson received an eight-year sentence and was ordered to pay $4.5 million in restitution on his conviction of bank fraud.

Sometimes the bank regulatory agencies enter into a formal agreement, or issue a cease and desist order, that essentially tells the crook who stole millions of dollars not to do it again, and to figure out a way to repay the bank for its loss. However, if a bank robber who stole $3,000 is caught, the penalty may be 20 years. There is something inequitable about an insider who steals millions of dollars and gets a minimal sentence, and a bank robber who steals a few thousand dollars and gets 20 years. Some, albeit small, equity is granted in that insiders may be tried under other laws as well (see Table 2.1).

Prior to 1989, once a case had been prosecuted (say under Title 18 USC. 656, which was enacted in its basic form in 1877), the *maximum* penalty was $5,000 and/or imprisonment for not more than five years. Congress then enacted the Financial Institutions Reform, Recovery and Enforcement Act of 1989, which increased criminal and civil penalties for certain financial institutions offenses. For 18 USC. 656, for example, the criminal penalty was increased to a fine of $1 million and 20 years imprisonment. The civil penalty may be $5 million or more. The act also has provisions for criminal and civil forfeiture in connection with Title 18 U.S. Code offenses affecting financial institutions.

The following consists of several examples of losses and penalties given to insiders before the passage of the 1989 act:[25]

- Gary Lewellen embezzled $16.7 million from the First National Bank, Humbolt, Iowa. No money was recovered, no fine imposed, no restitution made, but he was sentenced to 20 years. If he serves the full sentence, which is not likely, that works out to $835,000 per year.

- Harry Fagen embezzled $4.8 million from Guaranty Bond State Bank, Redwater, Texas. No money was recovered, no fine imposed, no restitution made, and he was sentenced to eight years, which amounts to $600,000 per year.

- John Vergo, President of Midtown National Bank of Pueblo, Colorado received two years for a $1.6 million loss to the bank ($800,000/year).

- Jake Butcher and C.H. Butcher Sr., caused the failure of 11 banks in Tennessee and Kentucky, and hundreds of millions of dollars of losses to the FDIC. Jake was sentenced to two concurrent 20-year sentences. C.H. Butcher and others were ordered to pay $19.3 million in damages for a plot to hide his wealth when the banking empire collapsed. The Butcher brothers banking activities are examined in Chapter 10.

A 1989 study of 44 criminal convictions of insiders of failed institutions revealed widely disparate sentences.[26] Burton M. Bongard, former president and director of Home State Savings Bank in Cincinnati, Ohio, was ordered to repay $114 million in restitution and $800,000 in court costs. He is serving six years in prison. Jeffery A. Levitt, former president of Old Court Savings, Baltimore, Maryland, was ordered to pay $14.6 million in restitution and is serving a 30-year term in prison. These are the upper extremes. At the other end of the spectrum fines were as low as $50, and there were work release programs and community service in lieu of jail.

Recently, bank frauds have been tried under authority of the Racketeer Influenced Corrupt Organization Act of 1970 (RICO, Title 18, Section 1961 and other sections), which, broadly interpreted, includes most ongoing patterns of racketeering (criminal) activities.[27] The key features of this law are that the fraud must involve an organization (two or more people) and a pattern of criminal activities (two or more crimes). U.S. Attorneys must get permission from the Department of Justice before prosecuting a case under RICO. The logic behind this is that, for example, a U.S. Attorney in Jackson, Mississippi may want to charge someone whom he considers a world class racketeer, but in the overall scheme of things does not qualify under RICO. The first bank related case tried under RICO involved Mario Renda, his wife, and the 14 corporations they controlled.[28] Renda and others were prosecuted for bank fraud. Under an agreement which settled the charges, the FDIC obtained $10.5 million in property for liquidation, which included funds from a Swiss bank account, an apartment building on Park Avenue in New York City, a shopping center in Hawaii, a 101-foot yacht, a 26-passenger executive jet, two Persian rugs, a silver inkwell, and a silver cigar box.[29] Mario Renda's escapades are examined in Chapter 7.

The maximum sentence that can be given under RICO is 20 years and $250,000 on each count. But the convicted felon can get a life sentence if the RICO offense is linked to another predicate crime that calls for a life sentence. Given the sentencing guidelines, however, it is not likely that a bank robber would get that harsh of a sentence.

In this chapter we have shown that crime pays. Major frauds against banks are profitable for perpetrators because they are relatively easy to commit, hard to detect, difficult to prove and prosecute, and the penalties may be slim to none. Major frauds will continue as long as there are people, greed, and money in our system; and the likelihood of that changing is also slim to none. The best solutions to the problem are early detection of the frauds and prevention. Early detection is the subject of the next chapter, and prevention is covered in the appendices.

Endnotes

1. U.S. House, HR 3388, Financial Institution Restitution Act of 1992. This act was not enacted into law.

2. "Bank Fraud: Bulletin of Fraud and Risk Management," Rolling Meadows, IL: Bank Administration Institute, Vol. 4, No. 1, February 1989.

3. "Bank Fraud: Bulletin of Fraud and Risk Management," Rolling Meadows, IL: Bank Administration Institute, Vol. 4, No. 2, February 1989.

4. "Central Bank Worker Sent $175,000 to Self," *Birmingham Post Herald,* March 8, 1989.

5. This is based on various news articles by Tom Jennings, Herb Jordan and others, that appeared in *The Mobile Press Register,* October 10, 1987–February 11, 1988.

6. U.S. House, *Adequacy of Federal Efforts to Combat Fraud, Abuse and Misconduct in Federally Insured Financial Institutions,* Hearing before the Commerce, Consumer, and Monetary Affairs Subcommittee of the Committee on Government Operations, 100th Cong., 1st. Sess., November 19, 1987, p. 605.

7. U.S. House, *Fraud and Abuse by Insiders, Borrowers, and Appraisers in the California Thrift Industry,* Hearing before the Commerce, Consumer, and Monetary Affairs Subcommittee of the Committee on Government Operations, 100th Cong., 1st. Sess., June 13, 1987, prepared statement from John K. Van De Kamp, State of California, Attorney General, pp. 81–82.

8. U.S. General Accounting Office, *Failed Financial Institutions: Reasons, Costs, Remedies and Unresolved Issues,* Statement of Frederick D. Wolf, before the Committee on Banking, Finance and Urban Affairs, House of Representitives, January 13, 1989, (GAO/T-AFMD-89-1).

9. The operations of loan brokers and deposit brokers are explained in Chapter 4.

10. U.S. House, *Federal Response to Criminal Misconduct by Bank Officers, Directors, and Insiders, Part 2,* Hearings before a Subcommittee of the Committee on Goverment Operations, 98th Cong., 1st. Sess., May 2 and 3, 1984, p. 30.

11. U.S. House, Hearing, November 19, 1987, p. 934.

12. Ada Focer, "Bank Insiders Who Bend to Greed," *Bankers Monthly,* September 1988, 16; Conversation with Robert Serino, June 29, 1989.

13. U.S. House, Hearing, June 13, 1987, p. 370.

14. U.S. House, Hearing, June 13, 1987, 455; U.S. House, *Combating Fraud, Abuse, and Misconduct in the Nation's Financial Institutions: Current Federal Efforts Are Inadequate,* p. 72; Report by the Committee on Government Operations, House Report 100–1088, October 13, 1988, pp. 95–96; U.S. House, Hearing, June 13, 1987, pp. 320–323, 553–555; Lee Berton, "An S&L in California Dumped Peat Marwick for Congenial Auditor," *The Wall*

Street Journal, May 9, 1989, pp. A1, A11; Conversation with William J. Crawford, 5/17/89.

15. U.S. House, Hearing, June 13, 1987, 456; U.S. House, House Report 100–1088, p. 149.

16. U.S. House, Hearing, June 13, 1987, 367, 427; Also see U.S. House, *Federal Response to Criminal Misconduct and Insider Abuse in the Nation's Financial Institutions,* 57th Report by the Committee on Government Operations, House Report 98–1137, 98th Cong., 2d Sess., October 4, 1984, p. 8.

17. Ibid., 135, 114–115; Also see U.S. General Accounting Office, *Bank and Thrift Criminal Fraud,* GAO/GGD-93-10FS, October 1992.

18. U.S. House, Hearing, *Federal Response to Criminal Misconduct by Bank Officers, Directors, and Insiders (Part 1),* Hearing before a Subcommittee of the Committee on Government Operations, 98th Cong., 1st Sess., June 28, 1983, p. 26.

19. U.S. House, Hearing, June 13, 1987, 456. Also 471–472, 482–486, 516–518; U.S. House Report 100–1088, pp. 95–101.

20. U.S. House, House Report 100–1088, October 13, 1988, pp. 84–85.

21. See U.S. Department of Justice, *United States Attorneys' Manual, Criminal Division, Title 9,* for details.

22. U.S. House, Hearings, Part 2, May 2 and 3, 1984, pp. 31–32.

23. Liz Galtney and Thomas Moore, "The Judicial Aftermath," *U.S. News & World Report,* January 23, 1989, 43; Kathleen Day, "S&L Fraud Seen Going Largely Unpunished," *The Washington Post,* February 4, 1989, p. A 14.

24. "Former Bank Chairman Sentenced to Prison," *Times,* Kerrville, Texas, July 21, 1989.

25. U.S. House, Hearing, November 19, 1987, pp. 1087–1088.

26. Pat Allen, "The Verdict's In: Crooks Are Out," *Savings Institutions,* March 1989, 36–42. Also see U.S. General Accounting Office, *Thrift Failures: Costly Failures Resulted from Regulatory Violations and Unsafe Practices,* GAO/AFMD-89-62, June 1989, pp. 52–53.

27. Some states are passing RICO laws. See Fred Strasser, "Rico and the Man," *The National Law Journal,* March 20, 1989, pp. 1, 34; Richard S. Dalebout and K. Fred Skousen, "RICO and Accountants," *CPA Journal,* August 1987, pp. 83–87. RICO is Title 18, Sect. 1962.

28. Federal Deposit Ins. Corp. v. Renda, 692 F. Supp. 128 (D. Kan. 1988).

29. FHLBB and FDIC Joint News Release, PR-42-89 (2-28-89).

3   BCCI—THE BANK OF CROOKS AND CRIMINALS INTERNATIONAL

It was an accident that Senator John Kerry learned about the Bank of Credit and Commerce International (BCCI). During the course of the 1988 Senate Subcommittee on Terrorism, Narcotics, and International Operations hearings involving drug smuggling, it was revealed that smugglers were using U.S. banks. BCCI was named as one of the principal banks used by General Manuel Noriega for laundering $23 million in drug money and for keeping it safe from those who might want to share in his wealth.[1]

Pandora's box was opened, and the secrets about BCCI started to trickle out. It moved slowly because U.S. Custom's sting Operation C-Chase was in progress. A Senate investigation at that time might have endangered the lives of undercover agents. In the years that followed, Senator Kerry learned that BCCI was a "drug-corrupted, money laundering bank which had, as a matter of corporate policy, the seeking out of drug money and other fast-moving funds...," and that BCCI "...surreptitiously entered the U.S. market and improperly took over at least two U.S. banks."[2] Moreover, at least $4 billion in capital is missing from BCCI. Part of the $4 billion included Treasury funds from more than 30 countries and the funds of more than 1 million depositors around the world.

Senator Hank Brown described BCCI as "...one of the smartest, deadliest, criminal organizations yet assembled. From the outside, it appeared to be full of successful bankers with impressive ties to some of the nation's most powerful leaders. No other law enforcement agency in the world had penetrated BCCI's guise when our Customs agents and Federal prosecutors in Tampa uncovered the bank's grisly depths."[3] Unfortunately, as Senator John Kerry pointed out, "Federal law enforcement officials handling the 1988 drug money laundering indictment of BCCI failed to recognize the importance of the information that they received concerning BCCI's other crimes...As a result, they failed to adequately investigate these allegations..."[4]

The History of BCCI

BCCI was founded by Agha Hasan Abedi, who grew up in northern India but fled to Pakistan shortly after the two countries were partitioned in 1947.[5] His father worked for the Rajah in northern India. It was at the Rajah's court that young Abedi learned two important lessons: First, access to wealth could be had by anyone who was indispensable to the person who controlled that wealth. Second, legal obstacles to any goal could be eliminated if they interfered with the plans of sufficiently important political figures. His connections with wealthy, influential political figures who were used to subvert laws were the cornerstones of his BCCI strategy.

One way to gain support of political figures was to bribe them. Bribes took many forms, including charitable contributions, payment of commissions, business expenses, soliciting business from BCCI, and so on. For example, Abedi donated millions of dollars to charitable activities supported by President Jimmy Carter. Other recipients of Abedi's funds included Secretary of the United Nations General Javier Perez de Cuellar, Ambassador to the United Nations Andrew Young, former director of the Office of Management and Budget T. Bertrum Lance, Jesse Jackson, and other dignitaries throughout the world.[6]

Abedi became a prominent figure in Pakistani banking. He organized United Bank, which became one of Pakistan's largest banks. United Bank had overseas branches in the Middle East and elsewhere. Applying the lessons that he had learned, his board of directors and employees included key political figureheads, and his customers were high net worth individuals.

The nationalization of banks in early 1970 limited United Bank's growth in Pakistan. It was time for Abedi to move. His goal was to have a global, Pakistani-managed bank located outside Pakistan. He chose Abu Dhabi to organize his new bank—BCCI. He needed five things to start BCCI:

1. *Secrecy:* Bank secrecy, which was found in Luxembourg and the Grand Caymans.

2. *Capital:* Bank of America loaned him $2.5 million, and owned 24 to 30 percent of the shares at different times. Sheik Zayed of Abu Dhabi invested $500,000. There appeared to be no other cash infusions into capital. BCCI was seriously undercapitalized.

3. *Deposits/assets of $100 million:* Sheik Zayed deposited at least $50 million. Sheik Zayed's family owned and ruled Abu Dhabi. The Sheik and other Middle East shareholders had "hold harmless" agreements from BCCI that insured against the loss of their investments or deposits.

Later growth was fueled by large infusions of petrodollars from the United Arab Emirates as oil prices soared. The average price per barrel of oil imported into the United States in 1972 was $1.80. In 1972, it rose to $12.52, and by 1981 it reached $35 per barrel. The profits earned by exporting oil caused a massive redistribution of world income from industrialized nations to oil exporting nations. Abu Dhabi was one of those nations that benefitted from the shift.

4. *Pakistanis to operate the bank:* Many qualified individuals were available as a result of the nationalization of banks. Swaleh Naqvi, a Pakistani, was BCCI's chief operating officer and co-conspirator.

5. *Credibility in the international community:* This was provided by his relationship with Bank of America.

BCCI became a reality in 1972. Abedi and Naqvi made it one of the fastest growing banks in Europe. By 1990, it was the seventh largest privately owned bank in the world, with $23 billion in assets. Because it was a private bank, the exact composition of the ownership was not known for many years. Nevertheless, it was controlled primarily by Middle Eastern investors. By 1990, the Sheik Zayed, his family, and the government of Abu Dhabi which he controlled, were the principal shareholders.

The parent holding company, BCCI (Holdings), was chartered in Luxembourg. The bank (BCC S.A.) was split into two parts: BCCI S.A. in Luxembourg, and BCCI S.A. (Overseas) in the Grand Cayman Islands. Neither BCCI nor its subsidiaries conducted banking business in Luxembourg. Instead, they used their London office for most of its Middle East and European operations. The office in Grand Cayman was used to conduct business in other countries. Collectively, BCCI operated in 73 countries. In the United States, it had agencies licensed in California, New York, and Florida. BCCI also had interests in other banks, and a commodities futures firm, Capcom Financial Services.

Capcom had offices in Chicago and London. It was used to launder billions of dollars from the Middle East to the rest of the world. Capcom was controlled by Saudi investors, including Sheiks Abdul Raouf Khalil and Kamal Adham. Both men were senior Saudi intelligence officials and relatives of the King. Moreover, both men acted as liaisons with the Central Intelligence Agency (CIA) for more than two decades.[7] General Noreiga was one of Capcom's better known clients.

BCCI made extensive use of multiple layers of entities, nominees, banks-within-banks, and other devices to shield its identity and operations from the scrutiny of government regulators. Because of its structure of organization, BCCI had no primary bank regulator supervising all of its operations. It was chartered in Luxembourg which, at that time, did not supervise bank holding companies which did no banking business in that country. Nevertheless, regulators in some of the countries in which it operated periodically examined their facilities. Equally important, BCCI had no central bank that acted as a lender of last resort to bail it out when it got into trouble. Therefore, it was essential for BCCI to appear to be profitable, even if that required manipulation of accounts and falsified reports—which it did.

Dealing with BCCI's criminal activity is a formidable task. The alleged crimes include fraud, money laundering, illegal purchase of banks, bribery, support of terrorism (i.e., Abu Nidal), arms trafficking including the financing and procurement of nuclear weapons and technologies for Pakistan, smuggling, management of prostitution, tax evasion, and more.[8] Former Senate investigator Jack Blum said that BCCI had "3,000 criminal customers and every one of those 3,000 criminal customers is a page-one story."[9] Blum went on to explain that BCCI was not really a bank. It was an international criminal enterprise that ran a Ponzi scheme. It used new depositors funds to pay expenses and to repay other depositors. It created a pyramid of mounting obligations that ultimately led to its collapse. Its success depended on asset growth and Abedi's charisma. He encouraged his employees to be aggressive and generate assets. They found ways to get around laws that impeded their growth. Abedi suffered a stroke in 1989, and it was the beginning of the end of BCCI.

This chapter focuses primarily on two aspects of BCCI's operations. It first examines how BCCI secretly got control of a major U.S. bank holding company and other banks. It then examines BCCI's role in laundering drug money, and how its aggressive policies contributed to it getting caught in a sting operation. Information about BCCI's other illegal activities is presented in Chapter 8 in connection with the Nigerians.

The Acquisition of First American Bankshares

In 1976, Abedi needed a foothold in the United States because Bank of America's relationship with BCCI was deteriorating. Bank of America sold its BCCI shares in 1980, but it continued to do business with BCCI until it was closed in 1991. Abedi wanted to obtain U.S. deposits to fuel the bank's growth and Ponzi scheme. But there were legal problems that he had to overcome. Because BCCI was a foreign bank, it could not accept deposits from U.S. citizens or become an FDIC insured bank. Equally important, because of Bank of America's equity interest in BCCI, it could not legally acquire a U.S. bank outside California. One way to get around the laws was to secretly acquire U.S. banks through nominees.

Abedi's first attempt was to buy Chelsea Bank, a national bank with a state-chartered holding company in New York. The nominee was a Pakistani national. He had no prior banking experience, and listed an annual income of $34,000. He also indicated that because of his lack of experience, he would be relying on BCCI for advice and counsel. The application was denied.

Spurned once, but not to be denied, Abedi tried again with a better qualified nominee. He was Ghaith Pharaon, a wealthy Saudi businessman whose secret partner in the ownership of the banks was BCCI. Supposedly, he studied at the Colorado School of Mines, Stanford University, and has a Harvard MBA. His acquisitions included National Bank of Georgia (Bert Lance's bank, 1978), Independence Bank in California (1985), and Cen-Trust in Florida (1989). Pharaon made Roy Carlson, a Bank of America officer based in Iran, president of the National Bank of Georgia.[10] Carlson had worked with Abedi for over a decade and maintained his relationship with him. National Bank of Georgia even financed Abedi's and other BCCI official's trips to the United States. Pharaon also placed a former senior BCCI officer in charge of the Independence bank. More will be said about Pharaon shortly.

Financial General Bankshares (FGB)

Financial General Bankshares (FGB) was a major bank holding company that Abedi wanted to control. It was one of the 50 largest bank holding companies in the United States and the largest in the Washington, D.C. area. FGB was a Virginia corporation that owned banks in Virginia, Maryland, Georgia, Tennessee, New York, and the District of Columbia.

In 1975, FGB sold controlling interest of National Bank of Georgia to Bert Lance for $7.8 million. National Bank of Georgia had problems in 1977, and Lance sold his shares to Ghaith Pharaon for $2.4 million. Lance also received $3.5 million from BCCI, which he used to repay a loan to the National Bank of Chicago and buy shares in FGB.[11] The sellers of the FGB stock did not know that BCCI was the secret buyer.

In 1977, a group of FGB shareholders discussed the sale of their shares with Abedi. He helped to arrange for four of BCCI's Middle Eastern clients to each purchase slightly less than 5 percent of the shares of FGB. Keeping the ownership under 5 percent was meant to circumvent Securities Exchange Commission disclosure rules and disguise the true nature of the transaction.

In February 1978, Lance announced at a stockholder's meeting that the BCCI group now controlled 20 percent of FGB's stock, and wanted even more. BCCI had failed to disclose their intentions as required by law. When the transaction was made public by the other stockholders, the Securities Exchange Commission (SEC) filed a complaint that the Middle Eastern Investors, BCCI, and other investors acting as a group had acquired more than 5 percent of the shares in violation of the Williams Act. In April

1978, the SEC issued a consent decree. The investors, without admitting guilt, agreed to divest their shares or make a tender offer for all of FGB's shares. The U.S. Court District Judge hearing the SEC complaint said that the investors relied heavily, if not exclusively, on Abedi and BCCI in deciding to purchase the bank's shares, and found that they had all acted as a group.

Commerce and Credit American Holdings (CCAH)

BCCI, on behalf of three of the original Middle Eastern investors and other clients, formed Credit and Commerce American Holdings, N.V. (CCAH), a Netherlands, Antilles holding company. They also formed Credit and Commerce American Investment, B.V. (CCAI) in the Netherlands as a subsidiary of CCAH. Both CCAH and CCAI were used to acquire shares of FGB.

In 1978, CCAH sought approval from the Federal Reserve Board for the acquisition; but it was denied because it was opposed by FGB and its subsidiary bank in Maryland where hostile bank takeovers are not allowed. Approval was denied.

In 1980, CCAH again applied to the Federal Reserve Board for approval to acquire FGB, but their tactics had changed. BCCI's modus operandi in 73 countries around the world was to hire well-respected and experienced lawyers, politicians, accountants, and public relations firms to accomplish their goals. Accordingly, the new board of directors of CCAH included former Senator and Presidential candidate Stuart Symington and former Secretary of Defense Clark Clifford, Robert Altman, and Retired General Elwood Quesada. The Middle Eastern investors promised to be passive and not take an active role in the management of FGB.[12]

Attorney Clark Clifford, and his law partner Robert Altman, represented BCCI from their first attempts to acquire FGB in 1978 through the late 1990s, including the indictment in Tampa for money laundering. Clark and Altman also represented Bert Lance and Ghaith Pharaon at various times. Both attorneys claimed that they were deceived by BCCI, and they denied any wrongdoing. However, a Senate Committee investigating BCCI found that even if they were deceived, both men had participated in some of BCCI's deceptions in the United States, withheld critical information they possessed about BCCI's ownership of First American, and concealed how BCCI financed their share ownership of First American.[13] Clifford and Altman's law firm received $17 million in legal fees from BCCI and its related entities for legal services rendered. In addition, BCCI paid $18.9 million to their firm in 1988 to defend them in the Tampa money laundering indictment. Finally, in 1986, 1987, and 1989, Clifford and Altman purchased $15 million in stock in CCAH. The stock purchase was financed by BCCI.[14] In 1988, Clifford and Altman sold some of their shares at three times the purchase price, realizing a gain of $11.3 million for Clifford and

$5.6 million for Altman. The stock was purchased by a front man for BCCI.

First American

Clark Clifford and Robert Altman made representations to the Federal Reserve Board that BCCI would not fund the acquisition. They went on to say that all holdings in CCAH constitute personal investments. Based on those representations and other information, the Federal Reserve Board approved the acquisition in August 1981. However, the acquisition was delayed pending approval from the New York State Banking Department who were involved because of FGB's New York banks. The acquisition was consummated in April 1982. In August 1982, Financial General Bankshares was renamed First American Bankshares. Clark Clifford was Chairman of the Board, Robert Altman was President. Stuart Symington became Chairman of the Board of CCAH in 1982. Altman was secretary and director.[15]

During the 1982-1990 period, investors added more than $12 million in capital to First American, and they received no cash dividends. Post 1990 bank examinations found no evidence of First American abusing its credit facilities for the benefit of BCCI or entities.[16]

Following BCCI's 1988 indictment for money laundering, the Federal Reserve Bank of Richmond examined the relationship between CCAH and BCCI in connection with CCAH's application to acquire a bank in Florida. First America purchased the Bank of Escambia, Florida. Their examinations could not substantiate any involvement between the two groups. Nevertheless, there was growing concern about the ties between BCCI and CCAH/First American. Later they discovered that First American had 40 accounts with BCCI.

Ghaith Pharaon

Abedi wanted to merge National Bank of Georgia into First American because of financial difficulties at the Georgia bank. It was generally understood that this was a consolidation of BCCI's activities in the United States. He arranged for CCAH to secretly buy Pharaon's shares in late 1986.[17] Pharaon received over $100 million for his shares.[18] Recall that a decade earlier, he had purchased them from Bert Lance for $2.4 million.

BCCI and Pharaon were also involved in the purchase of CenTrust, the largest State Savings Bank in Miami, Florida. In early 1987, Pharaon, BCCI, and CenTrust colluded to create a profitable market for CenTrust subordinated debentures which made CenTrust appear to be in better financial condition than it was. In 1988, $150 million of subordinated debentures was sold to investors. Drexel, Burnham, Lambert was the underwriter of the bond issue. Pharaon and BCCI arranged for a BCCI branch in Paris, France to purchase $25 million of the debentures, thereby artificially propping up their market price. CenTrust agreed to repurchase the bonds bought by BCCI. In August 1987, Pharaon filed a statement with the SEC that he had purchased just under 25 percent of CenTrust's stock. The legal definition of control is the ownership of 25 percent or more of the stock. Over the next two years he did acquire control. The acquisitions were secretly financed by BCCI, and they occurred at the same time that BCCI-Tampa was under indictment for laundering drug money.

CenTrust failed, and it cost the taxpayers hundreds of millions of dollars. The Office of Thrift Supervision issued a cease and desist order on December 9, 1989 because CenTrust was $223 million short of its tangible legal required capital and it had losses of $26 million. The OTS also cited substantial dissipation of assets, and unsafe and unsound banking practices. CenTrust had more than $30 million in artwork, oriental rugs, and crystal. The OTS also claimed that David Paul, the Chairman, received excessive and inappropriate levels of compensation. He received a $310,000 bonus in October 1989.[19]

Laundering Drug Money

It was no secret that BCCI was involved in money laundering. In 1983, the U.S. Customs service learned that a Jordanian arms dealer was one of the largest customers of BCCI's Miami office.[20] He used fraudulent bills of lading and cargo manifests to carry out a massive smuggling operation. BCCI issued phony letters of credit to finance the smuggling.

A Colombian drug trafficker told a Senate Subcommittee that everyone who was in the drug trade knew about BCCI-Panama.[21] They all used it. The bank's officers were very attentive, and if the drug trafficker's deposits were frozen at the request of the United States, BCCI would make sure you got your money back. He spoke from experience. After his deposits were frozen, his Panamanian attorney told him that if he was willing to give up 10 percent of the amount frozen as bribes, the funds would be released. The drug trafficker agreed, and the Attorney General of Panama ordered the impounded fund to be released.

General Manuel Noriega was a customer of the bank, too. In 1982, he opened an account there in the name of the Panamanian Defense Forces, but he had sole control of the account. He also had a VISA account with the bank. Noriega laundered some of his drug money through BCCI. His daughter was hired by BCCI-Miami, were she learned banking BCCI style. Noriega was indicted by a federal grand jury in Miami in March 1988 on laundering drug money and conspiracy charges. Colombian drug kingpin Rodriguez Gacha was another BCCI customer. He had $90 million of his funds in BCCI accounts seized by the Drug Enforcement Agency.[22]

A May 1987 Federal Reserve examination of BCCI's Miami office found money laundering activities. The Federal Reserve made criminal referrals to the U.S. Attorney in Miami, the Federal Bureau of Investigation, and the Internal Revenue Service. Examinations of other BCCI offices in the United States revealed additional money laundering activities.

Sting Operation

In December 1986, two undercover U.S. Customs agents, who were part of a sting operation (Operation C-Chase) that was trying to trace the flow of cocaine proceeds from the United States to South America, formed a partnership with a Colombian money launderer from Medellin.[23] About $200 million in currency per month needed to be laundered out of the United States. The money launderer would notify the agents when large sums of drug money were available for pick-up. The agents deposited about $33 million in cash for the Colombians at various U.S. banks that were cooperating with the government. Then the agents transferred the funds to bank accounts that they had established in St. Petersburg, Florida. About $16 million was laundered through BCCI, and the remainder through other banks.[24]

When the Colombian money launderer requested the funds, the agents would send a check for the correct amount to Colombia. There, the checks were sold on the black market. The money launderer demanded that the agents set up an account in Panama, because checks drawn on Panamanian banks sold at a higher price on the black market than checks drawn on U.S. banks. The agents opened an account at BCCI in Panama City, Panama. BCCI was chosen because it had a branch in Tampa, Florida which facilitated the transfers.

An alert officer at BCCI's Panama City branch discovered the laundering in the account set up by the undercover customs agent. He phoned the agent in charge and said: "I see that you are moving a lot of money through your account; I think you're laundering money; and I think I can help you do it more efficiently."[25] He suggested that they meet in Miami to discuss how BCCI, being a full-service bank, could help the agent's business. The bank officer suggested that the agent stop using checking accounts to transfer funds because many checking accounts had been seized by U.S. drug agents. Instead, he suggested that the funds be sent by wire transfers to buy certificates of deposit at the Panama City branch of BCCI, or at BCCI Luxembourg or in the Middle East. The CDs could be used to collateralize loans for the same amount to a firm in Europe. Then the European firm could loan funds to the drug dealers. This scheme allowed the drug dealers to obtain their funds from a legitimate source and the agent to have greater secrecy. Since the original CD would remain in Panama, it would increase BCCI's deposit base. (This scheme for laundering money is sometimes called a back-to-back loan.) Alternatively, the CD could be used to back a letter of credit issued to some other corporation. The funds asso-

ciated with the letter of credit could be transferred to one of the two Colombian bank branches in Panama City that were used by the drug traffickers. The agent took the officer's suggestions and was introduced to other
high-ranking BCCI officers in Miami, London, and Paris. At one of those
meetings, the agent—a top BCCI official—discussed the fact that the funds
were being laundered for Colombian cocaine dealers.[26]

The records of the CDs and the back-to-back loans underlying much
of the illegal activities were located in Panama, Luxembourg, Switzerland,
and other countries utilized by BCCI. They were shielded by bank secrecy
laws from U.S. regulators. Had the undercover customs agent not been an
"insider" in these transactions, the government may not have been able to
make its case. The investigation culminated on October 11, 1988, when an
indictment was issued against BCCI (Holdings, Luxembourg), BCCI, S. A.,
and Bank of Credit and Commerce (Overseas), and five officers in its
Tampa, Florida agency. Simultaneous examinations revealed laundering of
drug money at other BCCI offices. BCCI and the two operating subsidiaries pleaded guilty to money laundering in January 1990, and BCCI made a
forfeiture of $15 million. The officers were imprisoned, without parole, for
terms of 3-12 years. On October 10, 1988, a Grand Jury in Tampa indicted
Capcom, the BCCI related Chicago-based commodities firm that laundered
money.

The Florida Comptroller of Banks refused to renew BCCI's agency
license, and its Florida offices were closed. On June 12, 1989, the Federal
Reserve issued a cease and desist order to BCCI (Holdings).

The Chronology of Criminal Investigations and Audits

During the Tampa investigation of money laundering in December 1988,
one of the defendants told an undercover agent that he thought BCCI
owned National Bank of Georgia and other American banks.[27] The information was passed on to the Federal Reserve. It provided no direct evidence because it was only a rumor. Nevertheless, the Federal Reserve
persisted in investigating BCCI and its links to American banks, including
First American. In the previous year, the Federal Reserve had discovered
BCCI's money laundering activities.

In 1989, New York County District Attorney Robert M. Morgenthau
began conducting a criminal investigation of BCCI that was instrumental in
its closure. In November 1990, the District Attorney found the critical financial link between BCCI and First American bank. It was a report prepared by BCCI's external auditor revealing that BCCI had made loans to
CCAH shareholders. More than $1 billion in nonperforming loans were
secured by CCAH stock. In fact, BCCI owned CCAH in violation of the
Bank Holding Company Act. This was the first solid evidence that the

Federal Reserve had, in addition to information received from a foreign bank supervisor concerning loans from BCCI to CCAH shareholders.

BCCI had concealed its ownership at the time of its 1980 application to acquire FGB. BCCI and their nominee investors had secretly done what they promised in writing and in testimony to the Federal Reserve that they would not do—they owned and controlled FGB, which was renamed First American Bankshares, and they repeatedly filed false reports with the Federal Reserve. Following an investigation, the Federal Reserve Board issued cease and desist orders requiring BCCI to divest its interest in CCAH and other bank stocks, ensuring that BCCI had sufficient assets to cover the liabilities in its U.S. agencies, and to leave the country.

Price Waterhouse U.K. was one of two BCCI auditors, and Ernst & Whinney was the other. Neither firm had access to all of their operations. Ernst & Whinney withdrew in 1986, leaving Price Waterhouse U.K. as the principal auditor the following year. However, Price Waterhouse was not given access to all of BCCI's affiliates, or to documents involving the guarantees against losses to selected shareholders. The compartmentalization of banking functions and audits assured secrecy of the bank's various activities.

In 1990, Price Waterhouse U.K. found that BCCI's financial position was precarious. Price Waterhouse U.K. had "advised the directors that there were uncertainties over the recoverability of a number of major loans..." and stressed the need for restructuring BCCI.[28] It also found "false and deceitful" financial transactions that BCCI had booked in the Caymans. It was recognized that BCCI had to be closed or restructured. The report was sent to the Bank of England. This was not the first warning that the Bank of England had about BCCI. A House of Commons Treasury and Civil Service Committee concluded that the Bank of England was aware of problems as far back as the 1970s.[29] There were numerous allegations and accusations at that time, but nothing was done to investigate them.

An agreement was reached between the Bank of England, Sheik Zayed and the government of Abu Dhabi, which owned 77 percent of BCCI's stock, to keep the bank from collapsing. The Sheik and Abu Dhabi were going to inject more capital. The Bank of England allowed BCCI to move its headquarters, officers, and records to Abu Dhabi in April 1990. In addition, the Bank of England kept BCCI's condition secret from its creditors and depositors so that it could be restructured and new capital could be injected.

In 1991, Price Waterhouse U.K. advised the Bank of England about BCCI's loan losses, poor banking practices, and widespread fraud and manipulation. U.S. investigators wanted to obtain the audits. However, Price Waterhouse U.K. was not permitted under English law to disclose the audits without permission of the Bank of England, which it did not grant.

Therefore, some critical information about BCCI was not available to New York County District Attorney Robert M. Morgenthau's investigation.

The Bank of England thought that District Attorney Morgenthau's investigation was going to result in an indictment which might cause a run on BCCI by its depositors. That possibility, combined with the information received from Price Waterhouse U.K. in June 1991, were among the key factors that the Bank of England considered when it closed BCCI on July 5, 1991. Bank regulators in other countries closed BCCI globally at the same time.

When the Bank of England closed BCCI, it criticized the auditing process because it let the fraud and poor management practices continue to exist for years before it was addressed in the 1990-1991 reports. Price Waterhouse U.K. claimed that BCCI deceived and mislead them.

On July 8, 1991, a court in Luxembourg disclosed that BCCI had lost more than its entire net worth. Recall that BCCI was a Ponzi scheme, and there was not much net worth at any time. A Price Waterhouse U.K. report stated that BCCI may never have been profitable in its entire history.[30]

On July 12, 1991, the Federal Reserve took enforcement actions against BCCI's illegal acquisition of Independence Bank. Abedi and Naqvi were named in the action. Later in July, additional actions were taken in connection with BCCI's other illegal banking activities in the United States.[31]

On July 29, 1991, an indictment was issued in New York County charging that BCCI was an international criminal organization that stole funds from poor countries and small depositors. Those funds were used to keep BCCI afloat. According to District Attorney Morgenthau, BCCI was a Ponzi scheme that "...relied on the reputations of prominent people to provide it with the aura of wealth and respectability it needed."[32]

Indictments

On July 29, 1991, a New York County grand jury returned an indictment against BCCI, Agha Hassan Abedi, and Swaleh Naqvi, the bank's chief operating officer until October 1990. Naqvi was instrumental in BCCI's criminal activities. The top count of the indictment, Grand Larceny in the First Degree, exposed Abedi and Naqvi to terms in prison up to 25 years. Abedi had moved to Pakistan, and Naqvi was in Abu Dhabi.

In November 1991, the principals mentioned in connection with BCCI, including Abedi, Naqvi, Ghaith Pharaon, and others were indicted in the District of Columbia for the sham purchase of $25 million of CenTrust securities. That indictment was superseded in May 1992 with additional charges including racketeering and fraud in secretly acquiring banks. Pharaon's whereabouts were unknown.

In January 1992, New York County District Attorney Morgenthau agreed to BCCI's forfeiture of all of its assets in the United States—about $550 million.

In July 1992, Clark Clifford and Robert Altman were indicted in the District of Columbia on charges of conspiring to defraud the Board of Governors of the Federal Reserve System and for concealing material facts in connection with their investigation of BCCI. In New York they were indicted in connection with BCCI's takeover of First American. The Justice Department dropped its charges to allow New York State to try them. A New York judge dismissed state charges against Clifford, age 86, because of his poor health. Altman was acquitted of state charges.

Kamal Adham, who was charged with acquiring shares of First American as a nominee of BCCI, paid a civil money penalty of $10 million and $3 million to reimburse investigative costs. He has been barred from banking in the United States.[33]

By the end of 1993, $225 million had been paid to New York, and the District Attorney Robert Morgenthau's probe into BCCI continued.[34]

In January 1994, an agreement was reached with Abu Dhabi officials to extradite Naqvi to face criminal charges in the United States.[35] Part of the agreement was to drop civil racketeering charges and a $1.5 billion lawsuit brought by the trustee for First American against Sheik Zayed, the ruler of Abu Dhabi who in later years owned BCCI. Furthermore, in the agreement the Sheik agreed to drop claims of $400 million that the government of Abu Dhabi had invested in First American. First American was sold to First Union Corp., Charlotte, North Carolina, in 1993.

The Government of Abu Dhabi agreed to pay $1.8 billion to the liquidators of BCCI to head off additional lawsuits from creditors. They also waived claims for funds it had invested or deposited in BCCI.

In July 1994, Swaleh Naqvi admitted responsibility for $25 million of BCCI's losses in the United States. In a plea bargaining agreement, he was expected to receive a sentence of six to nine years. New York District Attorney Robert Morgenthau, who pushed for vigorous prosecution of the case, called the deal too lenient.

Spokesmen for the Federal Reserve told a Congressional committee "...that one of the best ways to deter the kind of fraud that occurred at BCCI is through criminal punishment that sends a loud and clear signal to would-be offenders."[36] What kind of signal did we send?

References

Herring, Richard, "BCCI: Lessons for International Bank Supervision," *Contemporary Policy Issues,* April 1993, 76-86.

U.S. House, *The Bank of Credit and Commerce International (BCCI) Investigation-Part 1,* Hearing before the Committee on Banking, Finance and Urban Affairs, 102, Cong., 1st. Sess., September 11, 1991. Serial No. 102-69.

U.S. House, *The Bank of Credit and Commerce International (BCCI) Investigation-Part 2,* Hearing before the Committee on Banking, Finance and Urban Affairs, 102, Cong., 1st. Sess., September 13, 1991. Serial No 102-69.

U.S. House, *The Bank of Credit and Commerce International (BCCI) Investigation-Part 1,* Hearing before the Committee on Banking, Finance and Urban Affairs, 102, Cong., 1st. Sess., September 27, 1991, Serial No. 102-69

U.S. Senate, *The Bank of Credit and Commerce International and S. 1019,* Hearing before the Subcommittee on Consumer Affairs and Regulatory Affairs of the Committee on Banking, Housing, and Urban Affairs, 102nd Cong., 1st Sess., May 23, 1991. S. Hrg. 102-379.

U.S. House, *Federal Efforts to Combat Fraud, Abuse, and Misconduct in the Nation's S&L's and Banks and to Implement the Criminal and Civil Enforcement Provisions of FIREEA,* Hearings before the Commerce, Consumer, and Monetary Affairs Subcommittee of the Committee on Government Operations, 101 Cong., 2nd Sess., March 14 and 15, 1990.

U.S. Senate, *The BCCI Affair,* A Report to the Committee on Foreign Relations by Senators John Kerry and Hank Brown, 102 Cong., 2nd Sess., December 1992, S. Prt. 102-140.

U.S. Senate, *The BCCI Affair,* Hearings before the Subcommittee on Terrorism, Narcotics, and International Operations of the Committee on Foreign Relations, 102 Cong., 1st. Sess., Part 1, August 1, 2, and 8, 1991, S. Hrg. 102-350 Pt. 1.

U.S. Senate, *The BCCI Affair,* Hearings before the Subcommittee on Terrorism, Narcotics, and International Operations of the Committee on Foreign Relations, 102 Cong., 1st. Sess., Part 2, October 18 and 22, 1991, S. Hrg. 102-350 Pt. 2.

U.S. Senate, *The BCCI Affair,* Hearings before the Subcommittee on Terrorism, Narcotics, and International Operations of the Committee on Foreign Relations, 102 Cong., 1st. Sess., Part 3, October 23, 24, 25 and November 21, 1991, S. Hrg. 102-350 Pt. 3.

U.S. Senate, *The BCCI Affair,* Hearings before the Subcommittee on Terrorism, Narcotics, and International Operations of the Committee on Foreign Relations, 102 Cong., 2nd Sess., Part 4, February 19, and March 18, 1992, S. Hrg. 102-350 Pt. 4.

U.S. Senate, *The BCCI Affair,* Hearings before the Subcommittee on Terrorism, Narcotics, and International Operations of the Committee on Foreign Relations, 102 Cong., 2nd Sess., Part 5, May 14, 1992, S. Hrg. 102-350 Pt. 5.

U.S. Senate, *The BCCI Affair,* Hearings before the Subcommittee on Terrorism, Narcotics, and International Operations of the Committee on Foreign Relations, 102 Cong., 2nd Sess., Part 6, July 30, 1992, S. Hrg. 102-350 Pt. 2.

U.S. Senate, *The Bank of Credit and Commerce International and S. 1019,* Hearing before the Subcommittee on Consumer and Regulatory Affairs of the Committee on Banking, Housing, and Urban Affairs, 102nd Cong., 1st. Sess., May 23, 1991, S. Hrg. 102-379.

Endnotes

1. U.S. Senate, *The Bank of Credit and Commerce International and S. 1019,* Hearing before the Subcommittee on Consumer and Regulatory Affairs of the Committee on Banking, Housing, and Urban Affairs, 102nd Cong., 1st Sess., May 23, 1991, S. Hrng., 102–379, p. 3.; U.S. Senate, *The BCCI Affair,* A Report to the Committee on Foreign Relations by Senators John Kerry and Hank Brown, December 1992, 224–225. Also see Robert E. Powis, *The Money Launderers,* Chicago: Probus Publishing Co., 1992, pp. 129–143. Senator Kerry's staff was informed in 1987 about General Noriega's connection with the Colombian cocaine cartel.

2. *Ibid.,* U.S. Senate, *The Bank of Credit and Commerce International and S. 1019,* p. 3.

3. *Ibid.,* U.S. Senate, *The BCCI Affair,* Report, 189.

4. *Ibid.,* U.S. Senate, *The BCCI Affair,* Report, 188.

5. The history of BCCI is well documented in U.S. Senate, *The BCCI Affair,* Report, 23–46.

6. *Ibid.,* U.S. Senate, *The BCCI Affair,* Report, 64–65, 484–491.

7. *Ibid.,* U.S. Senate, *The BCCI Affair,* Report, 567–599, 692. Capcom used "mirror image" trading to launder some of its funds. That involves buying contracts for one account and selling an equal number from another account. Because both accounts are controlled by the same individual, the profit or loss is netted. It is almost impossible to find these transactions buried in the millions of legitamate transactions that occur daily. Sheik Adham was involved in scandals in the 1970s involving Boeing Aircraft and the receipt of bribes. Ibid., U.S. House, *Bank of Credit and Commerce International (BCCI) Investigation-Part 1,* 65, 231, 659. Khalil and Adahm were shareholders in BCCI and Commerce and Credit American Holdings (CCAH).

8. U.S. Senate, *The BCCI Affair,* A Report to the Committee on Foreign Relations by Senators John Kerry and Hank Brown, December 1992, 1, 47–73.

9. *Ibid.,* U.S. Senate, *The BCCI Affair,* Report, 49.

10. *Ibid.,* U.S. Senate, *The BCCI Affair,* Report, 8, 123, 135, 137, 161–162.

11. *Ibid.,* U.S. Senate, *The BCCI Affair,* Report, 135.

12. Other notables associated with BCCI's strategy of using prominent individuals include: former Senator John Culver; former White House aid Ed Rogers; former federal prosecutors Lawrence Wechsler, Raymond Banoun, and Lawrence Barcell; former Federal Reserve attorneys Baldwin Tuttle and John Hawke; former State Department Official William Rogers; Presidential Campaign Director James Lake; Bert Lance, and former President Carter. *Ibid.,* U.S. Senate, *The BCCI Affair,* Report, 11, 12, 136. Also see: *Ibid.,* U.S. House, *Bank of Credit and Commerce International (BCCI) Investigation-Part 1,* 644.

13. *Ibid.,* U.S. Senate, *The BCCI Affair,* Report, 369, 404, 408.

14. U.S. House, *Bank of Credit and Commerce International (BCCI) Investigation-Part 1,* Hearing before the Committee on Banking, Finance and Urban Affairs, 102 Cong., 1st. Sess., Serial No. 102–69, Sept. 11, 1991, 3, 31–33. Clifford argued that the profit was justified by the fact that the bank he chaired grew in assets from $3 billion to $11 billion, and his salary was only $50,000 per year, far below the going rate.

15. U.S. Senate, *The Bank of Credit and Commerce International and S. 1019,* Hearing before the Subcommittee on Consumer and Regulatory Affairs of the Committee on Banking, Housing, and Urban Affairs, 102nd Cong., 1st Sess., May 23, 1991, S. Hrng. 102–379, p. 85.

16. Testimony of J. Virgil Mattingly, Jr., General Counsel, Board of Governors of the Federal Reserve System, before the U.S. Senate, Subcommittee on Terrorism, Narcotics, and International Operations, May 14, 1992.

17. In 1981, Pharaon formed a holding company in which he owned National Bank of Georgia and had a cost-sharing arrangement with BCCI. The name of the holding company was changed to NGB Financial Corporation. It was those shares that CCAH/BCCI purchased.

18. *Ibid.,* U.S. Senate, *The BCCI Affair,* Report, 171.

19. U.S. House, *Federal Efforts to Combat Fraud, Abuse, and Misconduct in the Nation's S&Ls and Banks and to Implement the Criminal and Civil Enforcement Provisions of FIREEA,* Hearings before the Commerce, Consumer, and Monetary Affairs Subcommittee of the Committee on Government Operations 101 Cong., 2nd Sess., March 14 and 15, 1990, pp. 485, 556.

20. U.S. House, *Federal Law Enforcement's Handling of Allegations Involving the Bank of Credit and Commerce International,* Staff Report, Subcommittee on Crime and Criminal Justice of the Committee on the Judicial, 102 Cong., 1st Sess., September 5, 1991, p. 3.

21. *Ibid.,* U.S. Senate, *The BCCI Affair,* Report, 107.

22. *Ibid.,* U.S. House, *Federal Law Enforcement's Handling of Allegations Involving the Bank of Credit and Commerce International,* Staff Report, 12.

23. *Ibid.,* U.S. Senate, *The Bank of Credit and Commerce International and S. 1019,* pp. 215–225; *Ibid.,* Robert E. Powis, *The Money Launderers,* Chapter 6, provides a detailed account of Operation C-Chase.

24. U.S. Senate, *The BCCI Affair,* Hearings before the Subcommittee on Terrorism, Narcotics, and International Operations of the Committee on Foreign Relations, 102 Cong., 1st Sess., Oct. 23, 24, and 25, and Nov. 21, 1991, Part 3, S. Hrg. 102–350, Pt. 3, p. 722.

25. *Ibid.,* U.S. Senate, *The BCCI Affair,* Hearings, Part 3, S. Hrg. 102–350, Pt. 3, p. 722.

26. *Ibid.,* Robert E. Powis, *The Money Launderers,* pp. 214–215.

27. *Ibid.,* U.S. Senate, *The BCCI Affair,* Report 230; Testimony of J. Virgil Mattingly, Jr., William Taylor, and E. Gerald Corrigan, Federal Reserve System, before the U.S. House, Committee on Banking, Finance, and Urban Affairs, September 13, 1991, p. 29.

28. The Bank of England allowed BCCI to move its headquarters, officers, and records to Abu Dhabi in April 1990. One consequence of this move was to shield records and individuals from criminal investigation. Hearing before the Subcommittee on Terrorism, Narcotics, and International Operation of the Committee on Foreign Relations, 102nd Cong., 1st Sess., Aug. 1, 2, and 3, 1991, Part 1, S. Hrg. 102–350, Pt. 1, 481.

29. *Ibid.,* U.S. Senate, *The BCCI Affair,* Report, 359.

30. *Ibid.,* U.S. House, *Bank of Credit and Commerce International (BCCI) Investigation-Part 1,* 695, 762.

31. Testimony of J. Virgil Mattingly, Jr., General Counsel, Board of Governors of the Federal Reserve System, before the U.S. Senate, Subcommittee on Terrorism, Narcotics, and International Operations, May 14, 1992.

32. *Ibid.,* U.S. Senate, *The BCCI Affair,* Report, 249.

33. Statement of J. Virgil Mattingly, Jr., General Counsel, Board of Governors of the Federal Reserve System, before the U.S. House Committee on Banking, Finance, and Urban Affairs, Dec. 9, 1993.

34. "$225 Million Paid in BCCI Settlement," *American Banker,* Dec. 28, 1993, p. 4.; "BCCI: Justice May Finally Prevail, " *Business Week,* January 31, 1994, p. 59.

35. Joe Davidson, "Pact with Abu Dhabi in BCCI Scandal Is to Deliver Prime Suspect to the U.S.," *The Wall Street Journal,* January 10, 1994.

36. Testimony of J. Virgil Mattingly, Jr., William Taylor, and E. Gerald Corona, Federal Reserve System before the U.S. House, Committee on Banking, Finace, and Urban Affairs, Sept. 13, 1991, p. 9.

4 THE BANCA NAZIONALE DEL LAVORO (BNL)[1]

The Largest Bank Fraud in History

The largest bank fraud in history occurred at the Atlanta, Georgia branch of Banca Nazionale Del Lavoro (BNL-Rome, Italy), the largest state-owned commercial bank in Italy and one of the largest banks in the world. In 1989, BNL-Rome was the 36th largest bank in the world, with total assets of $104.4 billion. At the end of 1991, it ranked 37th, with total assets of $131 billion. In the United States, BNL-Rome operates offices in New York, Chicago, Los Angeles, Miami and Atlanta (BNL-Atlanta). From 1985-1989, more than $4 billion in secret and unauthorized loans were made at the BNL-Atlanta branch office for the benefit of Iraq.[2] To put the $4 billion in secret unauthorized loans in perspective, that amounts to about $267 for each of the 15 million people in Iraq.

About $2 billion of the loans were for agricultural purposes, most of which were guaranteed by the U.S. Department of Agriculture's Commodity Credit Corporation (CCC). An additional $2.155 billion was earmarked for the purchase of Western equipment, technology, and know-how through a secret procurement network of companies and individuals worldwide that were front companies and agents for Iraq.[3] The *Iraq procurement network* was used to acquire chemical, biological, nuclear, and missile development programs. Similarly, arms dealers bought the know-how to produce cluster bombs so that they too could be produced in Iraqi factories. The Iraq procurement network gained control of Matrix-Churchill Corporation, a Cleveland, Ohio based machine tool company, and its affiliate in England. Safa al-Habobi, Chairman of Matrix-Churchill, was a member of the Iraqi secret police. The company produced computer controlled lathes that can be used in the production of armaments. Matrix-Churchill was directly involved in the Iraqi ballistic missile program. The program to produce the "Condor" missile was called Project 395 by the Iraqis. The Condor was capable of carrying a conventional, chemical or nuclear warhead of 500 kilograms (1,100 lbs) up to 1,000 kilometers (625 miles). Through its dealings with that company, BNL-Atlanta provided $100 million for Project 395.[4]

The availability of more than $4 billion from BNL-Atlanta increased Iraq's credit capacity, which facilitated the purchase of arms that they used in the eight-year Iran-Iraq War, (which ended in the summer of 1988) and in the Gulf War. After the Iran-Iraq War, Iraq was the preeminent military power in the Persian Gulf. The Bush administration wanted to maintain and improve relations with Iraq. This relationship included $5 billion in credit guarantees between 1983-1990 to purchase U.S. agricultural products. Then, on August 1, 1990, Iraq invaded Kuwait. President Bush ordered the use of armed forces on January 16, 1991, and the Gulf War began.

Pietro Lombardi, Executive Vice President and Regional Manager for BNL in New York, which is responsible for North American operations, testified before Congress that although the transactions made by the Atlanta branch were unauthorized by BNL-Rome or New York, they were not illegal or in any way inconsistent with the policy of the United States.[5] The U.S. Department of Justice thought otherwise. The FBI raided BNL-Atlanta in August 1989. On February 28, 1991, a grand jury indicted three employees of BNL-Atlanta, the Rafidain Bank, four Iraqi officials, Entrade International, Ltd., in New York, and its manager. Entrade is an indirectly owned subsidiary of the Enka Holding Investment Company, a Turkish firm that is one of the most powerful firms in the world. Enka subsidiaries had extensive dealings with Iraq. The 347-count indictment charged the defendants with a scheme to defraud BNL-Rome by causing BNL-Atlanta to make about $4 billion in secret unauthorized loans, principally for the benefit of Iraq.[6] The loans were in contravention to BNL-Rome's policies; they were made to uncreditworthy borrowers, and in unacceptable loan concentrations that exceeded U.S. and Italian government limits for safety and soundness. Moreover, the indictment charged that the loans were hidden from BNL-Rome, and that false documents were supplied to the auditors and U.S. government agencies. Of the ten defendants charged, two of the BNL-Atlanta officials and Entrade pleaded guilty, and BNL-Atlanta's manager and vice president, Christopher P. Drogoul, went to trial. The remainder were fugitives (in 1992).[7]

The charges against Drogoul included conspiracy, mail and wire fraud, making false statements, interstate transportation of stolen property, trading with an enemy (financing the sale of Cuban sugar to Venezuela), money laundering, forgery, obstruction, and tax evasion. On June 2, 1992, Drogoul pleaded guilty to 60 felony counts, which carried a maximum penalty of 390 years in prison, millions of dollars in fines, and restitution of $1.8 billion. When the Clinton Administration took office, the Justice Department and the court reduced the indictment to 70 counts. In September 1992, Drogoul pleaded guilty to three counts including wire fraud and making false statements to federal regulators. The wire fraud included fraudulent representations in writings and signals sent to BNL-Rome to obtain their funds. The false statements count concerned the right of the

United States to examine foreign banks, and require truthful periodic reports from those banks. Drogoul's reports about the asset size of his branch bank to the Federal Reserve and to other government agencies did not accurately reflect the secret unauthorized loans. On December 9, 1993, Drogoul was sentenced to 37 months in prison. Counting the 20 months he had spent in prison awaiting trial, and with time off for good behavior, his total time in jail will be about 30 months. That amounts to $133.3 million in unauthorized loans for every month he served in jail.

Iraq defaulted on its external debts after the Gulf War. Consequently, BNL-Rome Italy estimated its losses to be $1.9 billion. BNL-Atlanta's $1 billion worth of U.S. Department of Agriculture CCC guaranteed loans made to Iraq are in default, and the Export-Import Bank stands to loose about $50 million.[8] U.S. taxpayers stand behind these loans.

How Did It Happen? Simple as A, B, and C.

The indictment and lawsuits involving the scandal included charges that BNL-Atlanta made secret unauthorized loans to Iraq government entities, private entities in Iraq, and to other entities in the United States and in other countries. BNL-Atlanta also participated in the U.S. Department of Agriculture's CCC programs in excess of levels approved by BNL-Rome. It engaged in other unauthorized activities, including purporting to commit BNL to fund various commodity exports to foreign countries, secured only by the commodities shipped, agreeing to discount drafts under letters of credit issued by commercial banks at below market rates, and more.[9] For example, Iraq was charged a commission of 0.2 percent instead of being charged 15 percent as a poor credit risk.

BNL-Atlanta did not have authority to make loans in excess of $500,000 per customer, or $2.5 million in the aggregate, without BNL-Rome/New York's approval, even if the transaction was fully collateralized by cash. Nevertheless, since 1986, BNL-Atlanta had been lending more than its limit to Iraqi government-owned Rafidain Bank. Most of the $2.14 billion loans to Rafidain were under the U.S. Department of Agriculture's Commodity Credit Corporation's (CCC) programs. There were also loans extended to the Central Bank of Iraq and to the Ministry of Industry and Trade that were supposed to be used to finance industrialization.

To distinguish the means by which the secret funds for the benefit of Iraq would be disbursed, BNL-Atlanta devised options A, B, and C.

Option A. The Central Bank of Iraq (CBI), acting on behalf of various Iraqi government ministries, telexed the requests for letters of credit from Baghdad to BNL-Atlanta. BNL-Atlanta confirmed more than $809 million in letters of credit to CBI, to pay designated amounts to exporters identified in the letters of credit.

Option B. BNL-Atlanta disbursed about $693 million on the basis of telex requests from CBI on behalf of the Iraq government to pay for goods with limited descriptions and no supporting documentation. The disbursements were made through clearing accounts maintained by CBI. The use of the clearing accounts concealed BNL-Atlanta as the source of funds and the identities of the recipients.

Option C. BNL-Atlanta disbursed more than $107 million on the basis of telephone instructions from Raja Hassan Ali, acting on behalf of the Iraq Ministry of Industry and Military Production. These disbursements were also made through clearing accounts.

To disguise BNL-Atlanta as a secret source of funds for Iraq, the bank would telex Morgan Guarantee Trust Company in New York and instruct them to deposit those funds in Iraqi bank accounts at Manufacturers Hanover Trust, Irving Trust Company, Bankers Trust Company, and Chase Manhattan Bank.[10]

Option A resulted in a lot of paperwork and questions from other BNL branches. Options B and C reduced the paperwork and the likelihood of BNL-Atlanta being linked to Iraqi financing.

BNL-Atlanta also secretly made $88 million in standby letters of credit on behalf of companies exporting to Iraq, $300 million for firms exporting elsewhere, and more than $500 million in uncollateralized, low-interest commercial loans. For example, BNL-Atlanta made commercial loans to Entrade that were supported by illusory collateral. In addition, BNL-Atlanta also financed Entrade's sale of agriculture and consumer goods to Iraqi buyers. The sales to Iraq were financed by letters of credit issued by Rafidain Bank. Then BNL-Atlanta purchased the time-drafts drawn on the letters of credit, thereby financing Entrade's Iraqi sales. As part of the scheme, Entrade kicked back $8 million to Drogoul and others by transferring the funds to accounts controlled by him in Luxembourg and elsewhere.[11] Drogoul wire transferred $60,000 from Luxembourg to his Atlanta architect as a partial payment for renovating his house. Entrade also paid the architect $35,000 for Drogoul's benefit. More will be said about the payments for renovation shortly. Entrade also paid $53,708 unauthorized travel, entertainment, and other non-bank related expenses of BNL-Atlanta employees, which Drogoul had the bank improperly reimburse to Entrade.

Allegedly, Drogoul told BNL-Atlanta employees that he had BNL-Rome's approval to make the secret loans. Nevertheless, records of those loans were kept in a secret set of accounts, called the "grey book." The grey book consisted of computer records of the unauthorized Iraq transactions that were kept separate from authorized transactions. At first, BNL-Atlanta made false entries in their books and records to make it appear that authorized credits were extended to such parties, whereas in fact the loans were extended to parties whose identities were not disclosed. Later, BNL-Atlanta created bogus documentation, including faxes, invoices, and money confirmations. A fax machine was kept in the house of one of the co-conspirators to transmit bogus documents. Employees would keep hard copy records of the secret transactions in "floating banker's boxes," and moved them back and forth from their homes and cars to the bank as they were needed.[12] Most of the work on the secret transactions, including the funding, was conducted from the employee's homes. All boxes and computer records were removed from the bank prior to examinations and audits. Needless to say, the secret unauthorized loans were not included in reports submitted to the Federal Reserve or other government agencies, nor were the millions of dollars in profits reported to the Internal Revenue Service.[13]

In addition, it was alleged that some exporters inflated the value of commodities sent to Iraq under the CCC program so that kick-backs (more than $1 million) could be paid to Drogoul and BNL-Atlanta personnel, and that the CCC guaranteed loans contained guarantees for payments of "after-sales services," which is contrary to CCC regulations and U.S. law.[14] The after-sales service contracts were used to buy various types of equipment.

Secret Funding

BNL-Atlanta took advantage of BNL-Rome's AAA credit rating and borrowed in the money markets to finance their credit extensions to Iraq. They borrowed overnight and longer-term funds in the Euromarket as Banca Lavoro, presumably without the knowledge of BNL-Rome/New York. Some, but not all, of the Euromoney people took it on the word of BNL-Atlanta that they were permitted to borrow about $3 billion. The Euromoney people did not check with BNL-Rome on Atlanta's authority to borrow.

The Bank of Credit and Commerce International (BCCI), also known as the Bank of Crooks and Criminals, was one of the banks lending funds to BNL-Atlanta.[15] A Senate investigation revealed that BCCI was taking funds from its *overseas* branches for overnight use by BNL-Atlanta. The Senate report concluded that some larger arrangement between the executives of both banks must have existed for BCCI to place the overseas funds in the United States for the purpose of lending them short-term to BNL. BNL-Atlanta maintained more than a half dozen accounts at BCCI's offices in Miami. Moreover, Alfred Hartmann was on the board of directors of BNL-Atlanta and BCCI's secretly controlled Swiss affiliate, Banque de Commerce et Placements (BCP). Shortly after BCCI was closed in July 1991, BCP was sold to a Turkish group, Cukorova (part of the Enka Group), who also owned Entrade. BNL-Atlanta, BCCI, and the Enka Group were doing business in Iraq. In 1987, Iraq had defaulted on a $12 million loan from BCCI. In 1989, BNL-Atlanta made a payment of $6.9 million in connection with an Iraqi arms deal to M.M. Hammoud. This may be the same M.M. Hammoud that was a shareholder and front man for BCCI.

Once BNL-Atlanta had the funds, they would lend as Banca Lavoro in their grey book. Thus, there was no other record of the transactions.[16]

Audits

Peat, Marwick, Main & Co. (formerly Peat, Marwick, Mitchell, & Co.) was BNL-Atlanta's external auditor, and it conducted annual audits and examinations. BNL-Atlanta was also examined by the Georgia Department of Banking and Finance. Under the International Banking Act of 1978, the State of Georgia was BNL-Atlanta's primary regulator because it was a state-licensed agency and it was uninsured. The state shared their examinations with the Federal Reserve Bank of Atlanta. The Federal Reserve Bank conducted annual compliance reviews, and occasionally helped the State of Georgia review loans.

In July 1989, two BNL-Atlanta employees who were involved in the fraud went to federal authorities and reported the secret loans to Iraq in exchange for immunity from prosecution.[17] Subsequently, the U.S. Attorney's office in Atlanta advised the Federal Reserve Bank of Atlanta of the secret transactions. The Federal Reserve and the FBI commenced a surprise examination on August 4, 1989, to secure files, documents, and computer records reflecting those transactions. Examinations were conducted at all of the other BNL offices in the United States, but no secret transactions were found elsewhere.

BNL-Rome periodically conducted internal audits of its branches, and it relied on those audits and monthly reports from the branches concerning their lending activity. Both the internal and external auditors relied on representations made to them by BNL-Atlanta. Unfortunately for them, BNL-Atlanta withheld audit confirmations and created false audit confirmations for BNL-Rome and Peat, Marwick.

BNL-Atlanta's first internal audit since its inception in 1982 was conducted in September 1988, one year before the scandal broke. The person in charge of the audit, Louis Messere, had a background as a comptroller, not an auditor. Therefore, it is not surprising that routine audit procedures were not followed. Had they been, they might have discovered the secret loans. Despite these problems, the audit report revealed a bank that was out of control. It stated that: "Based on the audit findings, the Atlanta agency's operations accounting and internal controls were found to be in need of improvement in most areas... The accounting data preparation and its flow and input into existing systems does not comply with existing BNL practices and procedures and as such is deficient of sound practices and controls."[18]

The audit report was sent to BNL-New York, and then to Rome, but it was concealed from the U.S. bank regulators. When the Georgia Department of Banking and Finance asked for the report, they were told that it was still in progress and not available. The Department of Banking and Finance did not follow up to get the report, nor did it do a comprehensive exam until after the raid in August 1989. The Department gave BNL-Atlanta a clean examination report.

Did BNL-Rome Know and Authorize the Loans?

How can a branch manager make more than $4 billion in unauthorized loans and credits and the headquarter bank not know what is going on? U.S. District Court Judge G. Ernest Tidwell (U.S. District Court for the Northern District of Georgia, Atlanta) concluded that BNL knew, or should have known, what Drogoul was doing.[19] Drogoul claimed that he was a pawn in the scheme. Drogoul accused a former BNL-Rome director (Giacomo Pedde) and others of engineering that scheme to increase their lending to Iraq in 1982 when the Italian government terminated its relationship with Iraq, and wanted to cut off such loans. There was general knowledge at BNL that Drogoul was "Pedde's boy."[20] But that does not mean that Pedde knew about the grey book transactions.

In February 1988, Drogoul, Paul Von Wedel, a BNL-Atlanta employee, and Teodoro Monaco, BNL-Rome's co-director of their finance division, met in Baghdad while Drogoul was negotiating a $200 million credit facility with Iraq.[21] Monaco claims that the meeting was purely by chance. When they encountered each other in their hotel, Drogoul was at a loss to explain his presence 7,000 miles from Atlanta. Each gave vague excuses for being there and quickly parted company.

There is additional support for the view of BNL-Rome's knowledge and involvement. The Central Intelligence Agency produced reports that concluded that "managers at BNL headquarters in Rome were involved in the scandal."[22]

In 1988, Italian Minister of the Treasury Carli testified before the Italian Parliament that he knew of BNL-Atlanta's unauthorized loans, and that such loans were used to finance Italian exports to Iraq. Moreover, he made it clear that BNL-Rome and their regional office in New York were aware of some of the unauthorized transactions.[23]

According to BNL-Rome, the secret loans represented a "rogue" activity by BNL-Atlanta personnel, and that it had no knowledge of the loans to Iraq.[24] While it may or may not have been a rogue activity, there is no doubt that BNL-Rome knew about loans after the internal audit in September 1988, and there is speculation that they had previous knowledge of the loans. One wonders why BNL-Rome did not stop BNL-Atlanta's activities once it learned about them? A Federal Reserve report may have part of the answer.[25] The report stated that BNL-Rome lacked any credible controls and procedures that would limit and monitor the activities of its branches. Moreover, supervision of BNL-Atlanta by BNL-Rome/New York was unsatisfactory and ineffective. Banca d'Italia, the central bank of Italy, issued a report in March 1990 that blamed BNL-Rome's inadequate auditing and lack of internal controls for monitoring the Atlanta branch. Even if BNL-Rome knew about the loans to Iraq, there is no evidence that BNL-New York or Rome *authorized* the secret loans.

The U.S. Department of Justice (Washington-Main Justice) questioned whether BNL-Rome had been an unwilling victim of fraud. They concluded that BNL-Rome's audit procedures had been so ineffective as to constitute "willful blindness" to BNL-Atlanta's activities.[26]

Why Did It Happen?

Christopher P. Drogoul was born in the early 1950s. He is a national of the United States and France, and a graduate of Temple University in Philadelphia. From 1973-1981, he worked for Barclays Bank. An Italian Senate report alleges that Drogoul made unauthorized transactions while working at Barclays.[27]

He then went to work for BNL-Atlanta and was promoted to manager in 1985. According to Drogoul, when he took over as manager, the Atlanta branch had a loss of over $1 million, and he thought that the loss could be eliminated by growing the bank. He saw an opportunity for profits in CCC loans because many of his competitors did not understand that business. As a result of the contacts he had developed with major grain exporters, the CCC business mushroomed. Drogoul was invited by Iraq to participate in a portion of their CCC program. Later they asked him to take the entire program and syndicate out the portion that he did not want. When oil prices fell, Drogoul was unable to sell the Iraqi loans at a profit, and he elected to keep them on his books. BNL-Rome/New York would not give him approval to do it, so he did it covertly. However, according to Assistant U.S. Attorney Gale McKenzie, the scheme started before Drogoul became manager at BNL-Atlanta. He went "off book" and had started a slush fund under the former branch manager.[28]

Drogoul was known for his intense drive and competition. Paul Von Wedel, who worked with Drogoul at BNL-Atlanta, said that Drogoul was trying to grow the bank by getting around the rules and bypassing BNL-Rome's and New York's authority. For example, a change in management in New York resulted in a travel policy that restricted BNL-Atlanta to travel in the Southeast, even though they had clients in London, Baghdad, New York, and Minneapolis. Drogoul did not want to eliminate relationships that took five years to develop.

According to Von Wedel, the plan was to go to Rome, confess their sins, and present them with millions in earnings, and then do business as usual.[29] That view is in sharp contrast with a prosecution memorandum (April 23, 1990) that noted evidence that Drogoul planned to leave BNL-Atlanta and work for the Iraqi procurement network that helped to supply their war efforts.[30] An earlier prosecution report revealed that Drogoul and Iraq had planned for Iraq to default on the loans to BNL after Drogoul had gone to London to head a new Iraqi bank.

During the June 2, 1992 hearing, U.S. District Judge Marvin H. Shoob asked Drogoul what he got out of the scheme. The following are selected excerpts from the transcript.[31]

Drogoul: I received renovations to my home and a few other ancillaries as far as antiques and some others.

The Court: I don't believe that for a minute. You mean you made all these unauthorized loans, all these machinations took place, all these worldwide activities were going on, you were intimately involved in all of these, and all you got were remodeling expenses for your home? ... What about the eight million dollars, a part of which the government has seized, that was deposited in some bank in Europe in a company that you controlled?

Drogoul: I have not seen any documents regarding that matter. I am not aware.

The Court: I don't care about documents. I am not asking about documents. I said: what about it? Did you get it?

Drogoul: No: I did not get it.

The foreign company that received the money is Cumsud, a Luxembourg corporation. It was established by Pierre G. Drogoul, who is the defendant's father, and Yavus Tezeller, Executive Vice President of Entrade.

The Court went on to say, "He is not a very credible witness at this point when he tells me that all he received was expenses to repair or remodel his house after being involved in a five-billion dollar fraud. It doesn't take a rocket scientist to recognize that all is not being laid out on the table."

Drogoul later admitted to receiving more than $300,000 from Tezeller.

Individual BNL-Atlanta employees also received money, jewelry, antiques, family vacations, new houses, and international travel for their participation in the scheme. For example, Von Wedel received a $350,000 kickback from Entrade.[32]

Was It Politics?

A 1994 report by the Italian Senate Investigation Committee on the BNL-Atlanta case suggests that politics played a major role in the case.[33] The report asserts that the number, volume, and complexity of the transactions were too complex to be engineered by Drogoul alone. Instead, the use of BNL-Atlanta was consistent with BNL-Romes' objectives of continuing its long-term financial relationships with Iraq without the knowledge of the Italian government or those Italian companies which were creditors to Iraq. BNL-Atlanta was far enough away from Rome, and small enough to avoid

Rome's scrutiny on the deals that it conducted. BNL officials in England, France, and Venice were also implicated in financing arms deals to Iraq. Although politics may have played a role in BNL-Atlanta, the Italian Senate Investigation Committee found no illegal, unauthorized operations in any of the documents that they reviewed.

The Italian Senate report also suggested that politics in the United States played an important role in the BNL-Atlanta scandal. In 1992, Representative Henry B. Gonzalez, Chairman, U.S. House Committee on Banking, Finance, and Urban Affairs, said:

> As I have reported, our investigation has uncovered the use of U.S. credit programs—namely, the U.S. Department of Agriculture's Commodity Credit Corporation (CCC) and the Export-Import Bank's (Eximbank) insurance guarantee program—to grant credit to Iraq, a country that was viewed as uncreditworthy by the international banking community during a period of time when U.S. lending was at its highest. The Administration allowed and encouraged this at a time when it knew Iraq was also bent on developing super-range artillery and nuclear weapons. The Administration turned a blind eye to this and the BNL scandal that facilitated Iraq's quest to obtain terror weapons. The Administration wanted a friend in Iraq, however odious that friend was, and no matter what laws had to be overlooked or bent in the process of wooing Saddam Hussein.
>
> As part of this policy the Administration watched and did nothing as BNL participated heavily in the CCC program. BNL was also the second largest bank participant in the Eximbank program for Iraq. As the drive to befriend Saddam Hussein intensified, both the Department of Agriculture and the Exim bank were repeatedly pressured by top levels of the Administration to disregard their financial controls and safeguards in order to provide credit to Iraq. In fact, the financial experts at Eximbank vigorously warned that extensions of credit to Iraq did not offer a reasonable assurance of repayment. Unfortunately, their warnings went unheeded.
>
> Just as troubling is the irresponsible conduct displayed by officials in the State and Commerce Departments in approving and issuing export licenses to Iraq, many times over the heated objections of the Defense Department, for sensitive technology and goods that had obvious military applications.[34]

References

Commissione Di Inchiesta Sulla Utilizzazione Dei Finziamenti Concessi All'Iraq Dalla Filiale Di Atlanta Della Banc Nazionale Del Lavoro, *Bozza Preparatoria Della Relazione Finale.* Gennaio 1994.

Commissione Di Inchiesta Sulla Utilizzazione Dei Finziamenti Concessi All'Iraq Dalla Filiale Di Atlanta Della Banc Nazionale Del Lavoro, *Relazione Conclusiva.* 1994.

Kenneth Cline, "Guilty Pleas Fail to Clear Up Mystery Shrouding Lavoro," *American Banker,* January 7, 1994.

Kenneth Cline, "Lavoro Bank Scandal: The Inside Story," *Southern Banker,* June 1990, 6-8,10-11,20-22.

Kenneth Cline, "Lavoro Could Be the Big Loser in Aftermath of Iraqgate Case," *American Banker,* December 13, 1993.

Stephen J. Hedges and Bryan Duffy, "Iraqgate," *U. S. News & World Report,* May 18, 1992, 42-51

U.S. House, *Banca Nazionale Del Lavoro (BNL),* Hearing, Committee on Banking, Finance and Urban Affairs, 100th Cong., 2nd Sess., Serial No. 102-17, April 9, 1991.

U.S. House, *Banca Nazionale Del Lavoro Affair and Regulation and Supervision of U.S. Branches and Agencies of Foreign Banks,* Hearing, Committee on Banking, Finance and Urban Affairs, 101th Cong., 2nd Sess., Serial No. 101-178, October 16, 1990.

U.S. House, *Iraqi and Banca Nazionale Del Lavoro Participation in Export-Import Programs,* Hearings, Committee on Banking, Finance and Urban Affairs, 102 Cong., 1st. Sess., Serial No. 102-21, April 17, 1991.

U.S. House, *H.R. 4803, The Non-Proliferation of Weapons of Mass Destruction and Regulatory Improvement Act of 1992,* Hearing before the Committee on Banking, Finance and Urban Affairs, 102 Cong., 2nd Sess., Serial No. 102-121, May 8, 1992.

U.S. House, *Need for an Independent Counsel to Investigate U.S. Government Assistance to Iraq,* Committee on the Judiciary, 102nd Cong., 2nd. Sess., Serial No. 7, June 1992.

U.S. House, *Need for an Independent Counsel to Investigate U.S. Government Assistance to Iraq,* Hearings, Committee on the Judiciary, 102nd Cong., 2nd. Sess., Serial No. 43, June 2 and 23, 1992.

U.S. House, *The Role of Banca Nazionale Del Lavoro in Financing Iraq, the Failure of the Federal Reserve Under the Federal "Umbrella," Bank Regulatory Structure and Interference by the State of Illinois,* Staff Report, Committee on Banking, Finance and Urban Affairs, 102nd Cong., 2nd Sess., Committee Print 102-1, February 1991.

U.S. Senate, *The Intelligence Community's Involvement in the Banca Nazionale Del Lavoro (BNL) Affair,* Report, Select Committee on Intelligence, 103 Cong., 1st. Sess., S. Prt. 103-12, February 1993.

Endnotes

1. Author's note: The major thrust of the BNL scandal reported here deals with the fraud, how it happened, and what lessons we can learn from it. However, the scandal involves politics and intrigue that go far beyond the scope of this book. For those who are interested in these subjects, selected comments concerning them are provided in the text and notes, and references are presented at the end of this chapter.

2. The term loan, as used here, refers to loans, credit facilities, loan arrangements, and similar means of extending credit.

3. U.S. House, *Banca Nazionale Del Lavoro (BNL),* Hearing, Committee on Banking, Finance and Urban Affairs, 102nd Cong., 1st. Sess., Serial No. 102-17, April 9, 1991, 158-161, 208; U.S. House, *The Banca Nazionale Del Lavoro (BNL) Scandal and the Department of Agriculture's Commodity Credit Corporation (CCC) Program for Iraq, Part 2,* 102nd Cong., 2nd Sess, Serial No. 102-123, May 21, 1992, 310-315.

4. U.S. House, *The Role of Banca Nazionale Del Lavoro in Financing Iraq, the Failure of the Federal Reserve under the Federal "Umbrella," Bank Regulatory Structure and Interference by the State of Illinois,* Staff Report, Committee on Banking, Finance and Urban Affairs, 102nd Cong., 1st Sess., Committee Print 102-1, February 1991, 17. Two principals of Matrix-Churchill were charged and tried for exporting arms to Iraq. However, the prosecution was aborted when it was discovered that one of the principals was supplying intelligence information to the British, and that the British government gave its blessings to the exports. (*U.S. v. Christopher Drogoul,* U. S. District Court, Northern District of Georgia, Defendant's Sentencing Memorandum, 1:91-Cr. 078-01 (GET), p. 23.) Matrix-Churchill had extensive dealings with BNL-Atlanta; U.S. House, *H.R. 4803, The Non-Proliferation of Weapons of Mass Destruction and Regulatory Improvement Act of 1992,* Hearing before the Committee on Banking, Finance and Urban Affairs, Serial No. 102-121, May 8, 1992, 282-303. This section gives a chronology of BNL's role in weapons proliferation and its connection to Matrix-Churchill.

5. U.S. House, *Banca Nazionale Del Lavoro Affair and the Regulation and Supervision of U.S. Branches and Agencies of Foreign Banks,* Hearing, Committee on Banking, Finance and Urban Affairs, 101 Cong., 2nd Sess., Serial No. 101-178, October 16, 1990, 38, 113.

6. U.S. House, *The Banca Nazionale Del Lavoro (BNL) Scandal and the Department of Agriculture's Commodity Credit Corporation (CCC) Program for Iraq, Part 1,* 102nd Cong., 2nd Sess, Serial No. 102-123, May 21, 1992, 440-463 (the Grand Jury Criminal Indictment).

7. *Ibid.,* U.S. House, *The Banca Nazionale Del Lavoro (BNL) Scandal and the Department of Agriculture's Commodity Credit Corporation (CCC) Program for Iraq, Part 1,* 107-8, 261-263; and Part 2, 303-306. For a draft of the indictment, which differs from the one issued, see: U.S. House, *Need for an*

Independent Counsel to Investigate U.S. Government Assistance to Iraq, Committee on the Judiciary, 102nd Cong., 2nd Sess., Serial No. 43, July 2 and 23, 1992, 213-241.

8. U.S. House, *Iraqi and Banca Nazionale Del Lavoro Participation in Export-Import Programs,* Hearing, Committee on Banking, Finance and Urban Affairs, 102nd Cong., 1st. Sess., Serial No. 102-21, April 17, 1991, 1, 40, 73; *Ibid.,* U.S. House, *The Banca Nazionale Del Lavoro (BNL) Scandal and the Department of Agriculture's Commodity Credit Corporation Program for Iraq-Part 1,* 15. According to Congressman Jim Slatery, CCC guaranteed an additional $1 billion in loans to Iraq that are in default (p.15). Lawrence S. Eaglebuger, Deputy Secretary of State, stated that CCC's credit exposure to Iraq was about $455 million (p. 177). Henry B. Gonzalez, Committee Chairman, commented on the politics of the BNL scandal. Specifically, Deputy Secretary Eagleburger and National Security Advisor Brent Scowcroft both worked for Kissinger and Associates, which played in integral role in stimulating trade with Iraq (pp. 276, 364). The Chairman also charged that Scowcroft improperly intervened in the CCC program to appease Saddam Hussein (pp. 394-397). Mr. Kissinger had been a member of BNL's Consulting Board for International Policy (along with David Rockefeller, Pierre Trudeau, and other political dignitaries), and BNL was a general consulting client (p.365) of Kissinger firm. BNL was a client of Scowcroft when he was Vice Chairman of Kissinger and Associates, and Eagleburger's Yugoslavian business ventures (LBS Bank and Yugo automobile) relied on BNL-Atlanta for some of its financing (p. 364). Both individuals played important roles in the Bush Administration's policy toward Iraq. According to Kissinger, neither he nor his associates had personal knowledge of loans made to Iraq by BNL or its branches (pp. 376-378).

9. *Ibid.,* U.S. House, *The Banca Nazionale Del Lavoro (BNL) Scandal and the Department of Agriculture's Commodity Credit Corporation (CCC) Program for Iraq, Part 1,* 440-481; Part 2, 311. *Ibid.,* U.S. House, *Banca Nazionale Del Lavoro Affair and the Regulation and Supervision of U.S. Branches and Agencies of Foreign Banks,* 354 (*Banca Nazionale Del Lavoro v. Christopher Drogoul and Paul Von Wedel,* 1:89 -CV-2319 HTW). Von Wedel was responsible for the letter of credit operations in BNL-Atlanta.

10. U.S. House, *Banca Nazionale Del Lavoro (BNL),* 160.

11. *Ibid.,* U.S. House, *Need for an Independent Counsel to Investigate U.S. Government Assistance to Iraq,* 659-661; Kenneth Cline, "Guilty Pleas Fail to Clear Up Mystery Shrouding Lavoro," *American Banker,* January 7, 1994. Prosecutors estimated Drogoul's share of the kickbacks to be $4.2 million, of which he had withdrawn $2.5 million before the accounts were closed.

12. *Ibid.,* U.S. House, *Banca Nazionale Del Lavoro Affair and the Regulation and Supervision of U.S. Branches and Agencies of Foreign Banks,* 128.

13. Kenneth Cline, "Lavoro Bank Scandal: The Inside Story," *Southern Banker,* 11.

14. *Ibid.*, U.S. House, *The Banca Nazionale Del Lavoro (BNL) Scandal and the Department of Agriculture's Commodity Credit Corporation (CCC) Program for Iraq, Part 1,* 107-8, 261-263, 477; and Part 2, 303-306, 346, 350, 577. The U.S. laws violated are 15 U.S.C. 714 (M) and the Foreign Corrupt Practices Act (p. 492).

15. U.S. Senate, *The BCCI Affair,* A Report to the Committee on Foreign Relations by Senators John Kerry and Hank Brown, December 1992, S. Prt. 102-140, 70-71.

16. *Ibid.*, U.S. House, *Banca Nazionale Del Lavoro Affair and the Regulation and Supervision of U.S. Branches and Agencies of Foreign Banks,* 55-56.

17. *Ibid.*, U.S. Senate, *The Intelligence Community's Involvement in the Banca Nazionale Del Lavoro (BNL) Affair,* 9.

18. *Ibid.*, U.S. House, *Banca Nazionale Del Lavoro Affair and the Regulation and Supervision of U.S. Branches and Agencies of Foreign Banks,* 3, 56, 68. Statement of Henry B. Gonzalez, Committee Chairman.

19. Kenneth Cline, "Lavoro Could Be Big Loser in Aftermath of Iraqgate Case," *American Banker,* December 13, 1993, 5; U.S. Senate, *The Intelligence Community's Involvement in the Banca Nazionale Del Lavoro (BNL) Affair,* Report, Select Committee on Intelligence, 103rd Cong., 1st. Sess., S. Prt. 103-12, February 1993. At the sentencing hearing in September 1992, Drougol's attorneys raised concerns about CIA knowledge of the involvement of BNL-Rome in the fraudulent activities. These concerns are covered in the Senate Report, but are not addressed in-depth here. Nevertheless, the report found that the CIA had no knowledge, as a result of its operational activities, of the BNL-Atlanta's fraudulent activities before August 1989 (p. 43). Readers should recognize that there were significant political aspects of this affair. The Italian government conveyed to the U.S. Ambassador in Rome that indictment of BNL-Rome would damage bilateral relationships (p. 6). Also see: U.S. House, *The Banca Nazionale Del Lavoro (BNL) Scandal and the Department of Agriculture's Commodity Credit Corporation (CCC) Program for Iraq-Part 1,* 326-328.

20. *U.S. v. Christopher Drogoul,* U. S. District Court, Northern District of Georgia, Defendant's Sentencing Memorandum, 1:91-Cr.078-01 (GET), p. 86; and Government's Reply Sentencing Memorandum, p. 39.

21. *Ibid.*, Kenneth Cline, "Lavoro Bank Scandal: The Inside Story," 10; *Ibid.*, *U.S. v. Christopher Drogoul,* U. S. District Court, Northern District of Georgia, Government's Reply Sentencing Memorandum, 1:91-Cr.078-01 (GET), p. 39

22. *Ibid.*, U.S. Senate, *The Intelligence Community's Involvement in the Banca Nazionale Del Lavoro (BNL) Affair,* 28.

23. *Ibid.*, U.S. House, *Banca Nazionale Del Lavoro Affair and the Regulation and Supervision of U.S. Branches and Agencies of Foreign Banks,* 54.

24. *Ibid.*, U.S. House, *Banca Nazionale Del Lavoro Affair and the Regulation and Supervision of U.S. Branches and Agencies of Foreign Banks,* 10.

25. *Ibid.*, U.S. House, *Need for an Independent Counsel to Investigate U.S. Government Assistance to Iraq*, 572-574.

26. *Ibid.*, U.S. Senate, *The Intelligence Community's Involvement in the Banca Nazionale Del Lavoro (BNL) Affair*, 12.

27. Commissione Di Inchiesta Sulla Utilizzazione Dei Finziamenti Concessi All'Iraq Dalla Filiale Di Atlanta Della Banc Nazionale Del Lavoro, *Bozza Preparatoria Della Relazione Finale*. Gennaio 1994, pp. 6-7; the author is indebted to Maurizio Godorecci for translating sections of the report, which was written in Italian, into English.

28. *Ibid.*, U.S. House, *Need for an Independent Counsel to Investigate U.S. Government Assistance to Iraq*, 752.

29. *Ibid.*, Kenneth Cline, "Lavoro Bank Scandal: The Inside Story," 7.

30. U.S. Senate, *The Intelligence Community's Involvement in the Banca Nazionale Del Lavoro (BNL) Affair*, 49; *Ibid.*, U.S. House, *Need for an Independent Counsel to Investigate U.S. Government Assistance to Iraq*, 210.

31. *Ibid.*, U.S. House, *Need for an Independent Counsel to Investigate U.S. Government Assistance to Iraq*, 682-689.

32. *Ibid.*, U.S. House, *The Banca Nazionale Del Lavoro (BNL) Scandal and the Department of Agriculture's Commodity Credit Corporation (CCC) Program for Iraq, Part 2*, 346-347.

33. Commissione Di Inchiesta Sulla Utilizzazione Dei Finziamenti Concessi All'Iraq Dalla Filiale Di Atlanta Della Banc Nazionale Del Lavoro, *Bozza Preparatoria Della Relazione Finale*.

34. *Ibid.*, U.S. House, *H.R. 4803, The Non-Proliferation of Weapons of Mass Destruction and Regulatory Improvement Act of 1992*, Hearing, 264 -265.

5   MONEY LAUNDERING

Money laundering is widespread, as evidenced by recent front-page stories. The *American Banker* (December 21, 1993, p. 1) reported that a Swiss bank confessed to laundering drug money and forfeited $2.3 million to the United States. *The Wall Street Journal* (January 26, 1994, p. 1) reported that the mayor of a small Southern town was indicted for money laundering.

Money laundering is the conversion of the monetary proceeds of a criminal activity into funds with an apparently legal source and without revealing the true nature, source, or ownership of those proceeds.[1] It occurs in connection with criminal activities such as illegal drug trafficking, fraud, extortion, tax evasion, and other crimes.

Big Business

Illegal drug sales are a cash and carry business, and they generate a lot of cash. In 1991, estimated annual revenues from the sale of illegal drugs were about $300 billion worldwide and $100 billion in the United States.[2] That amount of cash in $20 bills weighs about 26 million pounds. In one money laundering operation in New York, a tractor trailer was required to haul $19 million in small bills. Moving bulk cash offshore is inconvenient. Customs officials have seized cash hidden in drums of textile dye ($1 million), in microwave ovens ($2 million), and in cryogenic containers that were supposed to be carrying bull semen ($6.4 million). Thus, it is easy to understand why drug traffickers are always looking for new and efficient ways to launder money.

Money laundering is an international business. According to Senator William V. Roth, Jr. (Republican, Delaware): "With the aid of modern technology, such as satellite telephones, pagers, and encrypted fax machines, the new international criminals instantaneously communicate with their associates across the globe. Using easily obtained phony passports and taking advantage of newly relaxed international travel restrictions as well the greatly increased volume of international trade, the new international criminals treat national boarders as nothing more than minor inconveniences to their criminal enterprises."[3]

Asian Crime Groups

International organized crime groups engage in a wide range of illegal activities which generate funds to be laundered. Asian organized crime groups, for example, engage in heroin trafficking, counterfeit credit cards, alien smuggling, loan sharking, kidnapping, and murder, to name a few of their activities. They are the quintessential crime groups engaging in every type of crime. Table 5.1 gives some idea of the size and geographic scope of selected ethnic Chinese crime groups, most of which operate out of Hong Kong. The Sun Yee Triad has more than 25,000 members and operates worldwide. The Wo Group has more than 20,000 members and has a major base of operations in San Francisco. Collectively, the Chinese groups listed in the table have more than 100,000 members.

The total number of Japanese organized crime groups (Yakuza or Boryokudan) members is estimated to be 88,600, but the number in the United States and Canada is not known. Nevertheless, an alleged Yakuza associate was involved in the purchase of Pebble Beach Country Club in California which was purchased for $841 million in 1990. Because of questions involving the purchasers' previous criminal activities, it was sold for $500 million in 1992 for $500 million to another group of Japanese investors.[4] In addition, Yakuza associates allegedly own casinos in Las Vegas.

Although the Italian La Cosa Nostra gets a lot of publicity on television, it is estimated to have only 2,000 active members in the United States. It is insignificant compared to the Asian crime groups.

The Asian crime groups do not have an international monopoly on money laundering or other crimes. Latin American and West African crime groups are active participants in money laundering and other crimes as well. The Latin American crime groups are most closely associated with laundering drug money. The West Africans are associated with laundering relatively small amounts of money resulting from credit card and commercial scams. Each scam is relatively small, but collectively they add to very large sums.

The Process of Money Laundering

Money laundering is a business specialty of the illegal drug industry. It is also used by other industries and individuals. Money laundering, like any business activity, has its own jargon. Some of the terms used by law enforcement authorities and drug traffickers include the following:[5]

Commingling. Obscuring the illegal funds by commingling (mixing) them with the proceeds of a legitimate business (front companies) so that the all of the funds appear to be income from the legitimate business.

Table 5.1: Ethnic Chinese Organized Crime Groups

Sun Yee Triad (Hong Kong)
- 25,000+ members.
- Associates in New York City, Los Angeles, Canada, Australia, and Thailand

Wo Group (Hong Kong)
- 20,000+ members within 10 subgroups.
- Wo Hop To Triad has a major base of operations in San Francisco.

14K Triad (Hong Kong)
- 20,000+ members and over 30 subgroups.
- United States, Canada, Australia, and the Far East.

Luen Group (Hong Kong)
- 8,000+ members in 4 subgroups.
- Luen Kung Lok Triad has a strong presence in Toronto, and associates in the United States.

United Bamboo Gang (Taiwan)
- 20,000+ members.
- Operations in Houston, Los Angeles, New York, and Vancouver.

Four Seas Gang (Taiwan)
- 5,000+ members.
- Operations in Los Angeles.

Big Circle Gang (PRC/Hong Kong)
- Membership unknown.
- Operations worldwide. Especially active in Hong Kong, Canada, and New York.

Source: U.S. Senate, *Asian Organized Crime: The New International Criminal,* Hearings before the Permanent Subcommittee on Investigations of the Committee on Governmental Affairs, S. Hrg. 102-940, June 18 and August 4, 1992, p. 139.

Complicity. Money laundering facilitated by financial institution's employees or owners. It is not limited to one bank. Various domestic and foreign banks may jointly be involved in laundering money. BCCI is one example.

Front company. The illegal funds are represented as income (commingled) of front companies such as legitimate real estate agencies and pizzerias. Front companies may also be dummy corporations, such as jewelry stores and precious metal dealers, established for the express purpose of money laundering. *Shell companies* are similar to front companies, but they are usually chartered offshore to hide their identity, and they exist on paper only. They can be used to transfer funds in what appears to be a legitimate transaction.

Integration. The provision of apparent legitimacy to the illegally gained wealth.

Layering. Separating illegal proceeds from their source by creating multiple layers of financial transactions designed to block the audit trail and hide the source of the funds.

Placement. The physical disposal of illegally obtained bulk cash proceeds.

Structuring/Smurfing. Structuring is the process of converting bulk cash into small amounts in order to evade CTR requirements. For example, $40,000 in cash can be structured into eight deposits of $5,000 each. The individuals who "place" or carry out the multiple, small transactions are called "smurfs."

The process of laundering money involves three steps: 1) placement, 2) layering and 3) integration. These steps may occur simultaneously, or they may overlap each other. The process is illustrated in Figure 5.1. The first step, placement, may involve structuring and/or smurfing to place bulk cash in traditional or nontraditional financial institutions. This step is labor-intensive and may involve hundreds of smurfs. Alternatively, the trafficker may get an exemption from a financial institution to engage in transactions in excess of $10,000. In either case, the deposited funds can be wire trans-ferred or sent by some other means to another location. Detection of the laundering process becomes difficult once it moves beyond the placement stage.

During the second step, layering, the funds are commonly placed in monetary instruments (cashier's checks, money orders, letters of credit, stocks, bonds, etc.), and wire transfers. Launderers prefer wire transfers—they are speedy and impose no limits on the amount of funds that can be transferred. Multiple wire transfers occur through numerous institutions, front companies and shell companies in order to deter detection. In addi-tion to these techniques, illicit funds are used to purchase assets such as real estate, cars, boats, and aircraft that can be used to further the launder-ers' activities.

The third step, integration, occurs when the laundered funds are put back in the economy in such a way that they appear to be legitimate. For example, the funds may be used to buy real estate, establish businesses, or to acquire other assets. Then the funds are recycled back into a criminal activity. One integration technique is overstating the value of exports and imports. For example, if imports to the United States are overvalued on the invoice, the difference between the actual value and the amount listed on the invoice is paid for from the proceeds from illegal activities. The over-valuation of exports provides justification to receive funds from abroad. BCCI used some of these techniques in Nigeria (see Chapter 9, "Credit Card and Telemarketing Frauds").

Common Traits of Launderers

The money laundering business is usually dominated by professional individual advisors whose laundering businesses are international in scope. Money launderers are generally intelligent, willing to take risks, overconfident, and they have a desire to outwit the system. Their backgrounds are in business, accounting, finance, and law. The leaders tend to specialize in particular fields such as precious metals, jewelry, and import/export. Even those who only work as low-level couriers tend to have good education and frequently have no prior criminal records. Some of the money launderers belong to groups that are bound by ethnic affiliations, nationality, family ties, and business connections. They are motivated by tax-free profits that come from laundering money.

A 71-year-old, who was known and respected as an international lawyer, a good neighbor, and president of his church parish was also part of a money laundering network that involved Colombians.[6] When a Los Angeles County SWAT team executed a search and arrest warrant and entered the bedroom of his home, the attorney fired a 9-millimeter handgun at them. They returned fire and he was mortally wounded. He had 61 weapons and $450,000 in cash in his house, as well as files on money launderers and drug dealers. His money laundering scheme used front businesses, including a liquor store. Money generated by the sale of drugs was used to cash customer's checks, which were then deposited in the store's bank account. Those funds were then wire transferred to Colombia. The liquor store laundered $1.85 million, and his other businesses laundered over $5 million in the short period of the investigation. The scheme was brought to the attention of law enforcement authorities when the bank became suspicious of the transactions.

Federal Legislation

Federal legislation has developed to address the fact that money laundering is a criminal activity. In order to detect the criminal activity, financial institutions and businesses must report money laundering and suspicious transactions to federal authorities. Those convicted of money laundering are subject to legal sanctions. Some of the federal legislation enacted to address money laundering concerns include the Bank Secrecy Act, the Internal Revenue Service's Form 8300, the Money Laundering Control Act, and the Annunzio-Wylie-Anti-Money Laundering Act.

Bank Secrecy Act. The Bank Records and Foreign Transaction Reporting Act and other provisions are commonly known as the Bank Secrecy Act (BSA) of 1970. BSA was the first federal legislation targeting money laundering and other white-collar crimes, including tax evasion. It is called the Bank Secrecy Act because it helps provide information to law enforcement agencies about

Figure 5.1: Money Laundering

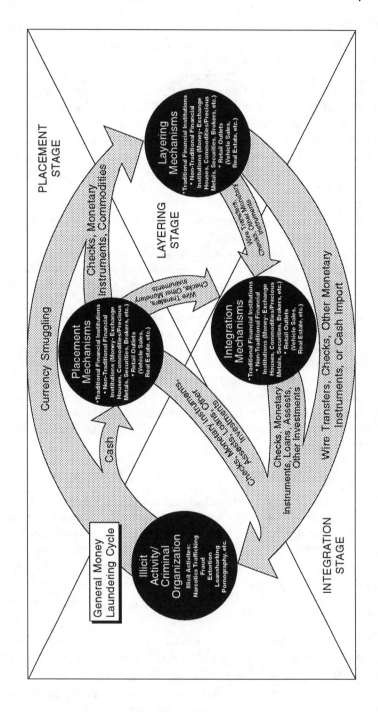

Source: FinCEN

the secret use of foreign accounts by U.S. customers by creating a "paper trail." While BSA aided in the tracking of money laundering activities, it did not make money laundering illegal *per se*. Nevertheless, some money launderers were prosecuted for violating the BSA and under the Racketeer-Influenced and Corrupt Organizations (RICO) statues.

The two principal parts of the BSA are: 1) requirements for financial institutions to keep records of certain basic records for five years; and 2) requirements for financial institutions to file Currency Transaction Reports (CTRs) for domestic currency transactions (deposit, withdrawal or exchange) in excess of $10,000, and Currency or Monetary Instruments Reports (Custom Form 4790, CMIRs). for international currency transactions in excess of $5,000. The Treasury, which implements part of the act, defines financial institutions to include banks (commercial banks, savings and loan associations, and credit unions), federally regulated securities brokers, currency exchange houses, funds transmitters, check-cashing businesses, and persons subject to supervision by state or federal bank supervisory authority. The act was amended in 1985 to include casinos in the definition of financial institutions.

Banks can grant exemptions to filing CTRs for certain legitimate firms that regularly engage in currency transactions with banks that exceed $10,000. The Treasury and IRS *Currency and Foreign Transactions Reporting Act Exemption Handbook* explains the requirements for special exemptions and unilateral exemptions.[7] Special exemptions require prior approval from the Treasury or IRS. Bowling alleys, car washes, dry cleaners, and other lines of business fall into this category. However, banks can unilaterally grant exemptions to certain retail businesses, bars, restaurants, hotels, and others listed in the handbook. The exemptions are for a specific time period, and for established dollar amounts. The handbook also explains reporting and recordkeeping requirements.

In July 1980, the Treasury closed a loophole in the law that provided for exemptions for cash transactions between domestic and foreign banks. In August 1980, the Bank of Boston exempted a deposit of almost $1.5 million that it handled as an international bank transfer, and it did not file the required CTR.[8] It was one of a series of deposits from front businesses that were laundering funds for an organized drug distribution network. In this connection, the bank accepted large cash deposits from a reputed mobster with underworld connections. The bank had no direct knowledge of the source of the funds, but it did not question their origin. The Bank of Boston pled guilty and was fined $500,000. A more important outcome of this case was that the concept of "knowledge" of criminal activity was expanded from "actual knowledge" to include *"willful blindness," "deliberate ignorance,"* and *"conscious avoidance."*

Internal Revenue Service

The Internal Revenue Service (IRS) also has responsibilities under the Bank Secrecy Act. The BSA (USC, Title 31), the Internal Revenue Code, Section 60501 (Title 26), and the money laundering criminal statutes (Title 18) require any person engaged in trade or business who receives more than $10,000 in a single transaction or related series of transactions must file a Form 8300, "Report of Cash Payments over $10,000 Received in a Trade or Business." Not everyone complies willingly. Recently, lawyers were required to divulge the names of clients who pay them more than $10,000 in cash.9 Less sophisticated businesses may not be aware of the filing requirements. However, ignorance of the law is no excuse, and the IRS is actively pursuing nonfilers and other violators.

In addition to CTRs (IRS Form 4789), the Bank Secrecy Act also gives the IRS responsibility for Currency Transaction Reports by Casino (IRS Form 8362, CTRCs). Casinos operating in the United States must file a report for each currency transaction in excess of $10,000. Finally, any person subject to U.S. jurisdiction who has a financial interest or signature authority in foreign accounts with a value of $10,000 or more must file a Report of Foreign Bank and Financial Accounts (Treasury Form TDF 90-22.1).

The IRS uses these forms to provide information about various illegal activities including money laundering. For example, the IRS Criminal Investigation Division recommended prosecution of an attorney who laundered more than $3 million in illegal drug proceeds for a client. The attorney pled guilty for failing to file CTRs, conspiracy to launder money, and drug conspiracy. He was sentenced to 15 years in prison.

Money Laundering Control Act

Money laundering (structuring) became illegal when the BSA was amended as Congress enacted the Money Laundering Control Act of 1986 (MLCA). BSA was amended again with the Money Laundering Prosecution Improvement Act of 1988 (part of the Omnibus Anti-Drug Abuse Act).

One outcome of the 1986 amendments was that financial institutions could no longer be "willfully blind" to the money laundering activities of their customers.10 A bank can be found guilty of money laundering even if it does not know the illegal origin of the funds, but should have suspected criminal activity based on the behavior of the customer. In other words, banks must *"know their customers."* What that means is that a bank must make reasonable efforts to determine who the borrower is, the credit history, the purpose of the loan, and other relevant information. Consider the following case. A bank made a one-year, $800,000 first mortgage loan to a Panamanian corporation. The loan was collateralized with a $1.1 million home owned by the corporation. After the loan was made, a government investigation revealed that the Panamanian corporation was owned by an illegal drug trafficker. The government seized the property claiming that it had probable cause to believe that the house was purchased with the proceeds from illegal drug sales. The government also claimed that the bank's president, who made the loan, should have known that the owner of the property was a drug trafficker.

Under federal law, property that has been acquired with laundered money is subject to seizure and forfeiture, even when it is collateral for a bank loan. If the bank was an "innocent" lien holder, the court may "pardon" the property. In the case of the loan to the Panamanian corporation, the court ruled that the bank was willfully blind to facts that it should have taken into account. These facts were that the Panamanian corporation was a shell corporation whose sole asset was the property, which was vacant, and up for sale. The bank did not know the purpose of the loan, or how it was going to be repaid. It did not do a title search on the property. The loan proceeds were transferred to Switzerland, and some of them were used to buy expensive gifts for the bank president's family. The bank lost $800,000 plus attorney fees.

Banks must have appropriate procedures to detect and forestall money laundering activities. Institutions that have failed to comply with laws have been fined and put on probation. For example, in 1990, the Bank of Credit and Commerce International (BCCI) was fined $14.8 million.[11] In July 1993, Dollar Savings and Trust Company, Youngstown, Ohio, agreed to pay a $1,182,639 civil penalty for failing to file CTRs as required by the BSA. Individual firms can be fined too. In April 1993, Essex Imports Inc., Deerfield Beach, Florida, agreed to pay a civil penalty of $50,000 for structuring currency transactions at financial institutions in order to evade BSA reporting requirements.[12] Although these fines send a strong signal to bankers and others, they are insignificant in comparison to the huge profits that can be made by money laundering.

Annuzio-Wylie-Anti-Money Laundering Act

Other pertinent legislation includes the Anti-Drug Abuse Act of 1988, the Crime Control Act of 1990 (Section 2532), The Federal Deposit Insurance Corporation Improvement Act (FIDICIA) of 1991 (Section 206), and the Housing Community Development Act of 1992 (P.L. 102-550, referred to as the Annunzio-Wylie Anti-Money Laundering Act of 1992). The Annunzio-Wylie Act permits the Secretary of Treasury to require any financial institution (including employees, officers, and directors) to file a Suspicious Transaction Report (STR) relevant to possible violations of law or regulations. The banks are prohibited from notifying the person who is the subject of the report. To protect the banks, the act limits their liability when filing such reports. In addition, all businesses must keep customer identification records for currency transactions between $3,000 and $10,000, and report suspicious transactions, regardless of their size. The suspicious transactions do not have to be linked to the drug trade.

Banks may not have *"flagrant organizational indifference"* to their obligations under BSA or to report suspicious transactions. All employees, officers, and directors must comply with it. Under the doctrine of *"collective knowledge,"* information known by employees, acting within the scope of their employment, can be attributed to that organization. Thus, a bank could face a criminal charge if an employee suspects that a transaction may be involved in money laundering but does not report it.

The Annunzio-Wylie Act strengthens the anti-money laundering efforts by giving federal bank regulators more latitude in investigating money laundering and allowing them to close or seize a bank, savings and loan association, or credit union under certain circumstances; or terminate its insured status. In deciding whether a institution should be seized, they must consider whether employees, officers, and directors were involved in the illegal activity, the bank's policies concerning money laundering, and other factors.

International Cooperation

There is international cooperation in dealing with money laundering. These efforts include:

- The United Nations Single Convention on Narcotic Drugs (1961). It established the International Narcotics Control Board to set up a system to regulate the manufacture of controlled chemicals. These controlled chemicals, such as ephedrine and lysergic acid, are used to refine natural narcotics such as cocaine and heroin. The 1971 Convention on Psychotropic Substances added dependency-causing synthetic substances to the list to be regulated.

- The Basle Supervisors' Committee Statement of Principles on Money Laundering (1988).

- A United Nations Convention Against Illicit Traffic in Narcotic Drugs and Psychotropic Substances (1988). This convention criminalized money laundering and added other measures to fight illicit drugs.

- The Financial Action Task Force (FATE), a group of 40 industrialized countries, made recommendations on money laundering and how to deal with it on a global scale.

- The Chemical Actions Task Force, under the Group of Seven economic summit partners (Canada, France, Germany, Japan, Italy, United Kingdom, and the United States), made recommendations for certain chemicals to be added to the UN Convention and for additional controls of illicit drug production and trafficking.

- A Caribbean Financial Action Task Force (CFATF) was formed to deal with money laundering problems involving Latin American nations.

- The European Community (EC) directive on money laundering (1991).

Although many countries have endorsed these programs and controls, not all of them have been instituted globally for a variety of reasons. One reason is that some countries fear that such controls would harm their economies, the banks that were required to make the reports, or the bank's employees or customers. Another reason is that it takes time to make legislative changes and to adopt an infrastructure necessary to carry out those changes. Some less developed countries may lack the resources or will to do it. For example, in the United States it costs between $3 to $15 to file a CTR.[13] By 1996, the number of CTRs could exceed 92 million. Stated otherwise, the cost of filing the reports could range from $276 million to $1.380 billion. To put the cost of filing CTRs in perspective, insured commercial banks had record earnings of $11.45 billion during the third quarter of 1993. If they earned $44 billion for the entire year, the cost of filing CTRs could amount to 3 percent ($1.38/$44 = 3%) of total bank earnings.

Creative Laundering

Despite the existence and enforcement of these acts and international efforts, money laundering is analogous to a balloon that has been squeezed in one place and bulges somewhere else. As laundering through banks becomes more difficult, drug traffickers and other criminals find new and creative ways to launder their funds. However, commercial banks are still directly and indirectly involved in money laundering. Chapters 3 and 4 deal with the Bank of Credit and Commerce International (BCCI) and Banca Nazionale Lavoro (BNL) and provide some examples of money laundering in connection with other criminal activities. Nevertheless, the federal laws have slowed the money laundering activities at banks and other financial institutions. Consequently, money launderers are making greater use of "nonbank" financial institutions. These include the following:

- Businesses that exchange money.

- Businesses that wire transfer money, cash checks, sell money orders and traveler's checks.

- Brokers and dealers in art, metals, and stones.

- Casinos and gambling establishments.

- Dealers in automobiles, airplanes, and boats.

- Real estate brokers and dealers.

- Insurance companies.

- Commodities brokers and dealers.

- Professionals such as attorneys and accountants.

- Illegal banking institutions.

The businesses that exchange money (casas de cambio), transfer money (giro houses), and money transmitters (agents of Western Union, American Express, and Travelers Express) provide payment services similar to those offered by commercial banks. Moreover, they are subject to many of the same anti-money laundering laws and regulations as banks. They are required to file CTRs and CMIRs just like banks. However, the activities of nonbank financial institutions are mostly unregulated, unsupervised, and are not monitored by federal and state authorities. Small budgets and lack of manpower are two reasons for the lack of supervision by state and federal authorities. Against this background of inadequate supervision, many of the small casas de cambio and giros do not register as businesses in the states in which they operate. Some of these two- or three-person operations are mobile, and they easily move from one location to another if they are bothered by authorities. In 1991, financial institutions filed 1.2 million CTRs, while nonbank financial institutions filed 30,406. Thus, the nonbank financial institutions may or may not file the required reports. Alternatively, they may file falsified reports. Money launderers, knowing how these firms avoid and evade the laws, use them extensively because they are less likely to be detected.

Casas de Cambio

Casas de cambio, Spanish for money exchange houses, are small businesses located along the U.S./Mexican border that exchange U.S. and Mexican currency. Casas de cambio are also located in Colombia and elsewhere in Latin America. When the Colombians adopted restrictive foreign exchange policies in 1967, casas de cambio were used to service the black market in foreign currency. They have been described as a parallel banking system offering a wide range of financial services. Other financial services they offer include accepting deposits, making loans, and wire transferring funds. Some launder money too. In the early 1990s, more than 1,000 such businesses were operating in Los Angeles alone.[14] The growth of casas de cambio was spurred by the devaluation of the Mexican peso. The exchange rate for $1 increased from 26 Mexican pesos in 1982 to 3,000 pesos in 1992. Other contributing factors were cross-border trade and the need to launder illegal drug revenues. According to a report from the Treasury Department's Financial Crimes Enforcement Network (FinCEN), each casa de cambio is capable of laundering $60 million per year. It is estimated that about 80 percent of the casas de cambio engage in some money laundering activity. That amounts to about $4.8 billion per year in laundered funds. Charles Lewis, Assistant U.S. District Attorney for the Southern District of Texas, described casas de cambio first as "an outlaw industry that exists primarily for the benefit of drug traffickers...," and second, to provide "false and misleading documents ... in order to launder moneys."[15] An owner of a casa de cambio agreed. He said that operating a casa de cambio would not be a good business if it were not for the laundering of drug money.

Laundering schemes can be simple. For example, an illegal trafficker gives the owner of a casa de cambio $100,000 cash to launder. The owner deposits that amount in the name of his company at a commercial bank.[16] The bank fills out the required CTR listing the casa de cambio as the owner of the funds. This breaks the link between the trafficker and the money because most casa de cambios do not keep records of where they got their cash, and the bank records the cambio as the owner. Once the funds have been deposited in a commercial bank, they can be wire transferred anywhere in the world. The laundering is complete because CTRs are not required on wire transfers.

Some illegal drug traffickers smuggle U.S. currency into Mexico. Typically, the traffickers use individuals called "smurfs" to do the smuggling and to carry out other illegal tasks for a fee. Because of the heavy traffic going South, it is unlikely that the smurfs will be stopped at the border. Then they come back to the United States with the cash. On the return trip, the smurfs file Custom's CMIR forms asserting that the money was earned in a legitimate business activity. Now the funds can be deposited in a commercial bank for wire transfer to other destinations.

An alternative is to deposit the funds in the casa de cambio's Mexican bank and have them wire transferred from there. The funds in the Mexican bank could be wired to an escrow company in the in the United States. The funds could be used to purchase real estate in the name of a nominee of the drug trafficker. Thus, there would be no records in the United States linking the drug trafficker to the laundered money. Mexican banks do not have similar reporting requirements involving cash deposits.

Giro Houses

Giro is Spanish for "wire," as in the term wire transfer. A giro house's primary business is to facilitate international business transactions between the United States and Colombia by coordinating and arranging for the transfer of funds. It is usually done by wire transfer or other electronic means. They also provide other services, including cellular phones, fax machines, answering services, private postal boxes, automobiles, and automobile insurance. Giros are usually found in major cities (i.e., New York or Houston) operating as part of other businesses, such as travel agencies. In the New York City metropolitan area, it is estimated that giro houses/travel agencies may be laundering about $1 billion per month.

Suppose that an illegal drug trafficker in the United States has $50,000 in U.S. currency that he wants to launder through a giro to obtain Colombian pesos. The giro will contact by fax or phone its Colombian counterpart, which has $50,000 in pesos that it is willing to convert into dollars. The two giros make the trade for a 7-10 percent fee which is split between them. In this case the dollars stay in the United States and the pesos stay in Colombia.

Sometimes the giros deposit the laundered funds in U.S. banks. Smurfs, using fictitious names, make deposits of less than the $10,000 CTR limit and then have the funds transferred.

Commercial banks account for most of the wire transfer traffic, both legitimate and illegitimate. Estimates are that daily large wire transfers amount to about $1 trillion.[17] Monitoring that amount of transfers for illegal traffic is a difficult task.

Check Cashers

A check casher's primary role is to cash payroll and government benefit checks for those who do not have regular bank accounts. They also sell money orders, provide wire transfers, and allow for payment of utility bills and rent on public housing. There are more than 4,500 such businesses in the United States. While they provide legitimate and needed financial services, some also provide illegal services. The Chairman of the New Jersey State Commission of Investigation stated that check cashers were "...being tapped at will by mobsters and other unscrupulous individuals ... whose objectives include such notorious activities as money laundering, income tax evasion, embezzlement, loan sharking, and other frauds."[18]

One way to launder money is for a drug trafficker to buy money orders or travelers checks from a check casher and then deposit those instruments in a bank. This avoids having the bank complete a CTR because no cash was involved. The check casher avoids the CTRs by breaking down the laundered money into small deposits and using fictitious names.

Check cashers also use "street cash" from drug sales, instead of cash withdrawals from a bank, as their source of funds to cash criminal customers' checks. The customers' checks can then be deposited in a bank and a cashier's check obtained for the customer, or issue his own business check. The criminal customer now has a "clean" check which can be deposited into his or her bank account. Alternatively, the check casher may use "street money" to cash the checks of legitimate customers. Those checks, in turn, can be sold to traffickers who buy them at a discount that ranges from 2 to 10 percent. The traffickers can deposit these checks in their bank accounts and avoid CTRs.

Money Transmitters

Some of the more than 100,000 agents of Western Union, American Express, and Travelers Express launder money. About 5,500 of the agents are also check cashers. All of the companies mentioned have anti-money laundering policies in effect, and they do not want their products used for illegal services. However, American Express, for example, does not run a criminal background check on its agents; nor does it ask them if they have been charged with a crime, such as money laundering; nor does it verify if its agents are filing CTRs as required by law.[19] It is not surprising that agents launder money on a regular basis.

Multiple wire transfers of funds below the mandatory $10,000 CTR threshold can also be used to launder money. The relatively small amounts are exchanged by smurfs for money orders, traveler's checks, and wire transfers. Most money orders have a maximum value of $1,000 or less, which means that the smurfs move a lot of paper. When funds are wire transferred say by Western Union, the transaction is identified by a number. The trafficker sends the number to the receiver who uses it to obtain a check from Western Union for the amount wired. No identification is required, and the check is deposited in a bank, thereby avoiding CTRs.

Even if the transaction exceeds $10,000, the agents, casas de cambio, and giros may not file the CTR reports, or they will disguise the name on the reports that they do file. Another method for avoiding detection is to split the laundered funds among several casas de cambios. Smurfs, who earn 2 to 4 percent, can easily launder " $250,000 in less than one hour at several nonbank financial institutions."[20] That amounts to $500 to $10,000 for an hour's work—not bad for a part-time job.

Illegal Banks

Illegal banking institutions offer banking services to money launderers and others without being chartered in the United States by federal or state banking authorities, or by exceeding the limits of their legal authority.[21] An example of the latter occurs when a nondeposit institution in one part of the country opens a branch office elsewhere, where it accepts deposits and requires customers to provide collateral in order to obtain letters of credit. Other illegal banks include counterfeit banks, phantom banks, shell banks, and ethinic-based banks.

Counterfeit banks. These are institutions that illegally use the names of legitimate banks to conduct their business. In one case, a counterfeit bank issued worthless letters of credit and promissory notes. Another offered high-yielding CDs.

Phantom banks. These are nonlicensed banks established to provide a cover for criminal activity. One phantom bank offered attractive loan rates and liberal lending policies to customers who paid advance fees of several thousand dollars.

Shell banks. Like shell corporations, they are typically based offshore in the Caymans, Bermuda, Luxembourg, Channel Islands, or Hong Kong, to provide the appearance of legitimacy when transferring funds abroad.

Ethnic-based banks. These unauthorized, uninsured institutions meet the needs of nondocumented resident aliens in the United States. They accept deposits, transfer funds, and provide other services.

Red Flags

The OCC published a list of red flags that bankers should look for in connection with money laundering.[22] Existence of the red flags or warning signs does not mean that money laundering is occurring, but it may be one explanation for the unusual activities.

1. *Activities that are not consistent with the customer's business.* One example is a retail business that deposits large volumes of checks, but does not withdraw sufficient cash to run that business. Another example is large volumes of deposits of cash, checks, and U.S. food stamps (frequently used to buy narcotics), and wire transfers that are not consistent with the nature of that business.

2. *Unusual characteristics.* Unusual characteristics include accounts outside the bank's normal service area. The accounts may have foreign addresses in Colombia, Luxembourg, etc. Requests for loans from a foreign company and loans collateralized by certificates of deposit may raise questions too.

3. *Attempts to avoid reporting requirements.* Attempts to avoid reporting may include asking for an exemption from CTR reporting, and then frequent increases in exemption limits. The customer may make frequent deposits of cash just below the reporting threshold. The deposits may be made at the bank or at automatic teller machines.

4. *Unusual funds transfer activities.* Receiving or sending large volumes of funds to or from foreign countries is a leading indicator.

5. *Customers who provide insufficient or suspicious information.* This includes businesses that are reluctant to provide information about the purpose of their business, prior banking relationships, etc. It also includes customers without references or identifica-

tion, and who refuse to provide the information necessary to open an account. Banks are not required to accept unsuitable customers.

6. *Bank employees.* Sudden changes in the lifestyle of certain bank employees may not be due to winning the Florida lottery. In addition, employees who are reluctant to take vacations may have sinister reasons for not doing so.

7. *Changes in bank transactions.* Significant changes in currency shipment patterns between correspondent banks, or increases in the amount of cash handled without a corresponding increase in CTRs, are reasons to be suspicious.

References

FinCEN, *An Assessment of Narcotics Related Money Laundering,* Redacted Version, July, 1992.

FinCEN, *Bibliography of Money Laundering and Related Topics,* October 1992.

FinCEN, *Trends,* published periodically by the Financial Crimes Enforcement Network (FinCEN).

Office of the Comptroller of the Currency, *Money Laundering: A Banker's Guide to Avoiding Problems,* June 1993.

U.S. General Accounting Office, *Illicit Narcotics: Recent Efforts to Control Chemical Diversion and Money Laundering,* GAO/NSIAD-94-34, December 1993.

U.S. General Accounting Office, *Money Laundering: Characteristics of Currency Transaction Reports Filed in Calendar Year 1992,* GAO/GGD-94-45FS. November 1993.

U.S. General Accounting Office, *Money Laundering: Treasury's Financial Crimes Enforcement Network,* GAO/GGD-91-53, March 1991.

U.S. Senate, *Asian Organized Crime: The New International Criminal,* Hearings before the Permanent Subcommittee on Investigations of the Committee on Governmental Affairs, S. Hrg. 102-940, June 18 and August 4, 1992.

U.S. Senate, *Drug Money Laundering Control Efforts,* Hearing before the Subcommittee on Consumer and Regulatory Affairs of the Committee on Banking, Housing, and Urban Affairs, 101 Cong., 1st Sess., S. Hrg. 101-492, November 1, 1989.

U.S. House, *Effectiveness of the U.S. Department of the Treasury Programs to Address Money Laundering and Related Federal Tax Evasion,* Hearings before the Subcommittee on Oversight of the Committee on Ways and Means, 102nd Cong., 2nd Sess., Serial No. 102-121, June 23 and 30, 1992.

U.S. House, *Money Laundering Legislation,* Hearing before the Subcommittee on Financial Institutions Supervision, Regulation and Insurance of the Committee on Banking, Finance and Urban Affairs, 101 Cong., 2nd Sess., Serial No. 101-88, March 8, 1990, pp. 1, 50.

U.S. Senate, *Current Trends in Money Laundering*, Report prepared for the Permanent Subcommittee on Investigations of the Committee on Governmental Affairs, 102nd Cong., 2nd. Sess., S. Hrg. 102-123, December 1992.

U.S. Senate, *Current Trends in Money Laundering*, Hearing before the Permanent Subcommittee on Investigations of the Committee on Governmental Affairs, 102nd Cong., 2nd. Sess., S. Hrg. 102-579, February 27, 1992.

U.S. Senate, *Drug Money Laundering Control Efforts*, Hearing before the Subcommittee on Consumer and Regulatory Affairs of the Committee on Banking, Housing, and Urban Affairs, 101 Cong., 1st. Sess., S. Hrg. 101-492, November 1, 1989.

Endnotes

1. U.S. Senate, *Current Trends in Money Laundering*, Report prepared for the Permanent Subcommittee on Investigations of the Committee on Governmental Affairs, 102nd Cong., 2nd. Sess., S. Hrg. 102-123, December 1992, p. 1; FinCEN, *An Assessment of Narcotics Related Money Laundering*, Redacted Version, July 1992, p. 3.

2. U.S. Senate, *Drug Money Laundering Control Efforts*, Hearing before the Subcommittee on Consumer and Regulatory Affairs of the Committee on Banking, Housing, and Urban Affairs, 101 Cong., 1st. Sess., November 1, 1989, S. Hrg. 101-492, pp. 6, 38. The estimate of drug revenues was made in 1991 by the Financial Action Task Force (FATF) of the "Group of Seven" industrial countries (United States, United Kingdom, Canada, France, Germany, Italy, Japan). The FATF was created to deal with illegal international narcotics trade.

3. U.S. Senate, *Asian Organized Crime: The New International Criminal*, Hearings before the Permanent Subcommittee on Investigations of the Committee on Governmental Affairs, S. Hrg. 102-940, June 18 and August 4, 1992, p. 6.

4. *Ibid.* U.S. Senate, *Asian Organized Crime: The New International Criminal*, pp. 52-53, 97.

5. U.S. Senate, *Current Trends in Money Laundering*, Hearing before the Permanent Subcommittee on Investigations of the Committee on Governmental Affairs, 102nd Cong., 2nd. Sess., S. Hrg. 102-579, February 27, 1992, pp. 215-216, 437-444.

6. *Ibid.*, U.S. Senate, *Current Trends in Money Laundering*, Hearing, pp. 169-170, 239.

7. For details see: U.S. Treasury, Office of Financial Enforcement and Internal Revenue Service, *Currency and Foreign Transactions Reporting Act Exemptions*, 1988.

8. For details on this case, see Robert E. Powis, *The Money Launderers*, Chicago, Probus Publishing Co., 1992, Chapter 1.

9. "Lawyers Lose," *The Wall Street Journal*, March 2, 1994, p.1; U.S. House, *Effectiveness of the U.S. Department of the Treasury Programs to Address Money Laundering and Related Federal Tax Evasion*, Hearings before the Subcommittee on Oversight of the Committee on Ways and Means, 102 Cong., 2nd Sess., Serial 102-21, June 23 and 30, 1992, pp. 18-28, 82.

10. *U.S. v. Bank of New England*, 821 F.2d 844, 1st Circuit, Cert. denied. 484 U.S. 943, 1987; the example is based on Cliff E. Cook, "Complying with the Spirit of BSA: 'Know Your Customer,' Policies and Suspicious Transaction Reporting," ABA Bank Compliance, Summer 1991, appears in *Ibid.*, U.S. Senate, *Current Trends in Money Laundering*, Hearing, pp. 328-329.

11. U.S. House, *Money Laundering Legislation*, Hearing before the Subcommittee on Financial Institutions Supervision, Regulation and Insurance of the Committee on Banking, Finance and Urban Affairs, 101 Cong., 2nd Sess., Serial No. 101-88, March 8, 1990, pp. 1, 50.

12. FinCEN *Trends*, Fall 1993, p. 6.

13. United States General Accounting Office, *Illicit Narcotics: Recent Efforts to Control Chemical Diversion and Money Laundering*, GAO/NSAID-94-34, p.6.

14. *Ibid.*, U.S. Senate, *Current Trends in Money Laundering*, Hearing, p. 107; also see: FinCEN, *An Assessment of Narcotics Related Money Laundering*, *Ibid.*, pp. 8-10.

15. *Ibid.*, U.S. Senate, *Current Trends in Money Laundering*, Hearing, p. 31.

16. There is a federal recordkeeping requirement that exchanges in excess of $1,000 must be recorded (31 CFR Sect. 103.37(b)(3)). However, the cambios break their transactions into small amounts to avoid recordkeeping.

17. *Ibid.* U.S. Senate, *Drug Money Laundering Control Efforts*, Hearing, p. 85.

18. *Ibid.*, U.S. Senate, *Current Trends in Money Laundering*, Hearing, p. 7.

19. *Ibid.*, U.S. Senate, *Current Trends in Money Laundering*, Hearing, p. 83.

20. *Ibid.*, U.S. Senate, *Current Trends in Money Laundering*, Hearing, p. 41.

21. FinCEN, "Criminals Use Different Types of Illegal Banking Institutions," *Trends*, April 1992, p. 8.

22. Office of the Comptroller of the Currency, *Money Laundering: A Banker's Guide to Avoiding Problems*, June 1993.

6   DETECTING FRAUD

Profiles of Insiders Who Abuse and Rob Financial Institutions

Insiders who abuse and rob banks tend to have certain patterns of behavior that when considered collectively form a profile. The following case studies of abuse and fraud illustrate the patterns.

Edwin T. McBirney III

Edwin T. McBirney III was an insider who abused his position as chairman of Sunbelt Savings Association of Texas, but whether he crossed the line between insider abuse and criminal misconduct will be up to the courts to decide.[1] He used brokered deposits and high-risk loans to fuel Sunbelt's growth from $90 million in assets to $3.2 billion within four years. Sunbelt expanded geographically and had real estate and other interests in California, Florida, Georgia, and Illinois. McBirney and the owners of a network of S&Ls allegedly wrote $100 million loans on butcher paper, while they were eating in restaurants, and sold parts of the loans (participations) to each other to avoid restrictions on making loans greater than the net worth of their respective institutions. The originator of the loans earned from 5 percent to 10 percent ($5 million to $10 million) on the front end for making the deals. The more deals they made, the more money they earned. In 1985 and 1986, Sunbelt paid more than $12 million in cash dividends, over half of which went to McBirney. To some extent he shared the wealth with others. Sunbelt paid $1.3 million for Halloween and Christmas theme parties. One party had a jungle theme, including a live elephant. Lion and antelope meat were served to the guests and McBirney was dressed as a king. Another party theme was a Russian winter with waiters dressed as serfs. McBirney also flew important guests to Las Vegas on a borrowed Boeing 727 for weekends of gambling and entertainment, including sexual favors for some. Amid all this extravagance, Sunbelt set an industry record by losing $1.3 billion in the first three quarters of 1988. Shortly, thereafter, the government took control of it.

In a civil court action to recover $500 million and receive $100 million in punitive damages, the FSLIC alleged that McBirney and other officers mismanaged Sunbelt and engaged in illegal activities. In addition, they had made loans to cover interest payments as well as the principal, thereby creating artificial profits to mislead bank examiners and others.

Donald A. Regar

Donald A. Regar was known as an aggressive, dynamic individual who promoted the idea of a king-sized bank for himself and the community.[2] Regar was president of Metropolitan Bank & Trust Company in Tampa, Florida, that had $261 million in assets when it failed due to mismanagement and fraud. The federal indictment of Donald A. Regar and Alan Z. Wolfson, the "wheeler-dealer mastermind" behind the fraud, charged that they overvalued the property pledged for loans and misrepresented the purposes of the loans. Wolfson had been convicted previously for defrauding another Florida bank. Nevertheless, through a private stock placement, he gained virtual control of the bank, and he became Regar's bad loan workout specialist. Wolfson and his friends accounted for almost half of the bank's $160 million loan portfolio, which was backed with grossly inflated real estate appraisals. Metropolitan made unsound loans to Wolfson and others to invest in a Miami option traders' get-rich scheme that cost the bank millions in losses. Wolfson and Regar also conspired to borrow funds from the bank to purchase the bank's stock illegally.

William G. Patterson

"The Swinger Who Broke Penn Square Bank," and "Wheeler-dealers Lead to Penn Square Bank," are the titles of articles that appeared in *Fortune* and *The Tulsa Tribune* after the Penn Square Bank failed.[3] These titles provide clues about the personalities of William G. Patterson, the 33-year-old director and senior executive in charge of Penn Square's (Oklahoma) oil and gas division, and Bill P. (Beep, or Billy Paul) Jennings, Penn Square's chairman. Jennings was an unindicted co-conspirator in the Four Seasons Nursing Centers of America stock scandal in the 1970s, although officially he was not guilty of anything. He was described as a cherubic, amiable, cigar-smoking entrepreneur. In an attempt to grow the bank faster than any other bank in Oklahoma, Jennings turned to Patterson.

Patterson, it was said, knew the oil business and was such a good salesman that he "could sell snowmobiles to Okies." He was not the stereotypical banker: He engaged in food fights in restaurants and drank beer from his boots. He occasionally appeared at the bank dressed in a Tyrolean outfit, a foam rubber lobster hat, or a Nazi helmet. Despite these personality traits, Patterson was very good at selling energy participation loans to large banks, and sell he did.

When making energy loans, however, Patterson ignored engineering estimates that resulted in oil and gas reserves being grossly overstated. For example, Penn Square loaned Kenneth E. Tureaud, president of Sket Petroleum Co., $27 million that was secured by leases on reserves that the bank's petroleum engineers appraised at $7 million, and Tureaud appraised at $33 million. According to Jennings, their engineering estimates occasionally differed from the estimates of their counterparts at other banks, but the differences were usually resolved in favor of the upstream banks when they sold participations. In another deal (Professional Oil Management, Inc.), Tureaud got into trouble with the Securities and Exchange Commission for overvaluing oil and gas property, diverting proceeds from the sale of securities for purposes other than drilling, failing to escrow drilling funds, and paying secret fees and commissions.

Under Patterson's reign, the bank's assets grew from $30 to $525 million in a six-year period, and the loan portfolio they managed exceeded $2.5 billion. Part of the growth was financed by Mario Renda, a money broker who was later convicted of fraud in connection with other banks. Renda was sued for fraud in connection with selling Penn Square's CDs to credit unions, but he won that case. The actions of Mario Renda and some of his associates are examined in Chapter 7.

To get around the legal lending limits to one customer, which was about $3.5 million, Penn Square originated large loans in excess of that amount, sold 80 percent or more of them to other banks, and kept the remainder. In doing so, they earned 0.5 percent to 1 percent origination fees when the loans were sold. The fees were not tied to the long-term performance of the loans. Thus, the front-end fees served as an incentive to sell more loans without regard to quality.

Penn Square had loaned oilman Carl W. Swan large sums to wildcat drill for oil. Swan was co-chairman of Continental Drilling Company and a director of the bank. He was also Jennings' partner in deals outside the bank. When Swan hit too many dry holes, the scheme to grow Penn Square rapidly by selling energy loan participations started to fall apart. For awhile, the bank shuffled the bad loans around, trying to hide them from examiners, but it didn't work, and the bank failed.

There are interesting similarities between the failure of Metropolitan Bank of Tampa and Penn Square Bank of Oklahoma City.[4]

- Both were suburban banks.

- Both were the fourth largest banks in their respective cities.

- Both had highly concentrated loan portfolios—energy for Penn Square and real estate for Metropolitan—and both were criticized for being overextended in those areas.

- Both had about 28,000 accounts.

- Both experienced phenomenal growth.

- Management caused the failure of both.

- Wolfson was involved directly with the failure of Metropolitan.

- Metropolitan was linked indirectly to Penn Square[5]

A sad ending to the Penn Square failure is that none of the principals involved went to jail because the government failed to prove Patterson had intended to defraud the bank.[6] It was a complex financial crime that baffled the jury.

Orrin Shaid, Jr.

Orrin Shaid, Jr., a 300-pound, flamboyant Texan was paroled after serving a five-year sentence for bank fraud at the Chireno State Bank (Texas), where he was the chairman. While on parole, he took control of the Ranchlander National Bank in Melvin, Texas. Not wanting to use his name in the deal, he claimed to be a financial consultant for Lynn Carruth Maree, a tall, attractive blond. Acting in her behalf, he purchased the troubled Ranchlander bank for $186,000, although her annual salary as a secretary was $7,200. Shaid financed the deal by purchasing two $1,000 CDs from Ranchlander. He altered the certificates to show a value of $100,000 each and used the bogus CDs as collateral for a $200,000 loan from Chandler State Bank. The alterations took place in front of Jean Moon, a former waitress and the next president of Ranchlander. As president, Moon made fictitious loans and cattle loans with nonexistent collateral.

Shaid used the same CD alteration scheme to purchase two Rolls Royce automobiles, two airplanes, and a yacht. He also diverted $6 million to the Cayman Islands where he eventually intended to escape, and acquired control of First State Bank, Wells, Texas, by paying a $50,000 kickback to obtain a fraudulent loan at that bank to finance its purchase.

When Shaid told Moon to destroy Ranchlander's records, she thought that he was going to kill her and she went to the FBI. His pyramid crumbled when FBI agents arrested him one month before the end of his parole from the previous conviction.[7] He was convicted of mail fraud and was sentenced to 35 years in prison. Moon planned to go back to work as a waitress in a truck stop.

Ernest "Pug" Vickers

Ernest "Pug" Vickers committed fraud.[8] After serving as a pilot in World War II, Pug became an automobile dealer and the mayor of Huntingdon, Tennessee. He borrowed money to buy an 80 percent, controlling interest in the Carroll County Bank of Huntingdon, which had about $8 million in assets. Pug installed his own people to run the bank, and they ran it into the ground. When Pug faced serious financial problems, he stole money from the bank using nominee loans and continuing overdrafts. Pug used his friends, including an auto mechanic at his dealership, to sign more than $500,000 in personal notes from the bank and give the proceeds to him with the assurance that he would repay the loans. When neither Pug nor his friends were able to pay off the loans, the bank failed.

A Typical Profile

Keeping these cases in mind, we can better understand the following profile of a modern day bank robber. The following is an excerpt from a U.S. House, House Report:

> *"The 'typical' insider bank thief ... is a male officer, director, or majority stockholder of a commercial bank, who either commits his crimes alone or in association with a few close associates or bank employees. He is often an outgoing, flamboyant businessman who runs his bank as if it were a sole proprietorship, such as a real estate office or automobile dealership. He spends, borrows, and lends money freely, often singlehandedly exercising control over the bank. The criminal schemes he uses may be simple or complex, depending upon his own ingenuity, but they usually involve a continuing series of related transactions that extend over a substantial period of time. The activities he engages in, while hidden from public view, are usually so abusive and involve such large sums of money that any reasonably alert board of directors should discern what is really going on inside the bank. Insider abuse and fraud cannot flourish in a vacuum."*[9]

Let's elaborate on the last point about fraud not operating in a vacuum. The Comptroller of the Currency found that policies, planning, and management were problems in 89 percent of the failed national banks they examined.[10] Poor management led to poor asset quality, which caused the failures. The boards of directors at the failed banks took one of two courses of action:

1. They were uninformed, had nonexistent or poorly followed loan policies, and inadequate systems for compliance with policies and laws.

2. They were overly aggressive, had liberal lending policies (that is, making 10-year loans on equipment that had an expected life of 5 years), and fostered excessive loan growth. The latter policies went hand-in-hand with making loans that were not supported by current financial statements of the borrower, poor collateral documentation, and overlending. In either case, the directors being uniformed or being overly aggressive contributed to the bank failures.

Most of the 162 national banks that failed were small; 79 percent had assets of less than $50 million, and 64 percent had assets of less than $30 million. A surprise finding of the study was that a disproportionately large number of recently chartered banks had failed. Small banks have fewer stockholders than large ones. Therefore, it is easier for a criminal to install a friendly board of directors in a small bank that has a few passive stockholders than it is in a large bank that has actively traded stock and is closely watched by analysts and investors. However, the stockholders and directors of large banks can be duped too. Consider Jake Butcher's United American Bank in Knoxville, Tennessee, which had $838 million in assets when it failed. A congressional investigation of that bank failure found "The UAB board of directors was, by every measure, a weak board that at no time provided an independent and critical review of bank management's actions."[11] Butcher minimized his contact with the board and the information they received about the bank's condition. Basically, they "rubber stamped" whatever he wanted to do. More will be said about the Butchers and director's responsibilities in this chapter and in Chapter 7.

Looking for Fraud and Abuses

Most major frauds and insider abuse involve more than one party and do not occur overnight. They consist of a series of financial transactions over an extended period of time. As they develop, clues may emerge about their existence. These clues, called *red flags*, are warning signs that further investigation is warranted. But unless someone observes the clues, and then does something about them, the fraud and abuse continue. This was the case for Butcher's United American Bank in Knoxville, Tennessee. Federal bank regulators knew that the bank engaged in unsafe, unsound, and possibly unlawful activities for more than six years before it failed, but they failed to act decisively to eliminate the abusive practices until it was too late. Substantial time lags also occurred before the federal bank regulators took action at Franklin National Bank, Penn Square, and Empire Savings and Loan.[12]

Reducing the Time Lag

To reduce the time lag between the recognition of fraud and abuse and the actions necessary to correct them, regulatory agencies, academicians, and consulting firms are trying to develop systems to predict which banks may fail and to thwart fraud. For example, efforts are under way at regulatory agencies to detect red flags by using statistical techniques to analyze financial statements that the banks are required to submit to them on a regular basis. David Cates, a financial analyst who had analyzed the data for Empire Savings and Loan before it failed, observed the following:

1. It was growing too fast to maintain sound credit administration, especially since many of its loans were of a commercial character.

2. The growth was heavily funded by jumbo CDs ($100,000 or more).

3. The growth was so rapid that it could not occur within its natural market. Cates went to say that Empires' financial performance "appeared to us so widely irregular—and so reminiscent of pre-failure performance at Penn Square, Midland, Abilene, etc.—that I promptly dubbed Empire "the Penn Square of the thrift industry."[13]

Although Cates was able to predict the failure of Empire, a recent study dealing with the statistical analysis of S&L failures concluded that the financial characteristics associated with failures are not constant over time.[14] Variables that were significant predictors in some studies were not significant predictors in others. The record high interest rates and negative spreads that caused bank failures in early 1982 affected balance sheet data differently than sophisticated, fraud-related failures. Therefore, such models may be of limited value in detecting failures in general, as well as failures associated with fraud. Empire Savings and Loan, which is examined in Chapter 6, gave the illusion of profitability until the day before it failed. Nevertheless, the OCC believes that off-site monitoring of a bank's balance sheet changes may lead to some early detection of problems.[15] Such balance sheet changes include:

- increased past due loans,

- loan growth,

- increased volatile liability dependence,

- change in loan mix,

- change in investment portfolio,

- increase in Other Real Estate Owned,

- excessive loan charge-offs compared to other loans of the same type, and/or

- increases in borrowings or account activity more than is warranted by the business.

Some additional early indicators of vulnerable or corrupt institutions are:[16]

- a rapid growth of deposits,

- recent changes of control,

- making out-of-territory loans, and

- an absence of outside audits.

In terms of deterrents, bank regulators are also trying to develop an artificial intelligence (AI) computer program for use by bank examiners.

The AI program will give bank examiners working in banks the insights of experienced examiners in the examination process. The FDIC has proposed requiring insured banks anticipating rapid growth of 9 percent or more in three months to give the agency advanced notice. The Government Accounting Office (GAO) has proposed independent audits. Finally, bank examiners and accountants should also be aware of the possibility of fraud.

Conducting an Audit with a Possibility of Fraud

Conducting an audit while being aware of the possibility of fraud is not the same thing as doing one with the intent of looking for fraud. If the cost of a regular audit is $100,000, the cost of one to detect fraud may be triple that amount. In addition to cost, audit problems arise when there are multiple, independent institutions involved in transactions. Auditors may not be able to track certain transactions in other institutions. Finally, the Right to Privacy Act stands as a barrier to such audits.

The fact that an audit is conducted by an independent Certified Public Accountant (CPA) does not guarantee the quality of the audit or the auditor's ability to detect fraud. The GAO reviewed the quality of audit reports performed by CPAs on 11 S&Ls before they failed.[17] According to the audit reports, which ranged from 5 months to 17 months before failure, the S&Ls had a combined net worth of $44 million. When they failed they had a combined negative worth of $1.5 billion. More is said about auditing in Chapter 12.

Profits and net worth can be overstated in several ways. One method is for an S&L to make a 100 percent loan (no down payment) on acquisition, development, and land loans (ADL) that covers all of the points, fees, and the first few years of interest (retained as interest reserve), plus an "equity kicker" (a share of the profits of the project). Because ADLs are risky they carry high interest rates. They are frequently made on a "without recourse" basis, which means there is no personal guarantee by the borrower; and they may only require interest payments to be made in the early years. Because of the high interest rates and interest reserves, the S&L gives the appearance of being profitable in the first few years, although the reserve is being drawn down as interest income. Moreover, the loans cannot become delinquent until the reserve is exhausted. Before that occurs, the loan can be sold. By using such devices, S&Ls appear to be profitable. In fact, Empire Savings and Loan in Mesquite, Texas, was one of the most profitable thrifts in the country up until the time it failed.[18]

According to the GAO study, the CPAs did inadequate audits on evaluating loan collectability and did inadequate reporting on regulatory compliance and internal controls. For example, in one audit a CPA firm was aware of a $30 million past-due loan that was guaranteed by two principal shareholders, but there was little evidence in their working papers that the S&L had evaluated the collectability of that loan. In another audit, the working papers did not indicate that $625 million in loans had been restructured during the period covered by the audit. Another CPA firm did not disclose that the S&L had several hundred million dollars of loans to the principal shareholders, secured by property in a limited geographic area. Finally, in two cases, CPAs did not point out that S&Ls had materially misstated their income. In fact, one of the S&Ls actually lost four times as much as it reported.

Why Don't Employees Say Something?

One may wonder why employees who have knowledge of insider abuse or criminal misconduct don't do anything about it. When this question was asked to groups of bank employees, the answer was that they believed that such reports would cost them their jobs. Therefore, they were unwilling to report fraud and abuse to their superiors, to officers, directors, or to the FBI. Job security was more important to them than honesty and justice. This type of defensive routine is common in organizations. According to Chris Argyris, an expert in organizational behavior, such "defensive routines are powerful and omnipresent," and they can have a counterproductive impact on the organization.[19] To change such defensive routines requires changes in the culture of the organizations, as well as changes in our culture at large. Since neither of these changes is likely to occur to a great degree in the short term, efforts to encourage "whistle-blowing" will probably not meet with great success.[20]

Fast Frauds

Most frauds take time to develop, which gives examiners, auditors, and others time to discover them. However, some frauds occur virtually overnight, making it difficult to detect and to deter them. For example, some individuals seek out small, weak banks that are in danger of failing. Specifically, these individuals want to acquire banks that are financed with loans secured by the bank's stock. Subsequently, the group goes to the correspondent bank that has loaned the funds and offers to buy the stock at 20 to 50 cents on the dollar. The correspondent is glad to make the sale because if the bank fails, they will get nothing. Once they have control of the bank, the group installs their own officers and directors. Money brokers are used to pump up deposits. Then fraudulent loans are made, backed by debentures of worthless corporations they control, falsified personal financial statements, and zero-coupon Treasury bonds. Once this is done, the newly acquired bank's funds are wired to the group's accounts in other banks located elsewhere. Consequently, the withdrawal of funds could result in the newly acquired bank's failure in a very short timeframe.[21] In one case, an alert cashier notified an OCC examiner that something was wrong. The OCC visited the bank that same day, traced the funds, and blocked the accounts.

Know Your Customer

Financial institutions are expected to "know their customers." Later chapters examine several cases where banks knew or should have known that their customers were crooks. The bank's desire to book loans or open large accounts sometimes results in banks being willfully blind to the fact that their customers are engaged in illegal activities. When this occurred, the banks were fined and property was forfeited.

Red Flags

In an effort to detect bank fraud and insider abuse at an early stage, the Federal Deposit Insurance Corporation published a list of red flags, or warning signs in their *Manual of Examination Policies (Appendix A)* for use by their bank examiners. The following red flags were taken verbatim from the FDIC's manual. They are listed for specific areas that represent potential problems. Keep in mind that red flags are indicators of possible cause for concern. The manual is careful to point out that generic terms widely used in law, such as "fraud," have a central meaning that must be applied to constantly changing factual circumstances. It goes on to say that many violations of laws and regulations are subject to legal interpretation.[22] Therefore, the presence of red flags does not mean that fraud or insider abuse is present. The subject areas covered by the red flags include:

- Linked financing and brokered transactions.
- Loan participations.
- Secured lending—real estate and other type collateral.
- Insider transactions.
- Credit card and electronic funds transfer.
- Wire transfers.
- Offshore transactions.
- Third-party obligations.
- Lending to buy tax shelter investments.
- Money laundering.
- Corporate culture ethics.
- Miscellaneous.

The red flags for linked financing and brokered deposits are presented here. The red flags for the other areas are presented in Appendix A at the end of this book. Red flags for linked financing and brokered transactions include:

1. Out-of-territory lending.

2. Loan production used as a basis for officer bonuses.

3. Evidence of unsolicited attempts to buy or recapitalize the bank coupled with evidence of a request for large loans at or about the same time by persons previously unknown to the bank. Promise of large dollar deposits may also be involved.

4. Promise of large dollar deposits in consideration for favorable treatment on loan requests. (Deposits are not pledged as collateral for the loans.)

5. Brokered deposit transactions where the broker's fees are paid from the proceeds of related loans.

6. Serious consideration by a bank of a loan request where the bank would have to obtain brokered deposits to be able to fund the loan.

7. Solicitations by persons who purportedly have access to multi-millions of dollars from confidential sources which are readily available for loans and or deposits in U.S. financial institutions. Rates and terms quoted are usually more favorable than funds available through normal sources. A substantial fee may be requested in advance or the solicitor may suggest that the fee be paid at closing but demand compensation for expenses, often exceeding $50,000.

8. Prepayment of interest on deposit accounts where such deposit accounts are used as collateral for loans.

Some additional red flags that apply to white-collar crime in general that are also applicable to banks include:[23]

- Employees exceeding their scope of responsibilities.
- Failure to rescreen employees.
- Marked changes in the lifestyle of employees.
- Open-ended contracts with suppliers.
- Outside business interests of employees.
- Personal financial pressures of employees.
- Poor money management by employees.
- Unexplained rising costs or declining revenues.
- Unusual reductions in, or loss of a regular customer's business.

Endnotes

1. Thomas Moore, "The Bust of '89," *U.S. News & World Report*, January 23, 1989, pp. 36-43; Liz Galtney and Thomas Moore, "The Judicial Aftermath," *U.S. News and World Report*, January 23, 1989, p. 43; Kathleen Day, "S&L Fraud Seen Going Largely Unpunished," *The Washington Post*, February 4, 1989, pp. A1, A15; McBirney is also mentioned in Chapter 4 in connection with stock loans at Vernon S&L.

2. U.S. House, House Report 98-1137, pp. 69-75; U.S. House, *Federal Response to Criminal Misconduct by Bank Officers, Directors, and Insiders, Part 1*, Hearing before a subcommittee of the Committee on Government Operations, 98th Cong., 1st. Sess., pp. 466-482; U.S. House, *Federal Response to Criminal Misconduct by Bank Officers, Directors, and Insiders, Part 2*, Hearings before a Subcommittee on Government Operations, 98th Cong., 2nd. Sess., May 2 and 3, 1984, pp. 1904-1945.

3. Roy Rowan, "The Swinger Who Broke Penn Square Bank," *Fortune*, August 23, 1982, pp. 122-126; Hearings, Part 2, pp. 2027-2029; also see U.S. House, *Federal Supervision and Failure of the Penn Square Bank, Oklahoma City, Okla.*, Hearing before a Subcommittee of the Committee on Government Operation, 97th Cong., 2nd. Sess., July 16, 1982, pp. 457-460.

4. *Ibid.*, p. 2025.

5. Wolfson was an investor in Chilcott Portfolio Management, Inc., which was involved in commodities fraud in Colorado. Chilcott had various loans and notes from Penn Square. Wolfson also tried to borrow from Penn Square but was denied a loan. Wolfson also was linked to Tureaud, who was a large borrower from Penn Square. *Ibid.*, pp. 2028-2029.

6. Mark Singer, *Funny Money*, New York: Alfred A. Knopf, 1985. See Chapter 21 for a discussion of the Patterson trial.

7. U.S. House, Hearings, Part 2, pp. 1954-1962; U.S. House, *Federal Response to Criminal Misconduct and Insider Abuse in the Nation's Financial Institutions*, 57th Report by the Committee on Government Operations, House Report 98-1137, 98th Cong., 2nd Sess., October 4, 1984. pp. 36-37, 45.

8. U.S. House, House Report 98-1137, p. 25; U.S. House, Hearings, Part 2, p. 2032.

9. U.S. House, House Report 98-1137, p. 26.

10. *Bank Failure: An Evaluation of the Factors Contributing to the Failure of National Banks*, Washington: Comptroller of the Currency, June 1988; Susan F. Krause, Fred C. Graham, and James E. Horner, "An Evaluation of the Factors Contributing to the Failures of National Banks," presented at the Conference on Bank Structure and Competition, Federal Reserve Bank of Chicago, May 13, 1988; Fred C. Graham and James E. Horner, "Bank Failure: An Evaluation of the Factors Contributing to the Failure of National Banks," appears in *The Financial Services Industry in the Year 2000: Risk and Efficiency*, Proceedings of a Conference on Bank Structure and Compe-

tition, Federal Reserve Bank of Chicago, May 11-13, 1988, pp. 405-435. There are some differences in the various versions of this study as different phases of it were released. An early draft of this study was dated January 1988.

11. U.S. House, *Federal Supervision and Failure of United American Bank (Knoxville, Tenn.)*, Hearing before the Commerce, Consumer, and Monetary Affairs Subcommittee of the Committee on Government Operation, 98th Cong., 1st. Sess., November 18, 1983, p. 45.

12. U.S. House, *Federal Supervision and Failure of United American Bank in Knoxville, Tenn., and Affiliated Banks*, 23rd Report by the Committee on Government Operations, House Report 98-573, 98th Cong., 1st. Sess., November 18, 1983, 16-29; U.S. House, *Federal Home Loan Bank Board Supervision and Failure of Empire Savings and Loan Association of Mesquite Tex.*, Report by the Committee on Government Operations, House Report 98-953, 98th Cong., 2nd Sess., August 6, 1984, p. 9.

13. U.S. House, House Report 98-953, p. 38.

14. Patricia M. Rudolph and Bassam Hamdan, "An Analysis of Post-Deregulation Savings-and-Loan Failures," *AREUEA Journal*, Vol. 16, No. 1, Spring 1988, pp. 17-33. Also see: "Warning Lights for Bank Soundness: Special Issue on Commercial Bank Surveillance," *Economic Review*, Federal Reserve Bank of Atlanta, November 1983; Booth, David E., Perzaiz Alam, Sharif N. Ankam, and Barbara Osyk, "A Robust Multivariate Procedure for the Identification of Problem Savings and Loan Associations," *Decision Sciences*, Vol. 20, pp. 320-333.

15. Robert L. Clarke, Comptroller of the Currency, Response to the Honorable Doug Barnard, Jr., concerning U.S. House Report on Combating Fraud, March 10, 1989, Major Findings, p. 5.

16. William F. Weld, Assistant Attorney General, Criminal Division, U.S. Department of Justice, Remarks before The Banking Law Institute, 4th Annual Bank and Savings and Loan Supervision, Enforcement and Compliance Conference, Washington, D.C., September 21, 1987.

17. U.S. General Accounting Office, *CPA Audit Quality: Failures of CPA Audits to Identify and Report Significant Savings and Loan Problems*, GAO/AFMD-89-45, February 1989. U.S. General Accounting Office, "The Need to Improve Auditing in the Savings and Loan Industry," Statement of Frederick D. Wolf before the Committee on Banking, Finance and Urban Affairs, House of Representatives, GAO/T-AFMD-89-2, February 21, 1989.

18. William K. Black and William L. Robertson, "Statement of the Federal Home Loan Bank, before the Subcommittee on Financial Institutions, Supervision, Regulation, and Insurance of the Committee on Banking, Finance, and Urban Affairs, House of Representatives," 100th Cong., June 9, 1987.

19. Chris Argyris, *Strategy, Change and Defensive Routines*, Boston: Pitman Publishing Inc., 1985, p. 34.

20. Janet P. Near, "Whistle-Blowing: Encourage It!" *Business Horizons*, January/February 1989, pp. 2-6.

21. OCC Advisory, November 21, 1988.

22. U.S. House, Hearings, Part 2, 1384. This section covers administrative actions by the FDIC.

23. Joseph T. Wells, "Red Flags: The Key to Reducing White-Collar Crime," *Corporate Accounting*, Spring 1987, pp. 51-53; Robert J. Lindquist and James E. Baskerville, "To Catch a Thief," *World*, July-August 1985, pp. 32-35.

7 CRIMES BY OUTSIDERS, PART 1

This is the first of two chapters dealing with crimes by outsiders. It examines patterns of deception by outsiders who prey on financial institutions throughout the country. The same groups of outsiders are involved in crimes nationwide. Usually, the crimes are committed by both national and international networks of criminals and organized crime figures who find flaws in the fabric of our financial institutions and then exploit those flaws to their advantage, sometimes resulting in bank failures. In most cases it is not the familiar names of organized crime—La Cosa Nostra, Mafia, Triad, "the mob," or drug dealers—who cause the failures. According to the President's Commission on Organized Crime, these are groups of criminals that are bound together by ethnicity and kinship. They are united in their drive for power and profits; and they maintain their power through protectors including financial institutions, lawyers, politicians, and others.[1]

Outside Foreign Conspiracy

There is the tendency for the public to think of bank crimes in terms of a sinister foreign conspiracy. This is so because the media has convinced the public that every crime committed by two or more people who eat in a pizza parlor and drink Chianti is Mafia related. However, there is no convincing evidence that a "conspiracy" by organized crime exists to systematically steal from banks or to cause their failure.[2] On the other hand, organized crime groups from China, South America, West Africa, and elsewhere commit frauds at financial institutions. In Nigeria, for example, it is rumored that there are training schools that teach foreign nationals how to commit various small-scale bank frauds involving checks and credit cards.[3] Frauds committed by organized crime groups are described in Chapters 5, 8, and 9.

Finally, not all outsiders who commit bank crimes are connected with the crime network. Some are ordinary and extraordinary individuals who figured out a way to steal from the system.

Our primary concern, however, is with individual crooks who know each other, or who know how to contact each other when an opportunity arises to rape a bank financially. To some extent, there is "guilt by association" between some of these criminals and organized crime. However, the guilt by association gives the misleading impression that there is a closer connection between bank failures and organized crime than may actually exist.

The Distance Factor

Another difference concerning crimes by outsiders is that the institutions they exploit may be thousands of miles apart, and because they seem unrelated it is difficult to uncover the linkages between the various crimes. In this connection, this chapter focuses on Mario Renda and some of his associates who were involved in varying degrees in bank frauds and bank failures in Florida, Kansas, New York, Wyoming, and elsewhere. Renda and his associates, however, are by no means unique in the geographic dispersion of their activities. For example, Frank Domingues and Jack Bona were real estate developers from California who made fraudulent loans from a number of California and Texas S&Ls by pledging properties with overinflated values as collateral.[4] These loans contributed directly to the failure of the San Marino S&L, San Marino, California. Participations in the fraudulent loans contributed to the financial distress of S&Ls in Florida, Massachusetts, Oregon, Pennsylvania, and elsewhere. Domingues and Bona were also under criminal investigation in connection with their takeover of South Bay S&L, Newport Beach, California, which also failed. Domingues also borrowed $815,000 from Vernon S&L (which is examined in Chapter 8) to buy stock in South Bay S&L. He was also a part owner of San Diego National Bank. Bona was a co-owner of the Atlantic City Dunes Hotel and Casino.

The Sequence of Events

Some of the same individuals are involved with institutions located throughout the United States because of the way they find their prey. Hypothetically, the sequence of events may begin with a corrupt loan broker who wants to find a bank to take loans on a $5 million real estate project that is probably (or definitely) going to be a bad loan. Loan brokers may be either individuals or firms who sell loans to banks. Most are honest, but we are interested in the crooked ones.

Corrupt individuals find that the ideal bank to buy a loan from is a small bank that is in trouble because it has inadequate capital, or for some other reason, and it needs loans to grow. To find weak banks, loan brokers use bank financial data that is published in *Polk's Bank Directory* and in other sources. A list of weak banks is selected and the broker calls each of them to talk to senior officers and directors to learn more about the bank and to determine what kind of loans they can sell to that bank. Once the bank has been selected, the loan broker explains that he has certain loans that he is willing to place with that bank. Moreover, he will also arrange for the "loan package" to include funds—brokered deposits—to finance the loans. The acquisition of loans conditioned on the purchase of brokered deposits is commonly called *linked financing*. The loans may be for 10 years or longer, while the deposits may only be in the bank 90 days or less. At this point, the loan broker is counting on the cooperation of the banker who is grasping for straws to keep his bank from failing. The banker sees an infusion of funds, fees, and loans. To get the loans and funds, the bankers may be willing to overlook correct underwriting procedures and ignore sound controls that are ordinarily in place.

To avoid the appearance of out-of-territory loans, local escrows and nominees may be used. If the bankers used common sense, they probably would not make such loans. However, they are under pressure to improve the performance of their bank. The loan brokers and crooks require the voluntary cooperation of some insiders and the unwitting help of others to close their deals. The loan brokers believe that bankers in this position are generally dumb, have ego problems, and are greedy. The fact that many bankers have fallen for such deals suggests that the brokers are correct in their assessment. When the deal is closed, the loan broker gets paid by the borrower, gets paid a finder's fee from the deposit broker, and is then no longer associated with the deal, leaving the bank holding loans that will go bad and that are financed with short-term brokered deposits. A weak bank, bad long-term loans, and hot money (short-term deposits) are the essential ingredients for failure. Even when regulators suspect something is wrong, there may be little they can do about it until it is too late to save the bank.

The Escapades of Mario Renda

Deposit Broker

Mario Renda, president and founder of First United Fund, Ltd., Garden City, New York, was a major player in various bank failures and frauds.[5] First United Fund was a holding company engaged in money brokerage, investments in government securities, real estate lending, discount brokerage, and other activities.

Renda—First United Fund—was a source of brokered deposits for the following failed banks: Penn Square bank (described in Chapter 6), Empire Savings and Loan and Mainland Savings (described in Chapter 10), San Marino S&L (mentioned at the beginning of this chapter), and failed banks in Kansas, Maryland, and Florida. He was also involved in one of the nation's largest pension fund scams. Several of his escapades and those of his associates are examined in this chapter.

Deposit Broker

First United Fund was one of the five most active deposit brokers, dealing with more than 1,000 financial institutions. A *deposit broker* is defined as "any person or entity engaged in the business of placing deposits for oth-ers, or in placing funds in accounts to be sold to others, an agent or trustee who established a deposit or member account in connection with an agree-ment with the institution to use the proceeds in the account to fund a prear-ranged loan."[6] This definition, however, excludes banks.

First United Fund brokered investments in the following manner. Em-ployees, officers, and agents of First United Fund solicited banks and other financial institutions and negotiated rates of interest and related terms on deposits. Then First United, or its agents, contacted its clients, advised them of the terms, and arranged for the investments to be made. When the deal was closed, First United demanded payment from the banks issuing the CDs. For example, suppose a credit union wanted to invest $5 million in CDs. The credit union would then wire the funds to a deposit broker who would then wire it in fully insured $100,000 blocks to the 50 banks paying the highest rates. Some brokers often invest more than $100,000 in banks and then subdivide the funds into amounts that provide full insur-ance coverage. Other brokers invest more than $100,000 and accept the risk of uninsured deposits. CDs of $100,000 or more with maturities in excess of one year are called *long-term jumbo CDs*.

Deposit brokers get better rates than individual depositors because of the large amounts of money they control. The credit union in the previous example gets insured deposits and the deposit broker earns up to $50,000 in commissions for the transaction. Deposit brokers' commissions usually range from 25 to 100 basis points, or $250 to $1,000 for each $100,000 of funds placed. In 1983, it is estimated that First United Fund placed over $2.5 billion in bank certificates of deposit and earned more than $3.2 mil-lion.

Deposit brokers may work with loan brokers to find target banks, or they may select their own targets. One way in which First United allegedly defrauded clients was with their so-called "special deal." One of the bro-kers selected a target bank from which to make a loan. The broker then solicited customers to invest in that bank by misrepresenting the rate of interest that they would receive. First United would procure the loan and make up the difference in interest rates paid by the bank and what was promised the investor with funds from the loan.[7]

In a 1985 survey by the FDIC of the largest suppliers of fully insured deposits to *troubled* insured banks, Merrill Lynch ranked 1st with $771.3 million and First United Fund ranked 13th with $28.1 million.[8] The survey did not include institutions that were financially sound.

There is nothing illegal about brokered deposits. They serve a useful function in the financial markets of facilitating the flow of capital. How-ever, abuses can occur and Renda and his associates excelled in this area. Similarly, there is nothing illegal about linked financing, but it too may lead to abuses which affect the soundness of a bank, as is illustrated by

Indian Springs Bank. Renda's First United Fund engaged in linked financing with 17 other banks, 14 of which ultimately failed. The combined deposits for all the banks was over $2 billion. Many, but not all linked financing deals are associated with real estate. For example, First Federal Savings and Loan Association of Beloit, Kansas, used brokered deposits to invest $5.6 million in a Hungarian movie, called "Predator," which was about a rock band chased by a man-eating bear. The movie was never finished and the loan went into default. Clifford R. Roth, esquire, an officer of First Federal Savings and Loan, was also the former general counsel at Indian Springs Bank.

Linked Financing: The Case of Indian Springs Bank

Indian Springs Bank was a small, one-office bank located between Wig City and Athlete's Foot on the lower level of a shopping center in Kansas City, Kansas. William Lemaster, president of the bank, wanted it to be a big bank. He hired Anthony R. Russo as a bank officer to help the bank grow. Russo, a former prominent criminal lawyer who represented reputed mobsters, was a convicted felon who had served a 16-month prison term in Levenworth Penitentiary for conspiracy to bribe and for promoting prostitution. Within an eight-month period after being hired by the bank, Russo was promoted from vice-president to executive vice-president. Because Russo was a convicted felon, the bank required FDIC approval for his employment. The FDIC gave its approval, but restricted Russo's activities to new business development. The new business he generated included accounts of and loans to reputed organized crime figures in Kansas City and Chicago. When a number of these loans failed, the FDIC put pressure on Lemaster to get rid of Russo. One such loan was for $300,000 made to Carmen Civella, son of Kansas City mob leader Carl Civella. To get around the FDIC, Russo was elected chairman of Indian Springs' holding company. In that position he was not an employee of a federally insured institution and was outside the FDIC's jurisdiction.[9]

    While on vacation in Hawaii, Russo met real estate developers Franklin Winker and Sam Daily. Mario Renda had a social and business relationship with Winkler and Daily in First United Management Co. Ltd. First United Management's articles listed Renda as president, Winkler as executive vice-president, and Daily as executive vice president and secretary. The company received $25,000 in management fees for managing the Hawaiian real estate development partnerships. Renda was also partners with Winkler and Daily in First United Partners Four, another real estate partnership.

    Winkler and Daily arranged a linked financing deal between their real estate development in Hawaii, First United Fund, and Indian Springs Bank. Brokered deposits from First United Fund were the key to the deal. In the early 1980s, Indian Springs' assets grew from about $6 million to more than $50 million. The growth was financed largely by brokered deposits. When the bank did not roll over maturing CDs, its assets shrank to $27 million in 1984—the same year it was closed. The bank's deposits included $9.3 million of brokered deposits; First United Fund provided about $6 million.

Indian Springs Bank agreed to accept $6 million in brokered deposits from Renda's First United Fund if certain loans were made on favorable terms in connection with the Hawaiian real estate development. The commissions on the brokered deposits were paid to First United Fund from an account set up by Winkler and Daily to distribute loan funds to the limited partners, instead of the commissions being paid by the bank. Also, First United Fund made payments to Indian Springs Bank to subsidize the high cost of the CDs, thereby creating an artificial market for them.

Indian Springs Bank got around its legal lending limit on large loans of 15 percent of capital, surplus, and undivided profits, plus half of the loan loss reserve to a single borrower, by making relatively small, unsecured loans to individual investors who would use the funds to invest in a Hawaiian real estate development, instead of making large loans to the real estate partnerships. Indian Spring's legal lending limit ranged from about $250,000 to $350,000. The bank loaned $3.7 million to about 30 individuals, who invested the funds in speculative real estate partnerships in Hawaii and to the partnership's organizers. Some of these borrowers were paid $2,000 to $3,000 by the real estate developers to fraudulently apply for the loans and then make the funds available to Winkler and Daily. This method of getting around the bank's legal lending limit is called *mortgage pulling*. Renda was the president of Southbrook Inc., which was one of the limited partners in the real estate development. The total loans in this venture exceeded Indian Springs Banks' lending limit by about 10 times! They accounted for about 16 percent of the bank's total loans.

Of the $3.7 million loaned by the bank, Daily and related companies received about $930,000. Winkler and related companies and trusts got $603,500; Renda's First United Fund and Southbrook got $78,000. That left $2 million for investments in real estate.

An FDIC examination of Indian Springs Bank in December 1982 uncovered large loans made outside its normal market area, and it ordered accelerated repayments of the Hawaiian real estate development loans. At a meeting between the FDIC and the bank's board of directors, the directors were told that the bank was near insolvency as a result of the loans on the Hawaiian real estate development. Until then, the directors were unaware of the details of these loans. Part of the bank's plan to resolve their problem consisted of making more loans on similar real estate development projects in Hawaii and Missouri that were organized by some of the same characters. The maturity on the original loans was approaching and the bank was not going to renew them.

The private placement memorandum for one of the limited partnerships advised prospective investors that the Hawaiian real estate development was a speculative security, and that it was going to purchase residential real estate that was subject to large cash flow deficits. The funds raised would permit the properties to be carried until they could be satisfactorily liquidated. Three limited partners in the real estate development refused to repay the loans to the bank, claiming that they were told by the general partners that the loans would never have to be repaid. Moreover, Lemaster told them that the loans would be rolled over when they matured at the end of one year, and that it was the general partners—not the limited partners—who would repay the loans. In July 1983, five days before the loans matured, Lemaster was killed in an automobile accident. His son thought that he might have been murdered. With the problem loans written off when the bank could not collect on them, the Kansas Banking Department closed the bank in January 1984.

The Federal Deposit Insurance Corporation and the Federal Home Loan Bank Board brought charges against Renda, his wife, and their related companies for bank fraud under the authority of the Racketeer Influenced and Corrupt Organizations Act (RICO). The FDIC claimed that the partnership interests were securities, and that through the use of mortgage pullers, securities were sold in violation of securities and racketeering laws. False representations were made to obtain the loans. There was a "conspiracy" and a "pattern of racketeering" to defraud Indian State Bank. The bank's failure was a direct result of the failure to repay the loans of the Hawaiian and Missouri real estate partnerships. As noted in Chapter 2, The FDIC and FHLBB sought treble damages of $63.5 million but settled with the Renda's for $10.4 million. The FDIC was also awarded treble damages of $61.2 million against Winkler. Collecting that amount is another matter. Daily filed for bankruptcy in Hawaii. He cannot be sued without the bankruptcy court's permission.

The linked financing schemes described in the Indian Springs Bank case also caused the failures of Coronado Federal Savings and Loan, which was located in the same shopping center as Indian Springs Bank, and Rexford State Bank, Rexford, Kansas. Indian Springs was the "pilot project" for the fraudulent schemes.

Linked Financing: The Case of Florida Center Bank

The principal participants in this case are Michael Hellerman, Charles J. Bazarian, John A. Bodziak, and Mario Renda. For simplicity, not all of the individuals involved in these and other schemes described in the book are mentioned by name. However, one individual who was indicted for fraud in connection with this and other banks, Jake Butcher, is discussed in Chapter 10.[10]

In the early 1970s, Michael Hellerman faced a long prison term for masterminding securities frauds. Instead of going to jail, he provided testimony that led to the conviction of organized crime figures in New York. Hellerman explained his links to organized crime in his 1977 book, *Wall Street Swindler*. His co-author, Thomas C. Renner, describes Hellerman in the book as having the "characteristics of a chameleon. He could and did create new swindles while playing the secret role of informer for federal prosecutors." Hellerman was "Driven by an almost insatiable desire for riches and luxury ... Hellerman was the very personification of the white-collar criminal."[11]

Under the federal witness protection program, created in 1970 by the Omnibus Crime Control Act, Hellerman's name was changed to Michael Rapp, and he moved to Florida.

The second primary figure in the Florida Center Bank case was Charles J. Bazarian. He had an eighth grade education but was the "consummate con man." He even conned the U.S. Attorney who prosecuted him into making a worthless investment.[12] In 1978, Bazarian received a four-year suspended sentence for mail fraud. Following a bankruptcy, he gained wealth and fame as he became one of the largest operators of low-income housing projects backed by HUD mortgages. His net worth was estimated to be $32 million, and he lived in a 23,000-square-foot house. At the time of this case, he was under investigation by the Justice Department for real estate activities in Oklahoma and California. Bazarian was also named in a FSLIC lawsuit in connection with the failure of Consolidated Savings Bank, Irvine, California. Consolidated made loans to Bazarian's Oklahoma-based corporation for about $9 million without appraisal or proper loan documentation.[13] In addition, he pleaded guilty to defrauding American Diversified Savings Bank in Costa Mesa, California. He was sentenced to five years in prison that was to run concurrently with the two-year sentence that he received in the Florida Center Bank case. In return for helping prosecutors, his sentence was reduced, and he was released from prison on probation. However, Bazarian violated the probation rules and was put back in jail. But Bazarian had one goal at this time—to see his daughter get married on September 4, 1993. A federal judge granted him a 24-hour furlough. Bazarian attended the wedding in Oklahoma, and he went on a honeymoon too. He disappeared. FBI agents found Bazarian on November 26, 1993, in Puerto Rico. He was watching a screening of "Carlito's Way." In this movie, Al Pacino plays a drug dealer trying to go straight.

The third figure in this case was John A. Bodziak, chairman of Florida Center Bank, Orlando, Florida. The bank had about $37 million in assets.

Rapp, aided and abetted by Renda and Bazarian, secretly purchased the controlling interest (51 percent) in Florida Center Bank from Bodziak and other shareholders. The bank was in poor financial condition and had been operating under a cease-and-desist order from the FDIC. The bank stock proved to be a poor investment for Bodziak, and Rapp was willing to pay him 10 times its actual value. The sale of the stock was financed by the proceeds of a bogus $30 million, 10-year loan to PaceCom Inc., to install pay telephones. According to federal investigators, Rapp secretly owned PaceCom. Rapp offered to pay Clyde Pichford (a Virginia stockbroker who needed money to replace cash he had stolen from certain accounts) and Dallas, Texas, investors a $5 million fee to arrange a loan of $20 million for PaceCom, providing that Rapp's role be kept secret.[14] The terms of the loan called for no scheduled interest payments and no payment of principal until maturity. Moreover, the loan could not be declared in default during its term. The collateral for the loan was 2,000 pay phones and a 10-year CD, on which the bank prepaid all of the interest to PaceCom. Rapp obtained an opinion letter from a Miami lawyer stating that the loan conformed to regulations, laws, and guidelines.

At the time the loan was granted, the bank received large inflows of brokered deposits (which accounted for 40 percent of total deposits before it failed). Mario Renda met with Rapp, Pichford, a Texas investor, and Bazarian who wanted to "rent" $20 million for one day to buy a CD that could be offered as security for the loan. The funds would be loaned, provided that they never left Bazarian's possession. When the transaction was completed, Bazarian wired $100,000 to Renda's attorney for Renda's use.

Some of the funds from the loan were used to pay for the stock and to make a capital injection into the bank. Pichford never got his $5 million. About half of the loan funds had been disbursed before the regulators blocked the transaction. The bank was closed shortly thereafter.

Rapp received a 32-year prison term and a $1.75 million fine. He was also indicted for defrauding Sun Bank of Miami in a check-kiting scheme. The Hellerman (a.k.a. Michael Rapp) story is not over. We will examine how Hellerman and organized crime figures contributed to the failure of The Aurora Bank, Aurora, Colorado, and his role in the failure of Flushing Federal Savings and Loan, Queens, New York.

Bodziak was sentenced to 10 years in prison and was fined $50,000. Renda and Bazarian were each sentenced to two years in prison and were fined $100,000.

Pichford was sentenced to 25 years in Virginia for embezzlement and bank fraud in that state.

Pension Fund Scandal

Martin Schwimmer was a financial consultant and agent of First United Fund. He was also an investment adviser registered with the SEC. As such, he served as an adviser to and agent for the employee benefit plans of Union Locals 38 and 810. Local 38 of the Sheetmetal Workers International Association of the AFL-CIO and Local 810 of the International

Brotherhood of Teamsters, Chauffeurs, Warehousemen and Helpers of America were both of New York. As their consultant, Schwimmer advised them to invest in long-term jumbo CDs brokered by First United Funds. Renda actively engaged in the solicitation of banks and savings and loans, and in the negotiations and terms concerning the long-term jumbo CDs. First United Fund raised more than $100 million in funds from two union employee benefit plans. These funds were used to purchase long-term jumbo CDs at 18 banks and S&Ls. The failure of at least two of the S&Ls, Old Court Savings and Loan in Baltimore, Maryland, and Mainland Savings Association in Houston, Texas, was associated with fraud in those institutions.

Schwimmer and/or Renda opened six non-interest bearing checking accounts in the name of First United Fund and First United, Inc., that were not recorded on First United's books, which is generally called *off-the-book accounts*. These off-the-book accounts were located in banks in California, Connecticut, Iowa, New Jersey, and New York. The off-the-book accounts were concealed from First United's auditors and from the trustees of the union's employee benefit plans. Renda also opened an account at European American Bank in Mineola, New York, which was recorded on First United's books.

Renda and his co-conspirators directed the banks and savings and loans to transfer more than $14 million in commission to the off-the-book accounts, telling them falsely that the funds would be used for the benefit of the unions' employee benefit plans. Similarly, $2 million was directed to be deposited in the European American Bank account. Eventually, Schwimmer and Renda used some of these funds for the benefit of themselves and others, including the purchase of stocks, bonds, and luxury items, and the transfer of funds to companies they controlled or in which they held an interest. Some funds were used to pay cash kickbacks to officials of Local 810 and its employee benefit plan. The commissions paid to the union officials were cash payments of about seven-eighths of a percentage point of the face value of each CD.

The indictment against Schwimmer and Renda charged that they created false documents to hide the existence of their conspiracy and impeded government investigators. It also charged that Renda embezzled $4 million in funds from Local 810's employee benefit plan and used it for his own use. This list of charges is by no means complete, but it does give some indication of the magnitude of their fraudulent dealings.

Anant Kumar Tripati: World Class Con Man

Anant Kumar Tripati was described by the United States Attorney for the District of Wyoming as "a world class con man."[15] Tripati, a native of India, allegedly was being investigated in Fiji for insurance fraud and in

London for a scam involving letters of credit. He was president and chief executive officer of Fort Lincoln Group, Inc., Santa Monica, California, a holding company for Fort Lincoln Life Insurance Company and Fort Lincoln Life Assurance Company of Minot, North Dakota. Tripati convinced the Insurance Commissioner of North Dakota that he personally had more than $300 million in CDs in a nonexistent London bank called Credit Internationale. The Insurance Commissioner believed him and certified this to be so.

Tripati's Fort Lincoln Life Insurance Company sold millions of dollars of annuities to three small banks, two of which failed.[16] The total dollar value of the annuities purchased by the banks exceeded their legal lending limits. Western National Bank of Lovell, Wyoming, had $1.4 million in capital and $16 million in annuities, and it failed. Community Bank of Hartford, South Dakota, had $3.3 million in capital and $10 million in annuities, and it failed. First National Bank & Trust Company, Wilbaux, Montana, survived its dealings with Tripati.

Tripati posed as a buyer of Western National Bank and First National Bank & Trust Company while he bought Community Bank of Hartford. All three banks were for sale. At First National Bank & Trust, Tripati staged a closing transaction by presenting a check for an undisclosed sum of money to one of the stockholders. Posing as the new or prospective owner gave him instant credibility at that bank and other banks, and dutiful bank officers and employees did as they were told. He promised Western National Bank Vice-President Michael Carter and First National Bank President James Carter (no relation to Michael Carter) promotions to boost their careers. He paid a $110,000 "finder's fee" to Raymond Dana, Community Bank's president. It was the two Carters and Dana who authorized the purchases of annuities from Tripati's insurance company.

To induce the banks to buy annuities, Tripati offered rates that exceeded current market rates of interest that were being paid on annuities. Another inducement was that the annuities had short maturities that ranged from one month to three years. When the first annuities matured, the insurance company sold additional annuities to pay off the first ones. Therefore, if regulators forced Tripati to pay off the annuities at one bank, he could sell annuities to another bank and use those funds to satisfy the regulators. The scheme had considerable potential for growth if everything had worked the way Tripati planned it.

The financial statements of Fort Lincoln Life Insurance Company shown to the banks were incomplete, since 14 of 21 pages were missing. Although the financial condition of the insurance company could not be verified, events showed that it did not have sufficient funds to pay off the annuities it sold.

The funds used to buy the annuities came from brokered deposits supplied by Mario Renda's First United Fund. At one time Renda and Tripati were partners owning a condominium in Florida. According to one report, Tripati instructed bank employees to use First United Fund to buy brokered deposits. The three banks involved in the scheme purchased more than $37 million in brokered deposits. Almost $26 million of those funds went into accounts controlled by Tripati to buy annuities. He used some of the funds from annuity sales to buy banks, and some he intended to send off-shore where it would be safe for him to retire when he tired of the scheme and left the country.

At Western National Bank, Tripati induced the bank to buy $15.9 million in brokered deposits from First United Fund. Western then purchased $9.6 million in annuities from Fort Lincoln Life Insurance Company. It is alleged that Tripati embezzled $6 million from the bank funds resulting from the sale of the annuities. Brokered deposits accounted for 64 percent of Western's total deposits. Some funds from the accounts Tripati controlled were used to purchase the bank.

The scheme began to fall apart during a routine FDIC examination of Imperial Bank in Los Angeles, where Tripati had an account. Bank examiners became suspicious of a $10 million check drawn on Community Bank of Hartford for the benefit of Fort Lincoln Life Insurance Company. Why would a small community bank write such a large check to an insurance company? The FDIC contacted banking authorities in South Dakota who began an investigation. The FDIC froze Tripati's account in Los Angeles, which made it impossible for him to cover the annuities coming due at Western National Bank, Wyoming. South Dakota bank officials closed the Community Bank of Hartford, and one week later the OCC closed Western National Bank, Wyoming. Therefore, First National Bank & Trust Company was able to back out of its deals with Tripati. Eventually, Tripati was convicted on 10 counts of bank fraud violations and was sentenced to 10 years in prison.

Gold Diggers

Dennis Nowfel, president of The Aurora Bank, Aurora, Colorado, was described as flamboyant, brusque, and hot tempered, but he was well-respected in the banking community.[17] Both Nowfel and his vice-president, William Vanden Eynden, had a problem; they liked to gamble. Unfortunately for them, they were losers. Between drugs, prostitutes, and hotel bills, they would spend up to $30,000 in a weekend at Las Vegas. They borrowed from other Denver banks to pay off their gambling debts and other debts.

Nowfel and Vanden Eynden met Faud Sam Jezzeny, a Las Vegas gambler, who proposed a deal that would make all of them rich. Part of the deal included paying Jezzeny's living expenses and gambling debts. The bankers introduced Jezzeny to Heinrich Rupp. Rupp had a metal recovery business in Aurora, Colorado. Allegedly, Rupp had been tried for Nazi war crimes, skied on the Swiss Olympic team, was a pilot for King Faisal of Saudi Arabia, and had a large stash of gold. Rupp opened the "Swiss American account" at Aurora Bank through which the fraudulent loan money was channeled. The bankers claimed that Rupp was the exclusive representative of five Swiss banks wanting to make large loans to American firms.

The cast of the principal characters is almost complete when the bankers and Jezzeny meet Michael Rapp in Florida. Michael Rapp, also known as Michael Hellerman, caused the downfall of Florida Center Bank that was described previously. Rapp introduced them to members of various East Coast crime families who were interested in getting loans from the Aurora and Swiss banks. John Napoli, a New York career criminal who was present at that meeting, told the bankers that by putting up $2 million, his mob contacts would pay them $9 million for the laundering of stolen cash or "hoist money."

Over a two-year period, the bankers made more than 100 loans for almost $10 million in the Swiss American account. The bank records falsely showed that the loans were made for use in Rupp's business, for tax shelters, and for a chain of delicatessens. Two loans to fund the stolen cash were made by Anthony DelVecchio and Jilly Rizzo, who will be discussed shortly.

According to Napoli, the bankers flew around the world, dropping off money to his friends and relatives while they waited for the elusive $9 million.[18] Some of the funds were used by Napoli and Joseph Chilli III, a reputed Bonanno mobster, to set up a delicatessen where other mobsters were invited to hang out, and the FBI was invited to film them, which they did. The FBI filmed mobsters, including Gambino capo Thomas Bilotti, who was later gunned down, talking about murder and other crimes. Napoli helped the FBI in their deli sting operation to get a reduction in a sentence in a drug con. Napoli and Frank (Frankie Butch) Guglieimini conned a drug dealer, who had previously conned Napoli, out of $180,000, only to discover that the drug dealer was working for the Drug Enforcement Agency. Napoli was sentenced to 10 years, and while on appeal decided to cooperate with the FBI.

Although the bankers delivered almost $2 million to the mobsters, they never got their $9 million in stolen cash. The bankers hid the mounting overdrafts from the bank's directors by altering the books and bouncing checks between other banks. At one point the overdraft in the Swiss American account amounted to $1.3 million. In a desperate move to cover their tracks, the bankers issued a $1.6 million note secured by drums of gold-bearing ore, valued at $2 million, that were buried in Rupp's backyard. The actual value turned out to be $1,200. When they could no longer hide their scheme, they reported it to the bank's directors and were fired. State banking authorities closed the bank, which by then had a negative equity capital of $2.05 million.

Nowfel pleaded guilty to bank fraud and got a two-year prison sentence, and Vanden Eynden pleaded guilty to bank fraud and tax charges and got a seven-year sentence.

Michael Hellerman (a.k.a. Michael Rapp), Anthony DelVecchio, and Jilly Rizzo were also involved in the failure of Flushing Federal Savings and Loan Association, Queens, New York. Flushing failed following two years of rapid and uncontrolled growth and risky lending practices. Hellerman and others who borrowed $8 million from Flushing were sued by the Federal Savings and Loan Insurance Corporation for violations of RICO. Hellerman, DelVecchio, and Rizzo were also named as defendants in a civil suit.

Endnotes

1. President's Commission on Organized Crime, Report to the President and the Attorney General, *The Impact: Organized Crime Today*, April 1986, Washington, Government Printing Office, p. 29.

2. Vincent P. Cookingham, "Organized Crime: The Corporation as Victims," *Security Management*, Vol. 29, No. 7, July 1985, pp. 28-31; "Bank Fraud and Embezzlement," *FBI Law Enforcement Bulletin*, February 1975, revised February 1978.

3. U.S. House, *Adequacy of Federal Efforts to Combat Fraud, Abuse, and Misconduct in Federally Insured Institutions*, Hearing before the Commerce, Consumer, and Monetary Affairs Subcommittee of the House Committee on Government Operations, 100th Cong., 1st., Sess., November 19, 1987, p. 868; Michael Violano, "The High-Tech Future of Foiling Fraud and Forgery," *Bankers Monthly*, April 1989, p. 37.

4. U.S. House, *Combating Fraud, Abuse, and Misconduct in the Nation's Financial Institutions: Current Federal Efforts Are Inadequate*, 72nd Report by the Committee on Government Operations, House Report 100-1088, 100th Cong., 2nd Sess., October 13, 1988, pp. 182-185.

5. Between August 1983 and March 1989, *American Banker*, published 55 articles dealing with Mario Renda and his associates. The most significant articles were written by Richard Ringer and Bart Faust. The information presented here draws heavily on those articles, but they are not cited individually. Similarly, Pete Brewton wrote a series of articles for *The Houston Post*, linking Renda to Herman K. Beebe, Sr., who is examined in Chapter 8, and to organized crime. These include the following: "Bank Fraud Investigators Looking for a National Plot," February 11, 1988; "S&L Probe Grew—and Grew Again," March 13, 1988; "Major Break Foreseen in Bank Fraud Probes," May 3, 1988; "Mafia's Involvement in S&L Failures Probed," October 8, 1988; "Bentsen Says He Has No Objections to Probe of Mob Role

in S&L Failures," October 9, 1988; "Conviction Won't Stop Probe into Bank Fraud," November 9, 1988—this article deals with Schwimmer who is discussed later; "Links to Mob Figures, Suspect Offshore Companies Abound," December 8, 1988, "Brokered Deposits Case Produces Prison Term," March 1, 1989 (Schwimmer); Other sources include: U.S. House, House Report 100-1088, October 13, 1988, *Ibid.,* pp. 185-186. U.S. House, *Federal Regulation of Brokered Deposits in Problem Banks and Savings Institutions*, Committee on Government Operations, House Report 98-1112 (Committee on Government Operations Report No. 52), September 28, 1984; U.S. House, *Federal Regulation of Brokered Deposits: A Follow-up Report*, 38th Report by the Committee on Government Operations, 1985, House Report 99-358; U.S. House, *Impact of Brokered Deposits on Banks and Thrifts: Risks versus Benefits*, Hearing before the Subcommittee on General Oversight and Investigations of the Committee on Banking, Finance and Urban Affairs, 99th Cong., 1st. Sess., July 16, 1985, Serial No. 99-36; FHLBB, FDIC Joint Press Release, PR-42-89 (2-28-89).

6. 12 CFR, 330, 561, 564.

7. *U.S. v. Schwimmer and Renda*, 692 F. Supp. 119 (E.D.N.Y. 1988). Although not discussed here, in Count 79 of Schwimmer's indictment, the government was going to introduce evidence that Schwimmer was involved with organized crime figures; *U.S. v. Martin Schwimmer and Mario Renda*, Eastern District of New York, CR 87-00432, Filed June 28, 1988. These were the primary sources for the discussion of the Pension Fund Scandal.

8. U.S. House, Hearing, July 16, 1985, p. 39.

9. Under the Financial Institutions Reform, Recovery and Enforcement Act of 1989, Sec. 910, civil money penalties can be imposed on institutions which willfully employ, without the permission of the appropriate banking agencies, persons convicted of certain crimes. This includes "persons participating in the conduct of the affairs of" an institution.

10. U.P. I., "Jake Butcher Indicted for Fraud in Florida," Sept. 1, 1989, p. 2; Press Release, U.S. Attorney, Middle District of Florida, August 30, 1989; Middle District of Florida. It is alleged that Butcher and others conspired to bilk $4 million from the Florida Center Bank. Butcher, who is currently in federal prison for bank fraud, is charged with 19 counts in the current indictment. According to Ricardo R. Pesquerza, Assistant U.S. Attorney, there was no link between Butcher and Hellerman (a.k.a. Rapp).

11. Michael Hellerman and Thomas C. Renner, *Wall Street Swindler*, New York: Doubleday & Company, 1977, p. ix.

12. "Travels with Charlie Bazarian," *Business Week*, November 15, 1993, pp. 156-158; "Sorry Charlie," *Business Week*, December 13, 1993, p. 95.

13. Allen Pusey and Lee Hancock, "Network Fueled $10 Billion S&L Loss," *Dallas Morning News*, December 4, 1988, p. 31A. This article deals extensively with Herman K. Beebe Sr. and others.

14. *U.S. v. Rapp,* 871 F.2d 957 (11th Cir. 1989).

15. U.S. House, *Adequacy of Federal Efforts to Combat Fraud, Abuse, and Misconduct in Federally Insured Institutions,* Hearing before the Commerce, Consumer, and Monetary Affairs Subcommittee of the House Committee on Government Operations, 100th Cong., 1st Sess., November 19, 1987, pp. 77-78. Other information about Tripati was taken from the articles cited in connection with Mario Renda. These sources differ on whether Tripati is a native of Fiji or India.

16. National banks may only invest in instruments for which they have express authority (12 U.S.C., #24 (Seventh); 12 C.F.R. part 1.). That authority does not include investing in single-premium retirement annuity contracts as an investment.

17. Sue Lindsay, "Aurora Gold Dealer Goes on Trial," *Rocky Mountain News,* November 29, 1987, p. 10; Sue Lindsay, "Final Chapter Opens in Bank's Downfall," *Rocky Mountain News,* November 29, 1987, p. 8, 26; Sue Lindsay, "5 Indicted in Fraud Scheme that Felled The Aurora Bank," *Rocky Mountain News,* April 23, 1987, p. 9. Telephone conversation with Sue Lindsay, 5/18/89. The Aurora Bank which is described here has no connection with The Bank of Aurora, Aurora, Colorado, which failed May 24, 1989 (FDIC News Release, PR-108-89, 5/24/89).

18. Jerry Capeci, "He Straddled the Fence," *New York Daily News,* date unknown.

8 CRIMES BY OUTSIDERS, PART 2

This chapter is about crimes committed by both outsiders and insiders. Outsiders sometimes require the aid of insiders (i.e., officers, directors, owners) in their schemes to defraud financial institutions. The chapter also deals with crimes committed by West Africans. These include crimes against financial institutions as well as crimes against businesses and individuals. The final part of the chapter examines worthless financial instruments and unauthorized banks.

Make Lots of Money Quick

Kickbacks

Kickbacks are usually relatively small amounts of money that by themselves do not qualify as a major bank fraud in the context used in this book. However, the practice is sufficiently common that the aggregate amount of kickbacks amounts to huge sums. By way of illustration, consider the case of Larry K. Thompson and Tyrell G. Barker.[1]

Thompson was a real estate and loan broker who agreed to buy a 366-acre tract of property in Midland, Texas. Tyrell "Terry" G. Barker was the owner and chairman of the board of State Savings and Loan Association in Lubbock, Texas. He was also the owner of Barker Development Corporation, a real estate development company in Dallas. Barker, who has dyslexia, could only read at a third-grade level according to a psychologist's report, but he was smart and learned to speculate in the real estate market. Barker, who knew little about banking, borrowed the funds to buy State Savings from Herman K. Beebe, Sr., owner of a Houston S&L and chairman of the board of AMI Inc., a firm in Shreveport, Louisiana, with interests in nursing homes, motels, and credit life insurance. One reason why Beebe financed the purchase of State Savings was to have the S&L sell his credit life insurance. Barker was not particularly successful at selling the credit life insurance, but he more than made up for it in real estate deals.[2] Barker was willing to lend on real estate projects where he got a 50 percent interest, and the borrowers were not required to invest any of their own money. More will be said about Beebe and Barker shortly.

Thompson asked Barker to coventure the real estate deal. Barker agreed and told Thompson that State S&L would fund the deal and that Thompson would take on six partners, all of whom were Barker's associates. At Barker's direction, the partners formed a partnership known as Make Lots of Money Quick (MLMQ #1). Their plan was to coventure with Thompson in order to purchase and develop the tract known as Northwood Venture. Barker arranged for State S&L to lend $2 million for the purchase and closing costs of Northwood Venture. From that amount, a $200,000 commission would be paid to Thompson, who would then wire $100,000 of it to Barker Development Corporation. Several of the MLMQ # 1 partners objected to the scheme and it was dropped. Instead, one of the partners, who was a real estate broker and business associate of Barker, would assume as assignee the partnerships' interest in the joint venture and would close the Northwood Venture deal. Eventually, Thompson received $200,000, which was identified in the closing documents as a commission, and wired $100,000 of it to Barker Development Corporation.

Both Thompson and Barker pleaded guilty to misapplication of funds, a violation of Title 18, U.S. Code Section 657 that carried a maximum sentence of five years and a $5,000 fine. Thompson received a three-year suspended sentence, 150 hours of community service, and a $2,000 fine. Barker received the maximum five-year sentence, with all but six months suspended. During the probation period, he had to perform 100 hours of community service annually, and make restitution of $100,000 to FSLIC. Barker was also convicted of misapplication of funds at Brownfield Savings and Loan Association, where he was also chairman.[3] In addition, he was convicted of fraud in connection with an attempt to acquire a Colorado S&L.[4]

Related Schemes

The kickback scheme just described was not an isolated case of two hapless individuals. Thompson was involved in another scheme to defraud individuals seeking loans. He, and others, claimed to represent foreign lenders who had large sums to lend at below market rates. Thompson and his associates induced a prospective borrower to advance them more than $2 million in connection with loan applications, yet no foreign money was forthcoming.

Barker was involved in various other fraudulent activities. In one deal, State Savings loaned $4.4 million to Beebe and an unnamed partner to finance a ranch near Vernon, Texas. The ranch cost $2.8 million, and the borrowers asked for $1.05 million as "working capital." The money was wired to Beebe's bank in Bossier City, Louisiana, where he used some of the funds to retire an outstanding loan from Barker. It was also alleged that the funds were used for payments to Beebe and other parties, including Woody F. Lemons, president and CEO of Dallas, Texas-based Vernon Savings & Loan. Woody Lemons was eventually indicted for defrauding Vernon with the intent of enriching himself.[5]

Beebe, whose criminal record was described as being "uglier than a mail-order suit," was convicted of defrauding the Small Business Administration of about $1 million.[6] He also pleaded guilty to two felony charges of wire fraud and conspiracy. In 1976, Beebe was a major figure in the scandal surrounding the failure of Citizens State Bank of Carrizo Springs, Texas. He has also been involved in the failure of at least 15 other failed banks.[7] A Public Broadcasting television special broadcast about financial fraud in Houston, Texas, mentioned Beebe in connection with the failure of Houston's Mainland S&L. Mainland Savings was referred to as "Gangland Savings" because of its connections to organized crime. Mario Renda's First United Fund, which was the subject of the previous chapter, was a major lender of brokered deposits to Mainland, and his associates were borrowers from that S&L.[8] On the television broadcast, it was alleged that Beebe was a "front" for Carlos Marcello, the head of the New Orleans La Cosa Nostra family.[9] In connection with State Savings and Loan Association, Beebe was charged with assisting with the submission of a false draw request on a loan made by State Savings and Loan, which wire transferred the funds to Bossier Bank and Trust Co., Louisiana, and with conspiracy to file false statements to obtain a loan from a Louisiana bank. He plead guilty and was sentenced to prison for one year and one day. Because of the close connections between Barker, Beebe, and Donald Dixon, we will examine Vernon S&L next.

Vernon Savings and Loan Association

Donald R. Dixon

Vernon S&L was owned by Donald R. Dixon and his wife Dana, who were close friends of Barker and Beebe. Beebe also helped Dixon finance the purchase of Vernon S&L in 1982. Through various complex transactions, he owned about one-third of the stock of the holding company controlling the S&L. Dixon had been a successful real estate developer in the Dallas area. When Dixon bought Vernon S&L in 1982, it had virtually no delinquent loans, but he changed that condition over the next few years. Although Dixon's only official capacity at Vernon S&L was to serve on its loan committee for a short period, he received $8 million in compensation and dividends between 1983 and 1986—not bad for a part-time job.

While Barker did not excel at selling Beebe AMI credit life insurance, Dixon did. He used the hard-sell approach. Prospective real estate borrowers who wanted to buy credit life from their own insurance agents were told to try to get their mortgage loans from those insurance agents. Subsequently, AMI netted $2.5 million from the sale of credit life insurance at Vernon.

After Dixon acquired Vernon S&L, the association commenced an aggressive growth strategy. Its assets grew 1,023 percent over the next five years, from $120 million at the end of 1982 to $1.3 billion at the end of 1986. The growth was financed through high-cost brokered deposits and jumbo CDs, which amounted to 28 percent of its total deposits. Most of these funds were used to finance speculative acquisition, development, and construction loans, which were characterized by deficient underwriting practices, including the lack of appraisals. Vernon S&L is also accused of swapping bad loans with another S&L, a practice called a *daisy chain*. Edwin T. McBirney, former chairman of Sunbelt Savings (discussed in Chapter 6), bought loans to help inflate Vernon's profits. Vernon made $20 million in paper profits from that deal. But when it was placed in receivership in March 1987, 96 percent of the loans were delinquent.10

A FSLIC lawsuit for $350 million charges that Dixon and six other officers "looted" Vernon's assets for their personal gain. Dixon and others hid real estate losses from examiners and reported profits, although Vernon S&L had a negative net worth of $350 million. Based on the sham profits, Dixon's holding company received $22.1 million in dividends and $15 million in bogus bonuses. There were also millions of dollars in losses from questionable loans. Dixon measured success in the number of toys he had. Vernon's toys included:

- A fleet of seven aircraft including a seven-passenger helicopter (to avoid crosstown traffic), a Lear Jet, a Cessna Citation, a Beechcraft King Air, and others.

- A $2 million beach house in Camino Del Mar, California (plus $800,000 operating expenses). Vernon S&L sold the house at a loss to a friend of Dixon's, and financed it 100 percent.

- $5.5 million in artwork at Vernon.

- $500,000 in furnishings at Dixon's Rancho Santa Fe home.

- A $10 million, 100-foot yacht, used for political fundraisers.

- A $22,000, two-week trip to Europe that Dana Dixon called "Gastronomique Fantastique." She described the trip as a "flying house party" of "pure unadulterated pleasure."11 The tour was arranged, in part, by Philippe Junot, the former husband of Princess Caroline of Monaco. Don Dixon made five other trips to Europe that were billed to Vernon S&L. During these visits, Vernon S&L set up an operation in Switzerland to attract foreign funds. Vernon S&L also loaned money on the purchase of a hotel sight in the "Sun Coast" of Spain and a restaurant in the Bordeaux wine region of France.12

Dixon had political ties to former House Majority leader Jim Wright (Democrat, Texas), who used Vernon's Lear Jet for his political campaign. Wright interceded on Dixon's behalf to keep the FHLBB from closing Vernon S&L. The Political Action Committee of Texas S&Ls gave Wright $250,000 to block unfavorable legislation, and the funds were laundered through Vernon S&L.[13] One check had the phrase "For Jim Wright" written on it. Pat L. Malone, former executive vice-president of Vernon S&L, admitted to establishing a system using Vernon's funds to reimburse $55,000 to the S&L's officers for political campaign contributions. Court records showed donations included unspecified contributions to Wright.[14] Wright's chief of staff claims that Wright does not know Dixon and that he was trying to help the entire S&L industry in Texas and the people they serve.[15] Nevertheless, an article in *Bankers Monthly* said that "The story of Wright and Dixon is a story of greed and selfishness, of abuse of power and wealth, of perversion of democracy. It's another example of how Texas politicians carry the water for the state's business tycoons and how they answer the call of constituents who say that they're being persecuted by unreasonable regulatory agencies."[16]

Other congressmen used Vernon's yacht for fundraising. This distinguished group included Senator Pete Wilson (California), former Senator Paul Laxalt (Nevada), and former House majority Whip Tony Coelho (California). Coelho called Wright's aide and asked for Wright's help in forestalling the FHLBB's closure of Vernon S&L.[17] Both Wright and Coelho resigned from their Congressional seats. Noted politicians who flew on Vernon's jets included former President Gerald Ford, Jack Kemp, Jim Wright, and Tony Coelho.[18]

Woody F. Lemons

Woody F. Lemons was the chairman of the board of Vernon Savings and Loan. According to the 13-count indictment returned against Lemons, he defrauded Vernon by arranging and inflating loans for the purchase and development of land in Arlington, Texas; and he received a share of the loan proceeds. The loan was inflated by $3.5 million, and he planned to use half of that amount for his personal benefit. Because of funding problems at Vernon S&L, however, he only received $200,000. Other counts involved conspiracy to defraud the United States because he concealed his receipt of the loan proceeds from the Federal Home Loan Bank Board, and other charges. On December 6, 1989, a jury found him guilty on all counts. He was subject to being sentenced up to 65 years imprisonment and to fines of $3,250,000. He was sentenced to 30 years in prison. However, the Fifth Circuit Court of Appeals reversed six of the counts, thereby reducing his sentence to 10 years. Their justification was that the bank fraud statutes impose punishment for each execution of a scheme, and Lemons was involved in one scheme.[19]

West Africans

Since the 1970s, some West Africans, principally Nigerians, have been involved in the gamut of financial frauds. These frauds include credit cards, checks, insurance, student loans, entitlements (i.e., food stamps, public housing, unemployment insurance, etc.), commercial frauds, and heroin trafficking.[20] One Western diplomat estimated that Nigerian gangsters defrauded foreigners of more than $1 billion in 1992, making fraud Nigeria's second largest export after oil.[21] Although the majority of West Africans are reputable citizens, the focus here is on the criminals, and there are plenty of them too.

Stolen goods and funds are often sent back to West Africa. One group tried to buy 80 typewriters and have them shipped to West Africa. Other purchases include fraudulently purchased guns and automobiles.

Some say that if the individuals are caught and returned to West Africa, their heads are cut off. Others say that they are retrained, given new identities, and returned to the United States to steal some more. While these are rumors, there is no doubt about their widespread crimes.[22]

Higher Education

It is alleged that some West Africans operate schools in the United States and in Nigeria which train foreign nationals how to commit various types of fraud.[23] Their training manuals include sections on credit card scams, counterfeiting cards, automatic teller machines, and more. Most of the crimes involve relatively small amounts of money. Collectively, however, they add up to millions of dollars annually. Those who commit the frauds may be connected with each other because of their ethnic heritage, or they may be part of an international organized crime organization.

Many of the West African perpetrators enter the country on student visas and are students pursing undergraduate and graduate degrees. Sometimes they arrange sham marriages with U.S. citizens to obtain INS green cards permitting them to stay here. Those who are students use their correct names to register at universities and to establish credit during their freshman and sophomore years. As juniors and seniors, however, they begin to defraud the system by obtaining loans and running credit cards beyond their limits. Subsequently, a substantial amount of their crimes occur in cities with universities and schools that have foreign students. Tracking these individuals is difficult because they move and have their mail forwarded through co-conspirators. Some have even worked in financial institutions and have helped others commit crimes by providing them with information for counterfeit credit cards.

Guaranteed Student Loans, administered by the U.S. Department of Education, are the main source of funding West African students. Many West Africans applying for such loans indicate that they are U.S. citizens.

Unfortunately, some banks do not determine the validity of the applications because the student loans are 100 percent guaranteed by the U.S. government. In addition, some West Africans claim to be from the Virgin Islands, which helps to explain their accents, and it also makes them eligible for welfare benefits. When they default on the student loans, the taxpayers pay for their education and their fraud.

Credit Card Frauds

According to a Senate hearing on credit card fraud, a group of Nigerians had been operating in South Florida since 1979.[24] The Nigerian nationals entered the country under student visas allegedly for the purpose of study. They "studied" prior to entering the country how to complete credit card applications with spurious information. The group was also involved in worthless checks, counterfeit traveler's checks, and the exportation of stolen automobiles rented with credit cards.

The Nigerian's U.S. connections supplied them with information on individuals with high net worth. They also made false applications for credit cards by using identities of individuals whose names are listed in telephone directories, college yearbooks, and other sources. Other information listed on the credit card applications is incorrect, but of sufficient quality to pass a point scoring approval. Once they receive their credit cards, they obtain driver's licenses by using false Nigerian birth certificates and their names imprinted on the new credit cards. In Nigeria, birth certificates are rarely used; and when Nigerains apply for student or tourist visas, all that is needed to obtain a birth certificate is a name and birthdate. South Carolina has been a frequent source for driver's licenses used in these scams. Using the false identification, they obtain charge accounts at stores and open checking and savings accounts at financial institutions. As with the flimflam example, the accounts are kited up and the funds are withdrawn. Checks with insufficient funds are used to pay merchants for the goods they buy, and the charges on the credit cards are never paid. Credit card and telemarketing frauds are discussed in detail in Chapter 9.

Flimflams

The unwritten legislative history of the Expedited Funds Availability Act of 1987 was that high-ranking government officials had to wait too long to have their U.S. Treasury pay checks cleared. Even if that is not true, it makes a good story. The 1987 Act, and Federal Reserve Regulation CC, presented a golden opportunity for check fraud. The act required banks to make funds available in two days for checks drawn on local banks, and in five days for checks drawn on banks elsewhere. Some banks offer overnight availability. Thus, those intent on fraud can deposit a check one day and withdraw funds the next day before the check may have cleared. In some cases, funds could be withdrawn the same day. On Fridays, for example, the business day ends at 3 p.m. Thus, a deposit made before 3 p.m. could be cleared by 4 p.m., which is technically the next business day. Usually the fraudulent checks are deposited at one location and the funds are withdrawn from another.

The following case is a "typical" West African flimflam operation that occurred at one bank located in Alabama. The scam was perpetrated in other Alabama banks and thrifts on or about the same time. One of a pair of roving foreign nationals, using false identification and American sounding names (i.e., Scott, Williams, Cole), opened a savings account for $100 in one of an Alabama bank's many branches. Their primary interest was to establish an account of any type. Shortly thereafter, a check for $4,900 was deposited in the account at a different branch. The deposit was a check stolen from Tennessee and drawn on a nonexisting account. The timing of the deposit would allow funds to be available for withdrawal before a weekend, but the check could not be returned until the following week. The perpetrator withdrew $100, thus recovering the initial investment and testing whether the account was operational. Then $4,500 was withdrawn from the account at another branch before the weekend. Since the fraud would not be discovered until the following week, the perpetrator had ample time to move to Florida, where the scam was repeated. After doing the flimflam there, the perpetrator returned to Alabama for repeat performances. This time, however, they were caught and arrested.

Letter of Credit Scams

Given access to high-quality color copiers, printers, and computers, it was only a matter of time before West African and Asian fraudsters were able to produce high-quality counterfeit letters-of-credit. A major bank and two law firms were stung on what appeared to be a legitimate letter-of-credit, but it was counterfeit.[25]

The Promise of Riches

Banks provide trade and longer-term finance in support of international commerce. In this connection, they may encounter fraudulent business proposals from Nigerians and others.

Money transfers. One common scam involves money transfers. Individuals posing as Nigerian businessmen sent letters to U.S. business concerns asking their help in transferring $37 million in unclaimed residual contracts from Nigeria that were awarded between 1979 and 1993.[26] For their efforts, the U.S. firms were promised a share of the income. One U.S. firm was offered a 60 percent commission to help an alleged official of a Nigerian petroleum company transfer $60 million from Nigeria to the United States. The firms were asked to provide letterheads, company invoices, and information about their bank accounts. Once provided, the information was used to transfer funds to Nigeria.

In a similar scam, letters, faxes and telex messages have been sent from Nigeria requesting funds to pay taxes and bribes to secure the release of large sums of money. The respondents are provided with false documents from the Ministry of Finance and Central Bank of Nigeria supporting the transaction. According to the Nigerian government, the fraudsters "...operate with the connivance of some insiders in these public and private establishments. The fraudsters use government facilities, impersonate public functionaries and leave huge accumulated telephone and postage bills unpaid."[27] A Canadian businessman was sold a fraudulent deal inside the Central Bank of Lagos.

Fraudulent orders. The fraudster may place a small order with a firm and pay for it with a genuine cashier's check drawn on a foreign bank. Next, a larger order is placed, also paid for with a genuine cashier's check. Once the businessman is hooked, he or she receives notice by DHL or another reputable courier that the Nigerian partner has an urgent need for a large order to be shipped immediately by air. The difference this time is that the cashier's check is fraudulent.

A variant of this scam is to order sample goods and never pay for them.

Charitable donations. The fraudster offers to make a donation to your organization and requests bank account information to facilitate the transfer. Instead of funds being transferred into the account, the account is looted.

Government contracts and crude oil. The fraudster claims that the Nigerian government wants to give your company a contract, or sell a "special allocation" of oil to you at a cheap price. However, you must pay certain "fees" before you can do business in Nigeria. Legitimate fees do not exceed $215.

Travelers beware. In some cases, businessmen are told by con-artists that they must travel to Nigeria to sell goods to the Nigerian government. Once there, the businessman may be told that his firm must "register" in Nigeria. The registration fees range from $20,000 to $30,000. Alternatively, the con-artist may show the businessman "proof" that he paid the funds for the victim prior to his arrival and now wants to be reimbursed. Of course, there are no registration fees or requirements to visit Nigeria to sell to their government. Nevertheless, greedy businessman go for the deal, and many put up more funds, in installments, in hopes of making millions of dollars in the future.

Business travelers to Nigeria may be told by con-artists that they do not require an entry visa, and that all of the necessary travel arrangements for the visit have been made. Therefore, there was no need for the traveler to contact Nigerian or U.S. authorities. When the victim arrives at the airport without a visa, he or she is met by the con-artist, and bypasses immigration and customs. Now the victim is in the country illegally—a serious offense in Nigeria. Equally important, the victim cannot leave Nigeria without a stamped entry visa. Unwilling to go, stay, or be charged with various crimes, the victims pay large sums to the con men in order to leave Nigeria.

Another ploy occurs when business visitors who travel to Nigeria may be met at the airport by a driver claiming to be sent to pick up the traveler. The visitor may then be taken to a convenient place and robbed.[28] That's one scenario; here is another. The business visitor gets a warm welcome from the local con-artist, who acts as a mentor to build up the victim's trust. At some point, the con-artist stops being a friend and becomes a businessman, claiming that he will lose his share of the front-end investment due to the visitor's intransigence. The con-artist threatens the victim with bodily harm, and the terrorized victims pay. According to the U.S. Embassy in Nigeria, this technique has been very effective.

The Department of State, Bureau of Consular Affairs, published a list of warning signs of possible scams. The list includes:

- Offers of percentages of large sums of money to be transferred into your account in return for your "discretion" or "confidentiality" concerning the transfer.

- Requests for signed and stamped blank letterhead or invoices, or other account information.

- Requests for payment in U.S. dollars in advance for taxes or fees.

- Statements that your name was provided to the fraudster by someone that you do not know, or by a "reliable contact."

- Resistance by your Nigerian partners for you to check with the U.S. Embassy.

Word to the Wise

Those who receive unsolicited business proposals from Nigeria should do the following:

- Contact the U.S. Department of Commerce, Nigeria Desk Officer, Room 3317, Washington, D.C., 20230, or call the Department's Nigeria Desk Officer at 202-482-4388 (Fax 202-482-5198), or write to the Commercial Section, U.S. Embassy, 2 Eleke Credcent, Victoria Island, Lagos, Nigeria (phone 234-1-261-0097, fax 234-1-261-9856).

- Do not travel to Nigeria until the *bona fides* are known, and only once you have a valid entry visa from the Nigerian Embassy or Consulates.

- Ship goods to Nigeria only on the basis of an irrevocable letter of credit, confirmed by a U.S. bank, even after the *bona fides* have been established.

- *Caveat emptor*—let the buyers and bankers beware.

BCCI[29]

Kickbacks. According to BCCI officials, few European or American businesses could do business in Nigeria without payoffs to officials. BCCI was no exception. Nazir Chinoy, a former BCCI official who was stationed in Nigeria in the first half of the 1980s, found pervasive corruption of the Nigerian banking system and ways that BCCI could profit from it. BCCI owned 40 percent of a Nigerian bank, and corrupt Nigerian officials owned the remainder. The bank was very profitable and was used extensively for laundering funds generated by Nigerians who received "commissions" from obtaining contracts with international firms, and they wanted to keep their money abroad. Commission means kickback. If the government approves a $300 million contract with a multinational corporation, 10 percent of that amount will be paid in commission.

Imports and exports. Another mechanism for paying off officials was to use over-invoicing of imports and under-invoicing of exports. When over-invoicing was used, the government paid for more than the actual market price. BCCI would disguise this through a series of shell corporations to make it appear legitimate. The bank would share in the profits. When under-invoicing occurred, the government would ship more commodities than were reflected on the invoices. The additional commodities would be sold at the same time, and the profits shared with the bank and the Nigerian official who kept his share of the ill-gotten gain overseas. For example, BCCI would loan $250 million to Nigeria for oil exports. Nigeria would charge OPEC prices, but would load 10 percent more oil than was called for on the invoice.

By bribing the receptionists and clerks at the Central Bank of Nigeria, BCCI was able to process its financial transactions much faster than Bank of America or Chase Manhattan. For example, BCCI officials would give the receptionist and clerks dresses and ties from London, $5,000 watches, silver canteens, and so on. The result was that BCCI's applications to get foreign exchange out of Nigeria or letters of credit were processed promptly, whereas it might take weeks or months for other banks.

Currency swaps. Nigerian officials and BCCI did currency swaps with government funds. The funds were placed in a BCCI account in London. BCCI would place the funds in another bank and swap it in different currencies or invest in stocks. If they made money, the first 8 percent would go to the Nigerian officials. Additional amounts would be split between Nigerians and the traders at BCCI. If they lost money, the cost was borne by Nigeria.

Letters of Credit. In 1981, the Central Bank of Nigeria required that letters of credit used in connection with imports be secured by 100 percent cash deposits. Banks were required to certify to the Central Bank that the payment had been made. Because this might tie up an importer's funds for months, it discouraged import activity. BCCI's solution to the problem was to create phony loans to the importers and deposit the "proceeds" from those loans in the BCCI bank. Then BCCI informed the Central Bank that the deposits had been made. When the import transaction was completed, the phony loan would be paid off. Through this scheme, BCCI generated letter of credit business, interest on phony loans, and foreign exchange profits from converting currencies.

Worthless Financial Instruments and Unauthorized Banks

Fraudulent Instruments

On a Connecticut radio station, a financial advisor told the audience how to make a return of several hundred percent in one year by investing in prime bank notes and other instruments that provided higher returns than stocks.[30] The investors were told that they could sell the prime bank instruments on a secret market. Other fraudulent securities "include standby letters of credit investments," and "ICC 3032 and 3039 investments." ICC stands for the International Chamber of Commerce. It is not a financial institution, nor does it secure or guarantee loans. Some instruments carry the names of legitimate banks. Fraudulent "Prime Bank Guarantees," and "Prime Bank Debentures" used Deposit Trust Company's (New York) name. However, Deposit Trust Company advises that these instruments have no legal validity. In addition, more than $600 million (U.S.) of "Prime Guarantee" and "Bank Guarantee" instruments were allegedly issued by the Bank of Bohemia A.S. (Prague, Czech Republic). However, the Central Bank of the Czech Republic (Ceska Narodni Banka) reported that the Bank of Bohemia disavowed and voided such instrument transactions.

Advertisements for such securities have appeared in *The Wall Street Journal* and the *New York Times*. The principal problem with them is that they do not exist. There are no such securities. Losses on them have amounted to more than $100 million, including $8.3 million by the Salvation Army.

The sales pitch is that large, creditworthy banks issue clean standby letters of credit worth $10 million or more each. These letters of credit are used to fund loans that banks do not want showing up on their balance sheets. For example, suppose that Citibank wants to make a $9 million loan, but wanted outside funding. Citibank could ask Bank of America to fund the loan, and then Citibank would guarantee it with a $10 million clean standby letter of credit at the end of one year. The bank's client gets the loan and is willing to pay the extra $1 million in order to keep the transaction confidential. Citibank gets an administrative fee, and Bank of America gets a good return on the loan. Instead of waiting for the loan to mature at the end of the year, Bank of America could sell the $10 million letter of credit for $9.5 million, and then use those funds to acquire more letters of credit. By continuously rolling over the letters of credit, the banks will make millions of dollars! It sounds too good to be true, because it is not true. There is no such market in standby letters of credit.

Check Frauds

Check flimflams were explained in connection with the West Africans. One unemployed cab driver used this technique to write more than $100,000 in bad checks in 14 Pennsylvania banks.[31] Experts say that banks' bad check losses exceed the combined losses from credit card fraud and from thefts and armed robberies. To combat check fraud, Wells Fargo & Co., Sanwa Bank, and Union Bank have developed the StarCheck database service. StarCheck flags overdrafts and checks drawn on closed accounts by comparing daily activity against their database of demand deposit accounts. Reports on the flagged accounts and other information are sent to participating banks by 8 a.m. the following morning.[32]

Counterfeit Checks

Counterfeit checks are a significant problem for both banks and business concerns. Machines that can encode phony checks with account and routing numbers cost about $25,000. Laser scanners to copy logos and computers and high-quality printers are also available at a low cost. Therefore, it is not surprising that counterfeit corporate, government, and cashier's checks are widespread.

To combat counterfeiting, John H. Harland Co., a large manufacturer of checks, has developed new security features. One of these is a holographic strip across the top of the check, which makes it difficult to copy. Another security device is a microprint signature line that reads "authorized signature," which will appear as a broken line when copied. Finally, checks can be manufactured to display the word "void" if it is photocopied.

Other schemes include fraudsters writing bad checks to merchants and then returning the merchandise for a refund. According to one source, about 42 percent of all retail returns are fraudulent.[33] Losses for illegal check schemes are estimated to be about $5 million in 1993, up from $4 billion in the previous year.

Worthless Money Orders

In 1993 and 1994, numerous banks received worthless Certified Money Orders that are "redeemable" at L.A. Pethahiah, P.O. Box 287, Tigerton, Wisconsin. Another address where they can be redeemed is Mount Calvary Fund, P.O. Box 9580, Warwidk, Rhode Island. None of the banks that received such money orders have collected any funds.[34] These are not the only counterfeit money orders in circulation.

Unauthorized Banking

A large number of organizations operate banking businesses in the United States without authorization from federal or state authorities. In some cases, they use names that are the same or similar to those of well-known international banks. By way of illustration, Barclays Bank PLC (P.O. Box 1089, Miami, Florida, 33003), is not part of Barclays Bank PLC, a multinational bank holding company headquartered in the United Kingdom. The legitimate Barclays (UK) reported that it did not have a banking office at that address. The Office of the Comptroller of the Currency publishes OCC Alert, which lists offshore shell banks and other banks that may be operating in the United States without authorization. The *OCC Alert 94-9 (April 4, 1994)* listed a warning for the following organizations:

- First American International Bank, Inc., Pawnee OK
- Mesa Grande Bank, San Diego, CA
- The Wellington Bank of Commerce, Los Angeles, CA
- VCC International Banking Group, Anaheim, CA
- Commerce Bank of Antigua, Ltd., Miami, FL
- General Merchant Bank, Los Angeles, CA
- Liberty Bank of the Republic of Georgia, New York, NY
- Diskont Handel Bank Agency, Ltd., Miami FL
- First American Insurance & Banking Corporation, New York, NY

This listing is not complete. The OCC Alert 94-2 (February 28, 1994) listed 55 organizations that may be in violation of banking laws by operating as banks.

Endnotes

1. *U.S. v. Larry K. Thompson*, Northern District of Texas, Lubbock Division, CR-5-88-002, CR-5-88-024; *U.S. v. Tyrell G. Barker*, Northern District of Texas, Dallas Division, CR-3-88-017-D.

2. Bill Powell and Daniel Pedersen, "Loan Stars Fall in Texas," *Newsweek*, June 20, 1988, pp. 42-45.

3. Allen Pusey, "5 Named in 1 Charge of Texas S&L Inquiry," *Dallas Morning News*, February 9, 1988, pp. 1A, 7A.

4. Michael Swaicki and Ross Ramsey, "5 Charged with Banking Fraud in Probe of Texas Institutions," *Dallas Times Herald*, February 9, 1988; *U.S. v. Tyrell G. Barker*, Northern District of Texas, CR-3-88-017-D, Filed February 8, 1988; *U.S. v. Larry K. Thompson*, Northern District of Texas, CR-5-88-002, CR-5-88-024, Filed May 20, 1988; *U.S. v. Herman K. Beebe, Sr.*, Northern District of Texas, Dallas Division, CR-3-88-124-D, Filed April 29, 1988.

5. *U.S. v. Woody F. Lemons*, Northern District of Texas, Dallas Division, CR3-88-234-T, Filed November 10, 1988.

6. William M. Adler and Michael Binstein, "The Speaker and the Sleazy Banker," *Bankers Monthly*, March 1988, p. 84; Bill Powell and Daniel Pederson, *ibid.*, p. 43.

7. Allen Pusey, "Problems, Players Surfaced in '70s Scandal," *Dallas Morning News*, December 4, 1988, p. 31A; Allen Pusey and Lee Hancock, *ibid.;* Pete Brewton, "He Saw the S&L Crisis Coming," *Houston Post*, May 14, 1989. This article links Beebe to 23 S&Ls.

8. *U.S. v. Martin Schwimmer and Mario Renda*, Eastern District of New York, CR 87-00423, filed January 28, 1988. Refer to the pension funds scandal in Chapter 4 for more information. However, funds from the pension plan were only a small part of First United's involvement with Mainland.

9. Dan Gifford, "Financial Fraud: A Special Report," Public Broadcasting, Houston, Texas, February 2, 1989; Conversation with Pete Brewton, Reporter, *Houston Post*, June 23, 1989. Pete Brewton wrote a series of articles for *The Houston Post*, linking Renda to Herman K. Beebe, Sr., and to organized crime. These articles include the following: "Bank Fraud Investigators Looking for a National Plot," February 11, 1988; "S&L Probe Grew—and Grew Again," March 13, 1988; "Major Break Foreseen in Bank Fraud Probes," May 3, 1988; "Mafia's Involvement in S&L Failures Probed," October 8, 1988; "Bentsen Says He Has No Objections to Probe of Mob Role in S&L Failures," October 9, 1988; "Links to Mob Figures, Suspect Offshore Companies Abound," December 8, 1988; Conversation with Jim James, formerly with the Texas Attorney General's Crime Strike Force, June 26, 1989; The President's Commission on Organized Crime, *The Cash Connection, ibid.*, p. 10.

10. Federal Home Loan Bank Board "News" ("FHLBB Places Texas Thrift into Management Consignment Program"), March 20, 1987; David LaGesse, "'Daisy Chain' Loan Swapping Described by Ex-Thrift Exec," *American Banker*, August 28, 1987; LaGesse, "FSLIC Alleges Vernon's Officers Lived High at Thrift's Expense," *American Banker*, April 29, 1987; LaGesse, "Vernon S&L's Yacht Was Used for Fund-Raiser," *American Banker*, June 19 1987; LaGesse, "FSLIC Charges Vernon Savings Was 'Looted'," *American Banker*, April 28, 1987.

11. William M. Adler and Michael Binstein, *ibid.*, p. 81.

12. Byron Harris, "S&L Stories 1987-1988," WFAA Television, Dallas, Texas, 1988.

13. "Wright's Troubles Seem Unrelenting," AP, Sherman, Texas, *Democrat*, May 7, 1989.

14. "Ex-VSL Officer to Plead Guilty to Fraud Charges," Vernon, Texas, *Record*, May 23, 1989.

15. "Speaking for the Speaker," *Bankers Monthly*, May 1988, p. 87.

16. William M. Adler and Michael Binstein, *ibid.*, p. 80.

17. "Wright, Coelho and the S&L Fiasco," *U.S. News and World Report*, June 12, 1989, pp. 21-22.

18. Byron Harris, *ibid.*

19. Marj Charlier and Wade Lambert, "Court Reverses Six of 13 Counts Against Ex-Head of Vernon S&L," *The Wall Street Journal*, September 5, 1991, p. B6.

20. Harold W. Evenson, "Pro-Active Approaches to Fraud Prevention," presented at the Bank Administration Institute's 1991 Bank Security & Fraud Prevention Conference, April 2-5, Orlando, Florida; U.S. Senate, *Emerging Criminal Groups*, Hearings before the Permanent Subcommittee on Investigations of the Committee on Governmental Affairs, 99th Cong., 2nd. Sess., September 17 and 24, 1986, S. Hrg. 99-1080.

21. Phillip Van Niekerk, "Fraud Big Business in Nigeria," *The Globe and Mail*, Windsor, Canada, July 26, 1993.

22. U.S. House, *Adequacy of Federal Efforts to Combat Fraud, Abuse, and Misconduct in Federally Insured Institutions*, Hearing before the Commerce, Consumer, and Monetary Affairs Subcommittee of the House Committee on Government Operations, 100th Cong., 1st, Sess., November 19, 1987, p. 868; Michael Violano, "The High-Tech Future of Foiling Fraud and Forgery," *Bankers Monthly*, April 1989, p. 37; Susan Faludi, "Credit Card Ring Charging Millions," *The Atlanta Journal*, February 1, 1984; Susan Faludi, "Calls Pour in on Nigerian Mafia Credit Card Ring," *The Atlanta Journal*, February 1, 1984; John Brady, "Foreigners Jailed in Credit Card Theft Ring," *The Atlanta Journal*, January 27, 1984; "Cultural Crime Ring," Inter-

national Association of Credit Card Investigators (IACCI) *News*, May/June 1989, pp. 5-6.

23. U.S. Senate, *Emerging Criminal Groups*, Hearings before the Permanent Sub-committee on Investigations of the Committee on Governmental Affairs, 99th Cong., 2nd. Sess., September 17 and 24, 1986, S. Hrg. 99-1080; pp. 174-175; U.S. House, *Adequacy of Federal Efforts to Combat Fraud, Abuse, and Misconduct in Federally Insured Financial Institutions*, Hearing before a Subcommittee on Government Operations, 100 Cong., 1st. Sess., November 19, 1987, p. 868.

24. U.S. Senate, *Credit Card Fraud*, Hearing before the Subcommittee on Consumer Affairs of the Committee on Banking, Housing, and Urban Affairs, 98th Cong., 1st. Sess., May 18, 1983, S. Hrg. 98-228, p. 32.

25. Barton Crockett, "A Big Bank and Two Law Firms Burned in Letter of Credit Scam," *American Banker*, February 2, 1994.

26. FinCEN, "Nigerian Scam," *Trends*, April 1992, p. 7; Office of the Comptroller of the Currency, Bank Issuance BC 258, February 27, 1992, Containing a Press Statement from the Central Bank of Nigeria concerning attempted fraudulent transfers of funds.

27. Phillip Van Nieker, *op cit.*

28. U. S. Department of Commerce, National Trade Data Bank, Business Scams in Nigeria, IM1911104, November 30, 1993. Also see U.S. Department of State, Bureau of Consular Affairs, "Tips for Business Travelers to Nigeria," July 1993; "Fraudulent Business Proposals From Nigeria Persist," *Business America*, January 25, 1993, pp. 22-23.

29. U.S. Senate, *The BCCI Affair*, A Report to the Committee on Foreign Relations by Senators John Kerry and Hank Brown, December 1992, S. Prt. 102-140, pp. 99-104.

30. Barton Crockett, and Jeanne Iida, "Phantom Instruments Sting Investors, Banks," *American Banker*, April 18, 1994, pp. 1, 4, and 5; OCC Alert 94-3, March 16, 1994,; OCC Banking Issuance BC-243-5, October 27, 1993.

31. Fred R. Bleakley, "Bad-Check Toll Rises As It Becomes Easier to Pull Off Such Fraud," *The Wall Street Journal*, December 2, 1993, pp. A1, A6.

32. *Financial Technology Review*, January/February 1994, p. 15.

33. Matt Barthel, "Illegal Schemes Involving Checks Expected to Increase This Year," *American Banker*, January 4, 1994, p. 16.

34. OCC Alert 94-5, April 6, 1994; Bank Issuance BC 243-4, October 27, 1993.

9 CREDIT CARD AND TELEMARKETING FRAUDS

Big Business

According to *Business Week*, "experts" estimated that U.S. credit card fraud in 1993 was $1 billion.[1] Most of the credit card frauds are accounted for by stolen, counterfeit, and lost credit cards. The total may be closer to $10 billion when the cost to the public is considered. Major credit card issuers, retail stores and oil companies all experienced large losses.

According to the Financial Crimes Enforcement Network (FinCEN), West African and Asian organized criminal groups have been the primary offenders. West Africans have stolen trays of legitimate credit cards at airports, from mail delivery trucks, and from other mail facilities. In Washington, D.C., nine postal employees were among 40 persons arrested and charged with intercepting and stealing credit card applications from banks for "pre-approved" credit cards and other items from the mail. Credit card issuers mail cards in bulk to select zip codes in order to reduce their mailing cost. The bulk shipments are easy targets for the fraudsters. To deter thefts of newly issued credit cards, Citibank, for example, requires their cardholders to call the bank to confirm receipt of the card before it can be used.

Not all stolen cards come from mail facilities. Fraudsters steal cards wherever they can get them. They prefer business credit cards and "gold" cards because of their higher credit limits.

Fraudsters avoid detection by re-encoding stolen credit cards with new magnetic stripes containing valid cardholder information. Magnetic encoding machines cost about $30, and they can be purchased from many stores selling electronic equipment. They also emboss new information on the cards. High-quality embossing machines cost substantially more, but they too are readily available.

Blank counterfeit credit cards have been produced by Asian organized criminal groups and have been shipped throughout the world. When the blank cards arrive in the United States, they are embossed and encoded with information that may or may not be valid. The information is obtained from stolen credit cards and sales slips, by bribing retail store employees for information, and from other sources. In California, a group was accused of stealing car rental contracts that contained legitimate credit card information. Some West Africans have been caught burglarizing a state division of Motor Vehicles to obtain information for embossing credit cards. Asians have been caught with similar information.

The counterfeit credit cards and identification are sent by courier service to the cities in the United States and elsewhere that have been targeted for the fraud. The use of courier services reduces the likelihood that the counterfeit cards and identification will be detected if the fraudster's luggage is searched entering the United States from abroad. The target cities are usually those that are easily accessible by air and have a high volume of tourist traffic.

The fraudsters, using the counterfeit credit cards and fake identification, make purchases and obtain cash advances. They commonly purchase high-value items such as expensive watches, jewelry, and electronics. The purchased items are shipped to another location where they will be sold. When the goods are sold, the proceeds are deposited into a local bank and then wire transferred to a foreign bank. For example, Asian gang members posing as affluent tourists are sent to various cities throughout the world to use their counterfeit credit cards.[2] Two Asian males were detained in Phoenix, Arizona, when they attempted to buy an expensive wristwatch. One suspect had two counterfeit credit cards. The same cards had been used for fraudulent purchases in Hong Kong and Guam.

Deterrents

Credit card issuers and card associations have devised a variety of security measures to deter thefts and counterfeiting. These measures include holograms, graphics, unique account numbers and validation codes, embedded computer chips, and other features. Thus, the technology of credit cards is becoming an increasingly important deterrent. After each technological innovation is introduced, it takes time for the fraudsters to overcome the new obstacle. When they succeed, the credit card issuers must escalate the level of technology. Each escalation raises the cost and level of sophistication for counterfeiting credit cards. It also raises the cost for legitimate credit card users and merchants.

Merchants, bank tellers, and others can help detect fraudulent cards by looking carefully at the following items.

- Mismatches between the printed four-digit number and the first four embossed numbers on the front of the card.

- Inconsistencies in the graphics, letter spacing, numbers, and indent printing on tamper-evident signature panels.

- Chipped, scratched, or discolored holograms, logos, or signature panels.

- Discrepancies in signatures, handwriting, or spelling.

One of the best deterrents is to ask for traditional identification, including picture, signature, general description, etc. Fraud education and awareness programs are important.

Credit card fraud is an expensive and never-ending battle. However, progress is being made due to fraud-fighting efforts at all levels in the card industry.

Domestic Fraudsters

Foreigners do not have a monopoly on credit card fraud; U.S. citizens do it too. For example, prisoners in some of our finer jails have access to telephones. The credit card fraudsters call jewelry stores in distant cities and use valid credit card information to buy expensive watches, such as Rolexs. The fraudster tells the store clerk a convincing story. For example, the fraudster may say that when he visited the store last week, he was very impressed with the high quality of their service and with their broad selection of watches and jewelry. When he returned home, he remembered his wife's birthday, which happens to be tomorrow. Therefore, he wants to surprise his wife with the Rolex watch that he so admired in the store. In addition, he also wants one for his sister and his daughter so that they won't feel left out of the celebration. Because the birthday is tomorrow, he wants the watches sent Federal Express today. He gives the clerk credit card information and the address to which the package is to be sent. The mailing address may be different than that of the legitimate credit card holder. For example, the prisoner may send the watches to his girlfriend, who is not in jail. Most jewelers will not use Federal Express to send watches to a federal penitentiary. However, if they do send the watches to an address other than that of the credit card holder, it is their loss. In some cases, the fraudster uses the address of the credit card holder. In that case, the fraudster may call the jewelry firm the morning that the Federal Express package is expected, and tell the sales clerk that he will not be home for the delivery of the watches. The fraudster might ask the clerk to please give the Federal Express air-bill number to him so that he can pick up the package at the Federal Express office.

This is one of dozens of schemes perpetrated on firms that have poorly trained sales clerks and weak internal controls. Merchants can be held accountable for not following the operating regulations issued by major credit card companies. For example, USAA Federal Savings Bank, the largest thrift insurer of credit cards, sued Grand Rent A Car Corp., which owns the Avis franchise at Los Angeles International Airport, for more than

$900,000 of fraudulent credit card transactions.[3] The suit was the first one to be filed under the Electronic Communication Privacy Act. The rental agency did not properly secure the credit card account holder information. The account numbers were sold to individuals who used them to create counterfeit cards and to make illegitimate transactions.

Telemarketing Fraud

Telemarketing means selling goods and services by interstate telephone calls or wire communications.[4] Most telemarketing firms are honest, but we are interested in those that commit telemarketing frauds. The frauds are designed to closely resemble legitimate business transactions in order to disguise their true nature. They may even buy legitimate businesses and join the Chamber of Commerce and Better Business Bureau to give the appearance of a well-established firm. They always include unfair and deceptive practices, but they do not always contain all of the elements of common law or criminal fraud. Thus, "telemarketing frauds," as used here, must be considered within a broad context.

Widespread activity. According to a 1993 survey conducted by Louis Harris and Associates, more than 92 percent of adult Americans have received some form of fraudulent solicitations from telemarketers during the previous two years.[5] Additional findings included the following:

- Seventeen percent of the respondents found it somewhat difficult to resist hard-sell telephone solicitations.

- Only one-third of consumers who responded to the solicitations ever received their promised "prize."

- Three percent, representing 5.5 million people, were victimized by fraudulent telemarketers. Retirees are common victims because they spend a lot of time at home where they can be reached by phone, and they are generally interested in increasing their income. Their memories tend to be poor, and they rarely ask for written guarantees or a prospectus.

Perhaps the most important characteristic of the widespread activity is that once most people realize that they have been cheated, they are often too embarrassed to tell their friends, relatives, or law enforcement authorities. By way of illustration, the testimony of Grace Singletary is presented in Figure 9.1. Telemarketers also target minorities, the elderly, and individuals with bad credit records.

Another study of telemarketing fraud perpetrated on businesses estimated that only 1 in 10,000 victims ever filed a formal complaint.[6] One

Figure 9.1

Testimony of Grace L. Singletary
before the Subcommittee on Commerce,
Consumer, and Monetary Affairs
House Committee on Government Operations

My name is Grace Singletary. I am 84 years old and live in Georgia. I am a retired schoolteacher and live on a limited income. When my husband died, he left $20,000 to me. That was our life's savings.

I had just returned from the hospital, after being treated for pneumonia, when I was contacted by phone for the first time in mid July 1989 by a Mr. Michael Ross. He spoke nicely and sounded like a gentleman. Mr. Ross tried to sell me a limited partnership in "Chariot 7" productions. I told him I wasn't interested. I didn't know him or his company and I wasn't investing at the time. After that first call, he called me daily, sometimes even twice a day. I still resisted. He sent me the prospectus and I didn't even look at it. Finally, I told him, that I could not invest because what little extra I had I was going to use to paint and repair my home. I made the mistake of telling him that I had $15,000 in savings.

During each of many daily calls, he said that the company was making a film about his life in the army, that he had been the sixth most highly decorated man in that war, and that he had steel plates in his body because of his many wounds. He was very touching and convincing and assured me that I would be part of a firm venture that would be meaningful as well as financially successful. He assured me each time he called that I absolutely would receive 2-1/2 times the amount of the investment.

Then, he said that he had just come from talking with Mr. Little, the president, who had told him, 'This partnership is going even better than the 2-1/2 times mentioned in the prospectus. It is, in fact, a 23 to 1 deal.'

Later, Mr. Ross said 'Grace,' (he spoke as though I had become his personal friend) 'if you can hold off on the house painting for just a couple of weeks, I can help you pay for it.' He said that I would have the money from "Chariot 7" by August 8. Then, he called and said Mr. Little had moved the date up and that I would have the money by August 1. All I had to do, Mr. Ross said, was sign the contract, and he would help me over the phone.

I looked the contract over. When I came to the part in the contract requiring my income and net worth, it indicated that I had to have $60,000 yearly income and a net worth of $100,000 exclusive of home, car and so on. I told Mr. Ross that I was not eligible to sign since I didn't have that income. He replied, "That's okay. I'll fix it. Just send the money." I sent a check for $10,000.00 dated 7-15-89 and the signed contract to him. A few days later, he called excitedly saying "All is going so well," and that if I could buy what little was left on hand, $5,000, the deal would be closed. But, he said, the money had to be in the California bank that day. So I did as he told me. I went to the bank and asked for a check to be wired to reach their California bank before closing that day.

Mr. Ross gave the bank name and an account number, which is on file in the District Attorney's office. That additional $5,000 brought my total investment to $15,000. I never signed the contract for the additional $5,000.

Well, the first of August came, and there was no check. I waited a few days and called Mr. Ross. He said, 'It has been mailed.' Still, no check. I called a few days later and asked him to call his bookkeeping department to see just when the check had been mailed. He replied by saying he would call me back. Then he said, 'No, wait a minute,' which I did. He returned to the phone and assured me that I would receive it no later than Wednesday.

Figure 9.1 (continued)

(This was after the promised August 8th date.) Of course, it never arrived. Neither did Mr. Ross call again, nor was I able to reach him or the president by phone. A business friend of mine attempted to reach Mr. Ross. He was told, 'Mr. Ross is in the field. Mr. Little is not in either.' I heard nothing more. By September 5, I realized that I had been taken.

Consequently, I suffered great mental and physical anguish. I had to go back under a doctor's care. I don't know if you can imagine how I felt. I then wrote to the District Attorney's office in California and in Georgia. Sometime in November, I had a call from Georgia Mezavani, a saleslady with "Chariot 7," saying that Mr. Ross had been in the hospital for some time suffering from cancer, and that she was taking his place. She was also very pleasant and sounded very concerned and friendly. At this time, she told me that the foreign rights to the motion picture had been sold and that I could expect a check around Thanksgiving. She called me several times to keep me informed on how the business was going and reassured me that my check would be in around Thanksgiving. I received a check on November 20, 1989, for $1,502.09. I received a second check on December 27, 1989, for $1,504.55. She also informed me that by the first quarter in 1990 and before April 15, I would have my whole investment back.

A few weeks later, she called me and told me that the company was going to film a comedy, with Jack Lemmon, the first of the year. She said it would outsell the other production 5 to 1. The only reason that a few units were still available, she said, was because Mr. Little had taken back some stock whose owners had lost everything in the recent earthquake. Georgia stated that 'Mr. Little is such a good man.' I was gullible again and mailed a check for $5,000, dated 11-25-89. My total investment was $20,000, the legacy left to me by my husband and our entire life's savings.

Because of the unfortunate circumstance I am here to discuss, I have been emotionally and mentally drained. I have not been able to sleep, and, while previously I thought of myself as a content person, now, I worry without stop about a future without any savings. That is why, even though I have not been well, I was determined to appear here today. I want to speak out against the people who took advantage of me, not only because of what they did to me, but because this Committee can take action to ensure that others will not be misled and cheated in this way.

I spent many years as a schoolteacher and think of myself as an intelligent person. The man who called me on the telephone about this business investment sounded like a gentleman, like someone I could trust. He said he had been with the company since it started. He was very convincing. He called every day. He invited me to visit them in their home and said, if I wanted I could have a position with the company, editing the scripts. He told me that the president of the company, a Mr. Little, was such a fine man, always addressing schools on the evil of drug abuse. He assured me that if I needed advice from an attorney or C.P.A., they had the best in the country. His daily phone calls and his persuasive manner convinced me. I am sick over this foolish deed, but I will not allow my personal embarrassment at having been taken prevent me from speaking out against these people so that others will not suffer as I have.

Thank you for giving me this opportunity to tell you about this terrible experience. I hope you will take action to stop this kind of sophisticated thievery.

Source: U.S. House, *The Nature and Extent of Telemarketing Fraud and Federal and State Law Enforcement Efforts To Combat It*, Hearings Before the Commerce, Consumer, and Monetary Affairs Subcommittee of the Committee on Government Operations, 101st Cong., 2nd. Sess. July 11 and 12, 1990, 11-15. The statement is a direct quotation, except for the deletion of her address.

reason for this might be that the merchandise is generally for relatively small dollar amounts.

Telemarketers frequently use a "boiler room" operation, which is a room full of telephones and salesmen, to make cold calls hoping to sell their goods. Salesmen's commissions range from 20 to 50 percent of the cash they bring in through the door. One salesmen earned more than $1 million during a three-year period. The boiler rooms may be located in Los Angeles or Las Vegas, and they solicit business in all other states. Doing business in distant locations makes it less likely that those state's authorities will interfere with their telemarketing operations. The boiler room salesmen sell the following:

- oil and gas leases
- commodities (precious/strategic metals)
- investments
- false charities
- business supplies
- travel
- vending machine franchises
- "you may have money waiting for you"
- "you have won a free prize"
- other products and services

An alternative to cold calls is to precede the call with a letter to the prospective customer stating, "You have won one of four fabulous prizes. To obtain your prize, you must call the following number within the next 48 hours." When the customer calls, the telemarketer confirms that they have won one of the prizes, but they must pay shipping and handling charges which can be billed to their credit card. According to the Louis Harris survey, only one-third of those who responded to the solicitation received the promised prize.

The telephone salesmen deceive prospective customers about the goods they have for sale by painting "word pictures in the mind of the consumer" which obscure the true quality or value of the good or service. For example, the lucky customer can buy jewelry, musical instruments, water purifiers, or packaged vacations that sound better than they are in reality. Moreover, the customer can pay for goods by providing the telemarketer with a credit card number.

When the sale is completed and the goods are shipped and received by the customer, the customer frequently discovers that the goods are of inferior quality, or they are not what the customer expected. The fancy musical organ they expected turned out to be a plastic toy. The outboard motor for a 16-foot boat is a small electric motor powered by two D-cell batteries suitable for powering toys in bathtubs. A $500 water purifier is a bag of charcoal, and so on. The customer "misunderstood" the word picture that was painted.

The fraudulent telemarketer's objective is to get a credit card number. The credit card number is used to record customer authorized sales, and in some cases unauthorized charges are made on the accounts. By using "electronic data capture," the telemarketers send account information to their banks electronically, leaving no paper trail, and funds are credited to telemarketer's account the next day. When paper credit card sales drafts are used, they can get cash within a few days. By the time the goods, if any, are shipped to the customer, the telemarketer may be in a distant location.

When the customer attempts to return the goods, he or she finds that the telemarketer has closed shop and has no forwarding address or phone number. When the customer refuses to pay the credit card bill because he believes he was cheated, the charge is returned to the clearing bank that had the credit card relationship with the telemarketer. If a customer disputes a charge transaction, the clearing bank is obligated to honor the customer's request to reverse the charge. Clearing banks typically depend on high volume and thin profit margins from their credit card clearing operations. If the telemarketer is unwilling or unable to reimburse the clearing bank for the reversed charge, the clearing bank absorbs the losses from the charge-backs. Charge-backs from telemarketing scams can be as high as 90 percent of the volume of credit card drafts deposited.

Reloading. Telemarketers know that there is no better customer than one who has been conned previously. "Sucker lists" of previous victims are available to them. Unscrupulous telemarketers call these people again to make additional sales. This activity is known as "reloading" or "double scamming." The salesmen emphasize that "this time" the victim has a better chance of winning the grand prize. Alternatively, the salesman may offer to help the victim recoup their financial losses. Of course the victim is asked to pay an up-front "recovery fee."

900-Number Telemarketing. The use of 900-numbers, or pay-per-call telemarketing, is another area of concern. Some, but not all, of the 900-number calls are based on false inducements or deceptive advertising on television, in the print media, or by telephone. Consumers incur a charge when they initiate the 900-number call, and then they pay a charge per minute of use. In addition, they may buy bogus goods or services.

Using the long-distance telephone companies and local carriers to bill and collect the proceeds from scams avoids the telemarketer's need for credit card laundering (known as factoring). Moreover, the telemarketer may not meet the criteria that major credit card issuers require for obtaining a merchant account at a bank.

Under the Telephone Disclosure and Dispute Resolution Act of 1992 (Public Law 102-556), the Federal Trade Commission must establish procedures similar to those found in the Truth in Lending and Fair Credit Billing Act (FCBA) for dealing with disputes involving billing charges arising from errors as well as those arising from deceptive acts or practices. The FCBA was enacted in 1974 to provide consumers with a means of disputing charges on their credit card bills.[7]

Deceptive telemarketers may enlist the aid of other professionals who materially assist in the fraud. In the case of the *Federal Trade Commission v. U.S. Oil and Gas Corp.*, banks, insurance companies, lawyers, accountants, and others were involved with this fraudulent scheme.[8] The scheme involved a federal lottery to win leases on oil and gas wells. The defendants promised investors that they had exclusive knowledge of the most valuable parcels of land and that they were going to win a federal lease. If for some reason they didn't win a lease, the defendants guaranteed that the investors would get their money back after seven years. Only a small fraction of the funds raised was used for filing fees on applications for the federal lottery of leases.

Other entities included an insurance broker who helped set up and administer a bogus insurance program whose beneficiaries were the defendants and not the investors. Two insurance companies provided the insurance for the scheme. A law firm helped design the bogus insurance program and helped one of the defendants loot $5 million in corporate assets. Two banks permitted the use of their names in the defendant's advertising materials, although they knew the program was fraudulent. Because of the bank's role in the scheme, they agreed to settle for $47 million in payments going to about 8,200 customers. Investors in this case were lucky. They are getting a return of about $0.90 on each dollar they invested. This large settlement sends a strong signal to banks and others to know their customers and not to knowingly aid and abet fraud.

Some banks did not get the message. Citicorp Credit Services Inc., allegedly provided processing of credit card charges for BankCard Travel Club.[9] Citicorp Credit Services knew or should have known about the club's deceptive sales practices. There were a high level of consumer complaints about the club, and its charge-back rate was 20 times the average rate in the industry. The FTC charged Citicorp Credit Services with aiding and abetting BankCard Travel Club's deceptive scheme. As part of the consent decree, Citicorp must investigate any of its clients with a high charge-back rate and terminate them if they are engaging in fraudulent, deceptive, or unfair practices.

Business accounts. The following is an example of another credit card ploy. A well-dressed man enters a bank to establish a business account and credit card relationship. He explains to the banker that he is a florist and that he has recently opened BlossomTime Flowers (or some other type of business). Furthermore, he intends to expand the business with telephone orders from throughout the United States. The banker, wanting to help a new business grow, provides him with the means for growth. However, the credit card sales drafts from BlossomTime may be a subterfuge used to pay for activities—such as prostitution, gambling, and drugs—that do not qualify for credit cards. The florist buys credit card charges for prostitution at a discount and then collects on them from the bank. The volume of credit card sales drafts from the florist may be reasonable at first, but then it grows to $200,000 or more. Then the florist withdraws all of his funds from the bank, either by wire transfer or by cash, and leaves town. It takes about 90 to 120 days before the full impact of the loss from charge-backs is felt at the bank. Once again, the bank is the loser.

Telemarketing fraud can also be directed against businesses.[10] A salesman calls a small business and asks to speak to the person in charge of buying supplies. He informs the buyer that the price of copier toner (or pens or paper) is about to be increased and offers the prospective buyer the remaining batch at the old price. After the goods are shipped and paid for, the salesman sends the buyer a "gift" to show his appreciation. The subsequent orders and the gifts increase in value until the buyer, also known as the "mooch," is hooked. One firm paid $29.95 for a box of paper clips and $1,346 for a box of paper worth $36. The gifts to the mooch turn into blackmail. The salesman threatens the mooch to continue with the orders or he will ask the boss if he too would like to receive a television in exchange for an order.

Factoring. Factoring, which is also known as credit card laundering, is a variation of a theme described previously. Factoring is when a telemarketer convinces a merchant, usually a small- to medium-size "mom and pop" operation, to handle the telemarketer's credit card sales drafts for a 3 to 10 percent commission. Banks usually charge merchants a discount of 2 to 4 percent, so the merchant expects to make money, depending on the volume of deposits. The telemarketer gives several thousand dollars worth of sales drafts to the merchant who sends them to the bank to be cleared. The dollar volume of the sales drafts increases over time. When it is sufficiently large, the fraudster withdraws the funds and leave the merchant to settle the charge-backs. If the charge-backs are sufficiently large, the merchant may go bankrupt, and the bank will then be the loser.

Many merchants are not aware that factoring is a violation of major credit card merchant/bank contracts. When factoring is used the merchant is responsible for all financial losses, and if fraud is involved the merchant could face criminal prosecution.

Debit Drafts.[11] Because of difficulties in factoring credit card sales drafts, some telemarketers are turning to debit drafts. The criminals open a business account at a bank, and they do not divulge that they are telemarketers or draft processors. Most bank customers do not realize that signatures are *not* required on the deposit drafts or debit cards to withdraw funds from their checking accounts. Nor do they realize that banks may not require verification before making payment on such claims. The fraudsters, however, know how banks operate, and they use debit drafts and automatic debit systems to make unauthorized withdrawals from the customer's checking account. By the time the customer gets his or her bank statement, both the money and the telemarketer are long gone.

The "originating bank," the one that accepted the deposit from the processor of the draft, has the responsibility for verifying the authorization to make payments. The "receiving bank," the one where funds are withdrawn from the customer's account, relies on the originating bank's verification procedures. Unauthorized withdrawals may be charged back to the originating bank.

Another scheme is that the telemarketer mails thousands of postcards to individuals offering them pre-approved credit. To obtain the credit, the victims must call a toll-free telephone number to get the details. They are led to believe that they are dealing with a bank or credit card company. They are offered a low-interest or secured credit card, but the annual fee must be paid in advance. The salesman advises the victims that they can draft their checking account for the fee. The victims are asked to provide the operator with the financial codes printed on the bottom of their checks. Armed with this information, the telemarketers, using their own magnetic encoding machines, encode bank deposit drafts with the victim's name, bank routing numbers, account number, *etc.* The magnetic ink characterization factor (MICR) imprinted at the bottom of the check is all that the telemarketer needs on the deposit draft. The telemarketers use the magnetically encoded deposit drafts to withdraw funds from the victim's account. The drafts may be deposited in large numbers just before the bank's closing time. Because the bank is dealing with bulk deposits, it may not verify if it has authorizations on file for the unsigned drafts. In some cases, the deposit drafts are processed electronically through the Automated Clearing House System. The funds are deposited immediately in the telemarketer's account, and then they are wire transferred elsewhere as soon as possible.

Interestingly, some of the encoding machines have been purchased from the FDIC when they auction equipment from failed institutions.

Figure 9.2 presents a typical script used by telemarketing salesmen asking for checking account information from a prospective customer or victim.

Many of telemarketing, credit card, and fraud losses of the types described here are preventable, if banks follow the guidelines and controls established by the major credit card companies. The message is simple: Failure to follow established guidelines and controls results in losses. The crooks find a bank or banker that is lax and exploit that weakness. One major weakness is that banks do not like to acknowledge that they have been victimized, and many do not cooperate with law enforcement authorities.[12]

Finally, information about credit card fraud and other scams is shared between financial institutions and law enforcement officers through the In-

---

Figure 9.2: Paper Debit Script for Telemarkeing Sales

Instructions for Salesman:

After you know that you have a good order and have exhausted all possibilities of a credit card sale, here's what you do.

Tell the Customer:

"Our company is connected to a nationwide payment system that allows us to take check orders over the telephone. This is done by a bank to bank transaction just like Visa or MasterCard or your money card so you can pay by your checking account."

"Are you serious about getting started right away?"

"I'll hold on while you get your checkbook so we can get the information to get you started right away.

"First I'll need the name of your bank and your branch."

"What is the check number? Could I have the numbers just underneath your check #: (there are nine (9) numbers with a /)"

"Okay, the last thing that I need is the long number at the bottom of your check (get all digits)." (The fraudster will check that the route code and check numbers are contained in this long number.)

Questions that Customers May Ask and Answers to Give

Q. "Why do I need to get a check?"
A. "I'll need some information from your check in order to process this order."
Q. "How will I know that you will be charging my bank the right amount?"
A. "You will receive a written confirmation from your bank."
Q. "I have never heard of this service. What is it?"
A. "This is the same type of service used by banks and other financial institutions.

Source: U.S. House, *Innovations in Telemarketing Frauds and Scams,* Joint Hearing Before the Subcommittee on Regulation, Business Opportunities, and Energy of the Committee on Small Business and the Subcommittee on Health and Long-Term Care of the Select Committee on Aging, June 21, 1991, Serial Nos. 102-28, 102-824, p. 161. Based on a draft prepared by National Consumers League. Reprinted with permission.

ternational Association of Credit Card Investigators (IACCI).[13] The IACCI publishes information about various types of fraud. They also refer questions to credit card companies. The credit card companies also give seminars at malls and chain stores to raise merchant awareness of credit card fraud.

Endnotes

1. "Stalking the Credit-Card Scamsters," *Business Week*, January 17, 1994, pp. 68-69. Also see: Lisa Fickenscher, "Fraudulent Cash Advances Decline as Visa and MasterCard Fight Back," *American Banker*, January 11, 1994, p. 16; U.S. House, *Telemarketing Fraud and Consumer Abuse*, Hearing before the Subcommittee on Transportation and Hazardous Materials of the Committee on Energy and Commerce, 102nd. Cong., 1st. Sess., May 9, 1991, Serial No. 102-14, p. 1.

2. U.S. Senate, *Asian Organized Crime: The New International Criminal*, Hearing before the Permanent Subcommittee on Investigations of the Committee on Governmental Affairs, 102 Cong., 2nd. Sess., June 18 and August 4, 1992, S. Hrg. 102-940, p. 39.

3. Mickey Meece, "USAA Sues Merchant to Recoup Credit-Fraud Losses," *American Banker*, March 14, 1994, p. 13.

4. The definition of telemarketing as it appears in the "Telemarketing Fraud Prevention Act of 1989," 101st Cong., 1st. Sess., H.R. 1354, refers to telephone sales across state lines. It does not include transactions where there have been personal meetings between the buyer and the sellers concerning the transaction. Board of Governors of the Federal Reserve System, et. al., Interagency Advisory, Credit Card-Related Merchant Activities, November 15, 1993; U.S. House, *The Scourge of Telemarketing Fraud: What Can Be Done Against It?* Fifteenth Report by the Committee on Government Operations, House Report 102-421, December 18, 1991.

5. *Ibid.*, U.S. House, House Report No. 103-20, *Consumer Protection Telemarketing Act*; U.S. House, *Consumer Protection Telemarketing*, Hearing before the Subcommittee on Transportation and Hazardous Materials of the Committee on Energy and Commerce, 103rd. Cong., 1st. Sess., H.R. 868, February 17, 1993, Serial No. 103-3, p. 17. Statement of the Federal Trade Commission before the Consumer Subcommittee on Commerce, Science, and Transportation, U.S. Senate, March 18, 1993.

6. U.S. House, *The Nature and Extent of Telemarketing Frauds and Federal and State Law Enforcement Efforts to Combat It*, Hearings before the Commerce, Consumer, and Monetary Affairs Subcommittee of the Committee on Government Operations, 101 Cong., 2nd Sess, July 11 and 12, 1990, p. 30.

7. For details on the FTC rules, see *Federal Register*, Part II, Monday, August 9, 1993, Federal Trade Commission, 16 CFR, Part 308.

8. *FTC v. U.S. Oil and Gas Corp.*, Case No 83-1702-CIV-Hoeveler (S. D. Fla.); and U.S. Oil and Gas Corp. Litigation, Case Nos. 83-1702-A1-CIV-Hoeveler and 83-1702-A2-CIV-Hoeveler (S.D. Fla.). Also see *Ibid.,* U.S. House, *The Scourge of Telemarketing Fraud: What Can Be Done Against It?* Fifteenth Report, pp. 92-93, 140-141.

9. *Ibid.,* Statement of the Federal Trade Commission, March 18, 1993, In re Citicorp Credit Services, Inc., Docket No. C-3413.

10. *Ibid.,* U.S. House, *The Scourge of Telemarketing Fraud: What Can Be Done Against It?* Fifteenth Report, pp. 22-23.

11. U.S. House, *Innovation in Telemarketing Frauds and Scams*, Joint Hearing before the Subcommittee on Regulation, Business Opportunities and Energy of the Committee on Small Business and the Subcommittee on Health and Long-Term Care of the Select Committee on Aging, 102nd Cong., 1st. Sess., June 21, 1991, Serial Nos. 102-28, 102-824.

12. *Ibid.,* U.S. House, *The Scourge of Telemarketing Fraud: What Can Be Done Against It?* Fifteenth Report, pp. 26-27.

13. International Association of Credit Card Investigators, 1620 Grant Ave., Novato, CA 94945, phone 415-897-8800.

10 CRIMES BY INSIDERS

Two cases are covered in this chapter: Empire Savings and Loan and the Butcher brothers' financial empire, in which United American Bank, Knoxville, Tennessee, played a key role. The Empire Savings and Loan case involved massive fraud and illustrates the use of land flips, nominee loans, kickbacks, and other abuses and misconduct by both insiders and outsiders. At the time of this writing, more than 100 people have been convicted for their involvement in the schemes that caused Empire's failure, and the court trials were still in progress. The mere magnitude of this case deserves attention.

The failure of the Butcher brothers' banking empire was the largest failure in U.S. banking history. Their schemes involved more than 60 interlocking corporations and partnerships that borrowed loans from Butcher-controlled banks. The Butchers used state-of-the-art techniques to juggle bad insider loans from bank to bank and to enhance their wealth.

Empire Savings and Loan Association

Empire Savings and Loan Association, Mesquite, Texas, was closed with losses of over $170 million.[1] Empire was the first federally insured S&L closed in Texas and FSLIC's largest disbursement to depositors in its 50-year history. The cost to pay off depositors was over $279 million. The cost would have been less if the Texas Savings and Loan Department and the Federal Home Loan Bank Board would have acted more swiftly and decisively when problems were discovered at Empire. However, Empire's books were in such disarray that their auditor, Coopers & Lybrand, was unable to meet their accounting deadlines nine times in 1982. The Federal Home Loan Bank granted each extension.[2] In October 1982, federal examiners gave Empire a CAMEL rating of "3C," which is not good, for imprudent lending practices in the areas of underwriting, appraisal, and risk exposure.[3] For instance, speculative type condominium construction loans accounted for 47.8 percent of total loans. Eventually, in August 1983, a special examination revealed virtual chaos at Empire and it was given a CAMEL rating of "4." By this time, construction loans accounted for over 65 percent of their total loan portfolio. The examination report revealed that borrowers had little or no equity in 27 condominium projects. Loans in excess of the sales price were made to speculators and secured by vacant land. And there were verbal commitments for $178 million in additional condo construction loans.[4] Empire Savings and Loan was closed in March 1984.

The principal characters in the schemes that led to Empire's demise included Spencer H. Blain, Jr.; James L. Toler; David L. "Danny" Faulkner; and Clifford L. Sinclair. Faulkner and Toler are alleged to have masterminded the schemes. Blain, Faulkner, Toler and others are accused of stealing more than $100 million from Empire. To do this, Empire, and its wholly owned real estate subsidiary Statewide Service Corporation, engaged in land flips, false appraisals, and questionable lending practices, such as financing speculative land loans.

The I-30 Corridor

About $1 billion in real estate investment in the Garland-Lake Ray Hubbard area was financed by Empire and other S&Ls. The area is referred to as the Interstate Highway-30 (I-30) corridor, and it is located about 20 to 25 miles east of Dallas. After Empire failed, only about one-third of the completed 2,200 condominiums in the city of Garland were occupied, and another 2,200 or more were still under construction. Building permits were issued for more than 6,400 condos and 232 apartments, despite the fact that the average sales of condos in east Dallas County were only 68 per month. Depending on which report one reads and which geographic area was covered by those reports, the supply of condos along the I-30 corridor was enough to satisfy market needs for the next 3 to 12 years. At one point, the vacancy rate in the area was 47 percent according to a Fannie Mae survey, and it was estimated that the condos were worth only 10 percent to 35 percent of what Empire had loaned on them.

Real estate developers enticed other prospective lenders to make loans in the overbuilt I-30 corridor area by promising them high rates of interest on their loans, fees as high as eight points (8 percent of the loan), and kickbacks of $0.50 per square foot of the project. The developers also arranged for the loans to be sold to other financial institutions, leaving the originating S&L with the fee income and no I-30 real estate loans on their books. The major problem was the lack of buyers and the large number of defaults on loan payments by those who did buy the condos.

Spencer H. Blain, Jr.

The first major player in this condo development is Spencer H. Blain, Jr., who acquired controlling interest in Empire in 1982 and became its chief executive officer and chairman of the board. Before that, Blain was president of a larger S&L in Austin, a former president of the Texas Savings and Loan League, and a director of the Federal Home Loan Bank of Little

Rock, serving as vice-chairman of the board and chairman of the executive committee. Therefore, he had outstanding credentials as a savings and loan executive.

Blain acquired controlling interest (67%) of Empire from Danny Faulkner, James Toler, and their associates. However, he failed to notify the regulators of a change of control prior to making the acquisition, as is required by law.[5] When he did file the notification, they approved it. To finance the stock purchase, he borrowed about $831,000 from Faulkner and Toler. Subsequently, he approved $40 million or more in loans on Faulkner-Toler real estate projects.

Blain's annual salary at Empire was $30,000 per year. Other remuneration from Empire was $251,458, most of which was a bonus.[6]

When Blain acquired Empire, his plans were to make construction loans, sell them in the secondary market without recourse, earn fees for making those loans, get larger by using jumbo deposits, be a limited partner in building condos, close the loans to buyers, and finally, sell the loans to Fannie Mae or Freddie Mac.[7] He achieved most of his goals.

In the year and a half that Blain was at the helm of Empire, he used brokered deposits to spur the growth of deposits from $17.3 million on June 30, 1982 to $308.9 million on January 31, 1984—a growth rate of over 1,700 percent in a year and a half! Empire often paid 2 percentage points higher on their brokered deposits than other banks and S&Ls. Empire continued to buy brokered deposits, in a desperate effort to survive, until the day before it failed. Brokered deposits of $262 million accounted for 85 percent of Empire's total deposits when it closed in March 1984. Mario Renda's First United Fund brokered most of those deposits.

In August 1983, Empire had assets of $340 million. Mortgage loans were $276.5 million (excluding $77.5 million sold in participations), and there was $181.3 million-outstanding in land and construction loans (excluding $61.2 million sold in loan participations).[8]

After Empire was closed, Blain testified before Congress. "I have never knowingly involved myself or lent to anyone else who was involved in what has been characterized as a 'land flip.' Although land flips are not illegal and not uncommon."[9] When Congressman Doug Barnard, Jr., asked Blain if he made any profits or commission on some of the properties that he financed, Blain answered "No, sir, I did not."[10]

According to federal prosecutors, Blain made more than $112 million in bogus condominium deals. Blain also made $21 million in real estate profits during his reign at Empire. However, he gave up most of it in settlements with the Federal Home Loan Bank Board to recover some of their insured losses. As part of the settlement, FSLIC got part ownership with Blain of 132 oil and gas wells. He acknowledged no wrongdoing. According to Blain, the impatience of the bank regulators, rather than any wrongdoing, caused the failure of Empire.[11]

David L. "Danny" Faulkner

The second major player in the bogus condominium deal is David L. "Danny" Faulkner, who quit school in the sixth grade, worked as a painting contractor, and became a self-made, multimillionaire, real estate developer. Faulkner wore Italian made alligator shoes, rode in a Rolls Royce, and wore a diamond studded Rolex watch. He was widely known in the Dallas area for his philanthropic activities. He was, by many people's standards, a pillar of the community. For example, he donated $1 million to build a church sanctuary for a young girl who was dying of cancer. However, some of his gifts raise questions about potential conflicts of interest. The regional head of Fannie Mae approved land purchases for Faulkner along the I-30 corridor while the official's wife was a Faulkner employee. In fact, she bought one of the condos and Faulkner gave her a Mercedes-Benz for a surprise birthday present.[12] Clifford Sinclair also testified that Faulkner ordered him to pay Texas State Senator Ted Lyon a $10,000 fee and give him a $26,104 Lincoln car for helping to settle a zoning dispute which increased the value of Faulkner's property by several million dollars.[13] In addition, Faulkner gave real estate appraiser Larry W. Hutson's wife a $5,000 fur coat. Hutson also received $387,000 for providing bogus appraisals on real estate.[14]

In 1979, Faulkner developed a condominium project called "Faulkner Point" on Lake Ray Hubbard. By 1982, he had stopped developing his own condominiums. Instead, he and James Toler bought options to purchase land in the area, and then sold the land at inflated prices to condominium investors. By using options (contracts to buy the land at a stated price during some specified time period), they invested little cash of their own. Faulkner and Toler and their associates handled the appraisals and development. Faulkner's profits amounted about $40 million and Toler's to about $38 million.[15]

James L. Toler

The third major player in the I-30 scheme is James L. Toler, former Mayor of Garland, Texas, and a land developer, who owned Lato Inc. and Zigga Inc. He was associated with Danny Faulkner and was one of the owners of Empire.

Clifford L. Sinclair

The fourth major player in the I-30 Corridor-Condo scam is Clifford L. Sinclair, who owned Kitco Developers Inc., a mortgage banking company, and Kitco Management. Currently serving a 13-year sentence for fraud, Sinclair had a long history of illegal activities. He successfully fought extradition to Alabama where he allegedly operated a phony mortgage brokerage firm, and a similar charge was pending in Arkansas.[16] Sinclair testified that he was a real estate promoter who found buyers to purchase the property owned by Faulkner and Toler in the I-30 corridor in Garland. Sinclair and his co-conspirators recruited more than 400 individuals to invest in the condominiums. He submitted false financial statements and credit applications for some of buyers. He even instructed employees how to change buyers' Social Security numbers to prevent discovery in a credit check.[17] He and his co-conspirators caused over 1,000 false appraisals to be made which were submitted to institutions funding the loans on the condominiums.

Sinclair, in financing the "Kirby Mills" development, made 39 loans from Empire for $39 million to purchase land. Each loan had a one-year term. Almost one year after they were made, no construction had begun on the project.[18] Construction loans of $105 million were planned, part of which would be used to repay the land loans. In connection with the "Faulkner on the Greens" condo project, Empire also made land loans of $23.7 million to finance the purchase of land from Sinclair and construction loans of $46.6 million.

Land Flips

In one transaction, Toler's Zigga Inc. bought land at $0.83 to $1.25 per square foot. Toler had a falsified appraisal made at $13 per square foot. The title to the land in such transactions would change from Toler (or his associates) to Faulkner (or his associates) at inflated prices on each exchange—a land flip. The same tract of land was sometimes flipped six times a day.

Consider the following example of land flips by Blain's Empire Savings and Loan and its real estate subsidiary, Statewide Service Corp. Statewide had a 25 to 50 percent limited partnership interest in many real estate development projects. Statewide purchased 36.4 acres of land from James Toler's Lato Inc. for $280,000. That same day, Statewide swapped that tract and other land. Then Blain bought 48.9 acres from Toler for $261,948, which included the Lato tract that Statewide had sold previously. Blain also purchased 16.95 acres of adjoining property for $424,500, which included the Toler Bay Condo Joint Venture owned by Toler and Faulkner. The total 65.85 acres cost $696,448, and were sold to Clifford Sinclair for $14.9 million in cash, plus two tracts of land in Steamboat Springs, Colorado, which were valued at $1.1 million.[19] Stated otherwise, he made $16 million in one prearranged land flip. That's not bad for a few days of work.

In another transaction, Statewide purchased about 82 acres for $0.52 per square foot, or $1.86 million. That same day it sold the same acreage to Faulkner and Toler for $0.85 per square foot, or $3 million. Then Faulkner and Toler sold 18.6 acres of that property to one of their associates, who in turn subdivided it into seven plots and sold them to condominium investors for $6.95 per square foot, or $5.6 million. In one day Faulkner and Toler made a profit of about $3.74 million, and still owned 63.4 acres of land.[20]

Empire and other lenders provided the financing for the land flips and the condominium investors. The land flips were financed with short-term land loans, and the proceeds were sufficient to cover 6 to 12 point (percent) loan fees, interest, and closing costs. When the land loans matured, construction loans were granted and additional fees were generated to cover all of the costs. According to a congressional report, "Empire could speculate in real estate development while increasing its paper assets with an artificially and fraudulently inflated loan and increasing its paper net worth with income from loan fees, interest, and closing costs that Empire itself was, in reality, paying."[21]

To illustrate the financing of flips, consider the following transactions.[22] Some land totaling 6.7 acres was sold for $392,113. On the same day the land was sold again for $1,379,469. Empire loaned the borrower $1,414,531. In another set of transactions, Kitco Developers (Sinclair) sold 3.6 acres for $156,816 to Ozark Service Corp. The same day, Ozark sold it again for $1,332,936 to Bob Ward Enterprises, Inc. It flipped one more time for $1,724,976. Empire eventually loaned $1,898,250 to a Mr. Carpenter on that transaction, and the price increased from $1.00 to $12.10 per square foot on the 3.6 acres in these transactions, which occurred over about a two-and-one-half month period.

Once a parcel of land had reached high values—as high as they were going to flip that parcel—it was divided into smaller plots and sold to a prearranged group of more than 150 condominium investors. Empire and other S&Ls loaned 110 percent of the value to the condominium investors, who were then paid "bonuses" from the funds they borrowed. The bonuses were as much as $43,000 depending on the size of the loans.

Many of the investors who bought the plots grossly exaggerated their net worths to qualify for the loans and bonuses that were mentioned previously. Carl Wren told Bell County Savings that he owned over $1 million in marketable securities when he owned none.[23] Brenda Stemwede told Lancaster First Federal Savings that she had cash value life insurance worth $130,000 when she had none. Jerry Buchingham told Empire he owned two houses, which was a lie. These people and others were greedy, and either did not realize the risks involved or were willing to take the risks to earn the bonuses. When the loans came due, and the investors at the bottom of the pyramid could not pay for them or sell the land at the prices they had paid for it, many of them went to jail.

The aftermath of the Empire Savings was that three of the principals involved were charged under Racketeer Influenced and Corrupt Organizations Act statutes:

- Spencer H. Blain, Jr., was sentenced to 20 years in prison and ordered to forfeit $22 million.

- David L. Faulkner was sentenced to 20 years in prison, and ordered to forfeit $40 million and pay a $215 criminal fine.

- James L. Toler was sentenced to 20 years in prison, and ordered to forfeit $40 million and pay a $220 criminal fine.

- Clifford R. Sinclair plead guilty on March 24, 1986 to conspiracy to commit bank fraud, making false statements to a federally insured lending institution, and making false statements to a government agency. As part of the plea agreement, he was sentenced to 13 years in prison, a fine of $40,000, and restitution of $600,000 to FSLIC. The court imposed an additional three years in prison.

- Arthur Formann, a real estate appraiser involved in the scheme was sentenced to 10 years in prison.

United American Bank (Knoxville, Tennessee) and the Butcher Brothers

Jacob "Jake" Franklin Butcher was a born salesman and an unsuccessful Democratic gubernatorial candidate in Tennessee in 1978.[24] His younger brother, Cecil Hilgie "C.H." Butcher, Jr., was a gruff, hard-driving businessman who called the hard financial shots for the two brothers. C.H. gained some banking experience working in his father's Union County Bank of Maynardville, Tennessee. In 1968, the Butcher brothers bought their first bank in Lake City. They arranged financing of the purchase through Jesse Barr, a banker at Union Planters National Bank, Memphis. By 1974, they controlled nine banks. By 1982, their assets amounted to about $180 million, and they controlled 14 financial institutions with more than $3 billion in deposits. The next year their financial empire collapsed.

Jake Butcher acquired approximately 51 percent of Hamilton National Bank of Knoxville in February 1975, and eight months later changed its name to United American Bank, N.A. (UAB Knoxville). He borrowed about $16 million to finance the purchase. Hamilton had a history of poor asset quality and above average loan losses. Hamilton's earnings had been depressed by high interest costs on time-deposits that were used to fund its growth.

In 1976, the Office of Comptroller of the Currency (OCC) expressed concern to UAB's board of directors that Jake's $200,000 salary was considerably more than that paid at comparable banks, and that he had diverted $98,000 from the sale of credit life insurance from the bank for his own use. Federal law prohibits insiders and employees at national banks from benefiting personally from the sale of credit life insurance to that bank's customers.[25] In November 1976, Jake converted the bank to a state charter to avoid that law, to avoid adding capital, to make bigger loans, and to free noninterest-bearing deposits from the Federal Reserve. He also withdrew the bank from the Federal Reserve System. The following year, Jake's income from credit life was $241,300. His gross income in 1977 was $2.3 million. His tax deductions for interest and other expenses amounted to $2 million. Butcher was reported to have said he made a lot of money fast because he owes so much.[26]

In 1980, the two brothers separated their holdings. Alleged reasons for their separation included the possibility of lending money to each other and to skirt federal regulations. Jake Butcher had controlling interests in UAB Knoxville, where he was chairman and chief executive officer. He also controlled United American Banks of Chattanooga and Memphis, Tennessee, and Somerset, Kentucky. Citizens Union National Bank and Trust Company of Lexington, Kentucky, became part of the UAB group in early 1982.

C. H. Butcher, Jr., had controlling interest in a chain of 30 smaller rural banks in four states. However, City and County (C&C) Bank of Knox County was his flagship bank. Other Tennessee C&C banks included C&C Bank of Anderson County, C&C Bank of Hawkins County, C&C Bank of Jefferson County, C&C Bank of Monroe County, C&C Bank of McMinn County, C&C Bank of Rhea County, C&C Bank of Roane County, and C&C Bank of Washington County. There were also C&C banks in Kentucky. Other C.H. Butcher banks that were not part of the C&C group included the Bank of Commerce in Morristown, Citizens Bank of Sneedville, United Southern of Nashville, and others. Both brothers had interests in family trusts that held bank stocks, including stock in UAB Knoxville.[27]

The Butcher's strategy was to borrow money to buy a bank, pay it off, and then buy another one. However, much of the Butcher banking empire was financed with loans made from one Butcher bank to another, sometimes with loans made by a bank to purchase its own stock. For example, UAB Knoxville loaned Anderson Trust, in which C.H. Butcher was the principal beneficiary, $1.5 million to buy stock in C&C Bank of Anderson County, which C.H. controlled. Similarly, UAB Knoxville loaned funds to Hamilton Bank of Memphis Trust, where Jake was the principal beneficiary, to buy stock in Hamilton Bank in Memphis. Finally, Jake told La Follette, Tennessee, grocer Robert L. Woodson, III, that he could buy more stockholders' shares in UAB Knoxville. Moreover, Jake offered to lend him the funds from his Kentucky bank to buy the shares and even to pay half of the interest on the loan. Woodson agreed, but he never received the shares because the other stockholder had pledged them as collateral against another loan.[28]

Jesse Alfred Barr was Jake's adviser and business associate. Barr was president of Service and Management Inc., a Butcher related company. He was also a director of C&C Financial Interstate Service, Inc., a data processing firm specializing in banking services and an umbrella corporation for C.H's business interests. Barr had resigned as executive vice president from Union Planters National Bank, Memphis, Tennessee, and was later indicted and convicted for embezzlement and misapplication of that bank's funds. Union Planters claims Barr's crimes cost them $30 million, and they got a $17.6 million civil judgment against him. Because of the 1976 conviction, Barr could not work in a bank again. However, he could and did serve as a "consultant" to the Butcher brothers. Barr also acted in Jake Butcher's name to approve loans and to shift them from bank to bank to avoid regulatory scrutiny.

In connection with the Butchers, Barr was convicted of conspiring to obtain fraudulent loans for Butcher from banks he or his family controlled, among other charges. One such loan was to buy a $460,000 yacht. At the sentencing, the Judge called Barr "the key player who made possible his [Butcher's] million-dollar thefts."[29]

Barr helped Jake try to acquire Union Planters Bank, but Jake shelved those plans in 1974 when he decided to run for governor. After Jake lost the campaign, he tried but failed to get a seat on the bank's board of directors.

Barr also helped Jake put together the 1982 World's Fair in Knoxville, with the help of President Jimmy Carter, Senator Howard Baker (Republican Tennessee), and former Budget Director Bert Lance. Lance was President Carter's budget director who resigned because of the banking scandal that was covered in Chapter 1. At one time, Butcher had loaned Lance money to buy a bank. Lance, his companies, and relatives had borrowed $4.1 million from Butcher banks. Millions of dollars in loans were made to state political figures.[30] Jake also donated to Carter's presidential campaign. It paid off to mix banking and politics. Eventually, the Butcher group persuaded federal officials to spend $295 million on the fair and related projects. Much of it was spent on construction contracts with firms that had close ties to the Butchers. According to the General Accounting Office, there was a lack of competitive bidding for these projects and the possibility of unwarranted private gains. Barr was a partner in a trust controlling at least one of the projects. Many of the loans to fair-related ventures defaulted in 1982, a year that was characterized by falling market rates of interest and a deep recession. One such defaulted UAB loan for $701,000 was to Barr's secretary, who organized a company to provide linen service to the fair.

Under Jake Butcher's reign, UAB Knoxville's assets grew rapidly, financed largely by interest rate-sensitive borrowed funds, such as large CDs, that were then commonly called "purchase money" or "hot money." The financial innovation of brokered deposits emerged in the late 1970s and grew rapidly in the early 1980s.

Over the six-year period the Butchers controlled the bank, it engaged in a pattern of unsafe, unsound, and unlawful banking practices such as forged notes, loans in the names of nominees, and misrepresentation of collateral values. According to William M. Isaac, former Chairman of the FDIC, UAB Knoxville "eschewed caution in favor of leverage, reasonable conservatism in favor of aggressiveness, and diversification in favor of real estate concentration and loans to insiders or quasi-insiders and their interests ... UAB was a bank bordering on being out of control."[31] In one case involving limited partnerships, a $15,000 investment by the partners in a project resulted in a $4 million loan loss by the bank. In another case, UAB loaned $300,000 to CC (Buddy) Pack, a resort developer. The bank took a second mortgage on Pack's property, which already had a $497,000 lien against it. Pack's company had reported losses of $690,000 for that year, and Pack had filed a pauper's oath in court several months before he received the loan. Finally, he didn't own all of the real estate he put up as collateral.[32]

The pattern of insider lending was a long-standing practice at the UAB Knoxville. Press reports in 1978 observed that Butcher's bank had a high percentage of insider loans that exceeded the bank's equity capital.[33]

Frequently the borrowers were close personal friends or associates of those making the lending decisions at the bank. Borrowers sometimes dictated the terms of their loans to the bank officers. Although friends, associates, and families of insiders are not insiders in the legal sense of the term, their loans amounted to $211.5 million, or 506 percent of total equity capital and reserve in 1982. All of these loans were adversely classified: $27.5 million was considered a loss, $62.3 million was classified as doubtful, and $121.7 million was classified substandard. Loans to insiders (officers, directors, and their interests) amounted to $38.1 million, or 62 percent of equity capital and reserves. Of this amount, $25 million was adversely classified. The bank's five largest borrowers, including their various interests, owed the bank $251 million. Such policies were reflected in the bank's low returns. In 1981, the return on assets was 0.50 percent, about half of what peer banks earned.[34]

The Butchers' chain and financial dealings involved about 40 loosely affiliated banks and five savings and loans that fell under the authority of seven different federal and state regulatory agencies. It also included more than 60 interlocking corporations and partnerships that borrowed millions from their banks. Some of the loans were legal, some were forged. For example, Franklin Haney, a real estate developer who was involved with Jake Butcher on several projects, claimed that a $2.7 million loan from UAB Knoxville was forged. Milton Turner, another real estate developer, claimed to know nothing about $2.4 million in loans made by UAB in Memphis and UAB in Somerset to one of his real estate companies in Texas. One note was signed by Gene Cook as an officer of that company. No Gene Cook was employed by that company. However, Jake's farm manager was named Gene Cook, and he said he did not sign the note.[35]

Lack of Regulatory Effectiveness

Lack of cooperation between government agencies seriously compromised the regulator's effectiveness, but made it easier for the Butchers' and their associates to subvert the system. The following example of check kiting $16 million illustrates the point. Because the FDIC and the Tennessee Department of Insurance did not communicate with each other, it was improbable that they would be able to detect the check-kiting scheme involving UAB Knoxville, Southern Industrial Banking Corporation (SIBC), Knoxville, and City and County Bank of Hawkensville County, although both banks were supervised by the FDIC. SIBC was chartered in 1929, and because of a "grandfather" clause in the law it was permitted to use the term "bank" in its name. It was founded by Cecil H. Butcher, Sr., the brothers' father, and associates, to finance furniture, automobiles, and farm equipment. C.H. Butcher, Jr., gradually took control of it. SIBC was a thrift—a finance company that made consumer and commercial loans funded by the sale of uninsured "investment certificates" to retail customers. It was supervised by the Tennessee Department of Insurance. The supervision consisted of checking to determine if SIBC met minimum capital standards. The Tennessee Department of Insurance does not classify loans.[36] Edward C. Browder was a director of both SIBC and UAB Knoxville. C.H. Butcher was the chairman of SIBC. C.H. also controlled City and County Bank of Hawkensville County. Cecil H. Butcher, Sr., served on SIBC's board of directors.

On October 8, 1982, UAB Knoxville sold, without recourse, $16 million in loan participations to SIBC. SIBC paid for the participations with a check drawn on its account at City and County Bank of Hawkensville County. However, SIBC only had $10 million in its account at City and County Bank at the time the check was drawn. On October 12, 1982, SIBC drew a $16 million check on its account at UAB Knoxville, when its balance was only $1.7 million, payable to City and County Bank. On October 14th and 15th, UAB Knoxville loaned SIBC a total of $13 million to cover the check that SIBC had drawn on the 12th.

SIBC was used as a "dumping ground" in the shell game of moving at least $25 million in bad loans from one Butcher controlled bank to another to avoid being discovered by bank examiners. Bad loans were exchanged for collectible consumer loans made by SIBC.[37] It was Jesse Barr who engineered the movement of loans between banks. Between November 11th and December 23rd, UAB Knoxville repurchased for its own account the entire $16 million in loan participations, even though it had no written commitment to do so. Some of the loans sold in these transactions were of such poor credit quality that they were adversely classified by FDIC examiners. While the FDIC was concerned about UAB Knoxville's repurchase of bad loans before the bank was closed, it may not have been aware of the check kiting scheme until a later date.

C.H. Butcher's SIBC borrowed funds from UAB Knoxville to help finance Jake's failed gubernatorial race. To help pay off $900,000 of those debts, SIBC loaned Financial Services Leasing $870,000. Financial Services Leasing was a shell company and was not even listed in the phone book. The same day as the loan was made, SIBC sold all of its furniture and equipment to Financial Services Leasing, and then leased them back at a cost of $12,500 per month for five years. SIBC transferred the $870,000 promissory note, without recourse, from Financial Services and $30,000 cash to pay off SIBC's loan from UAB Knoxville. Now Financial Services, rather than SIBC, owed UAB Knoxville $870,000. Then SIBC paid $12,358 per month to UAB Knoxville to reduce Financial Services' debt.

Financial Leasing was also used by SIBC to dump $500,000 of its bad debts and for other purposes. For instance, Financial Leasing made a $2.8 million loan to C.H. Butcher for undetermined purposes. It bought 74 houseboats from Jake Butcher's wife and leased them to Jesse Barr for $2.8 million. (They were to be used as floating hotels during the World's Fair.) It was $25 million in debt when it filed for bankruptcy. Most of it owed to Butcher-controlled banks. Unfortunately, Financial Leasing had no credit files and no collection system, so most of the debt will go uncollected.[38]

SIBC also engaged heavily in loans to insiders. Eight Butcher associates, including C.H. Butcher, had borrowed $28.5 million in loans, almost half of SIBC's loan portfolio.

In another set of transactions unrelated to SIBC, loans were used to pay off or increase other loans. On August 31, 1982, an unnamed S&L (supervised by the Federal Home Loan Bank Board) made a $2.5 million loan to a Butcher-related person. On September 1, a $901,402 loan at UAB Knoxville was repaid. Then UAB Knoxville purchased a $1,235,000 participation in the $2.5 million S&L loan. The net result was that rather than the loan at UAB Knoxville being repaid, it was increased by $333,598 ($1,235,000 − $901,402 = $333,598).[39]

Those in control of the S&Ls had close financial links to the Butchers. For example, one majority stockholder of an S&L borrowed the money to buy the stock from the Butchers. Others were business associates. The complex nature of these transactions made them difficult to uncover; and the fact that many regulatory agencies were involved frustrated the ability of some regulators to deal with the situation. Nevertheless, the U.S. House Committee on Government Operations concluded that UAB Knoxville, Penn Square, and Franklin National Banks failed, in part, because of indecisive actions by banking regulators.[40]

The House Committee also examined the role of Ernst & Whinney (E&W), a major independent public accounting firm which had audited UAB Knoxville's books since 1975. Net income (unaudited) for the first nine months of 1982 was $1.05 per share of common stock, compared to

$0.80 per share in the previous year. The profit picture changed in the fourth quarter. The net income for the entire year was a loss of $0.76 per share of common stock, compared to $1.17 per share earned in the previous year. E&W signed an unqualified audit report and certified that the financial statements fairly represented the financial position of the bank and conformed with generally accepted accounting principles applied on a consistent basis. The statements were released by the bank on January 28, 1983, and the bank was closed 10 days later. According to the FDIC, the financial statements were materially false and misleading.

This was not the first time the accountants had deficiencies in their auditing of banks. The FDIC sued Ernst & Ernst in connection with their auditing of Franklin National Bank, which failed.[41] However, Ernst & Ernst, now E&W, was not alone in their failure to find and report problems at banks. Peat, Marwick, Mitchell & Co gave an unqualified report for Penn Square Bank, Oklahoma City, Oklahoma before it failed.[42] More will be said about auditing in Chapter 12.

On November 1, 1982, the day after the World's Fair closed, 180 FDIC examiners (10 percent of their audit force) closed in on the Butchers' banks simultaneously so they could not pass bad loans from bank to bank. The FDIC would have moved in sooner, but all of the hotel rooms in Knoxville were filled with tourists from the World's Fair. On February 14, 1983, UAB Knoxville was declared insolvent. It had deposits of $838 million. It was the third largest commercial bank to fail in U.S. banking history, following the Franklin National Bank (deposits of $1.4 billion) and United States National Bank of San Diego (deposits of $932 million). Within the next six months, eight other banks owned or controlled by the Butchers failed. Collectively, their deposits amounted to $1.7 billion, making the Butcher-related failures the largest in U.S. history. Eleven other Butcher-related banks in Kentucky and Tennessee were sold or merged. On February 15, 1983, the FDIC announced that it had sold UAB Knoxville's deposit liabilities and assets to First Tennessee Bank, Knoxville, Tennessee.[43]

Jake Butcher was sentenced to two concurrent 20-year sentences. C. H. Butcher and others were ordered to pay $19.3 million in damages for a plot to hide their wealth when their banks failed.

Endnotes

1. U.S. House, *Adequacy of Federal Home Loan Bank Board Supervision of Empire Savings and Loan Association*, Hearing before the Commerce, Consumer, and Monetary Affairs Subcommittee of the Committee on Government Operations, 98th Cong., 2nd Sess., April 25, 1984, numerous press clippings appear in the hearings, pp. 550-587 and other pages; U.S. House, *Federal Home Loan Bank Board Supervision and Failure of Empire Savings and Loan of Mesquite, Texas.*, 44th Report by the Committee on Gov-

ernment Operations, House Report 98-953, 98th Cong., 2nd Sess., August 6, 1984; Other published reports dating from the early 1980s to the present include: Allen Pusey, "The Fall of Empire," Austin, Texas, *American-Statesman*, April 23, 1989; Bill Lodge, "Garland Man Recounts Land Sale in I-30 Trial," Dallas, Texas, *Dallas Morning News*, May 13, 1989; "Key Testimony Opens in Condo Fraud Trial," Sherman, Texas, *Democrat*, April 18, 1989; "Witness' Past Probed in I-35 Condo Trial," Sherman, Texas, *Democrat*, April 25, 1989; "FSLIC Gets Oil Well Interest in Empire Savings Settlement," *American Banker*, April 27, 1987; Andrew Albert and Richard Ringer, "Questions Raised by 'Penn Square of Thrifts' Get Scrutiny at Congressional Hearing Today," *American Banker*, April 25, 1984; Andrew Alber and Richard Ringer, "Regulators Evaluating Empire's Cost," *American Banker*, March 20, 1984; "In Empire's Wake, a Dynasty Shakes," *American Banker*, March 27, 1984; Rick Atkinson and David Maraniss, "Turning Anger into Action on Thrifts," *The Washington Post*, June 13, 1989, p. A1, claim FSLIC's loss on Empire is $165 million.

2. Rick Atkinson and David Maraniss, "Only Ambition Limited S&L Growth," *The Washington Post*, p. A18.

3. U.S. House, House Report 98-953, 6-27; U.S. House, Hearing, April 25, 1984, Report of Examination, p. 191.

4. U.S. House, Hearing, April 25, 1984, p. 254.

5. National Housing Act, Section 407(Q).

6. U.S. House, Hearing, April 25, 1984, p. 276.

7. U.S. House, Hearing, April 25, 1984, p. 155.

8. U.S. House, Hearing, April 25, 1984, p. 257.

9. U.S. House, Hearing, April 25, 1984, p. 152.

10. U.S. House, Hearing, April 25, 1984, p. 162.

11. "Failed Texas Thrift's Former Head Blames Agency's Impatience," *The Wall Street Journal*, April 27, 1984.

12. U.S. House, Hearing, April 25, 1984, p. 297.

13. "Witness Says Senator Got Cash and Car for Help," Bonham, Texas, *Favorite*, April 20, 1989.

14. Bill Lodge, "Witness Says I-30 Figures got Bogus Appraisals," *Morning News*, Dallas, Texas, June 26, 1989; Bill Lodge, "I-30 Defendants Prepare Case; Toler Set to Testify," *Morning News*, Dallas, Texas, July 3, 1989.

15. U.S. House, *Federal Efforts to Combat Fraud, Abuse, and Misconduct in the Nation's S&L's and Banks and to implement the Criminal and Civil Enforcement Provisions of FIREEA*, Hearings before the Commerce, Consumer, and Monetary Affairs Subcommittee of the Committee on Government Operations, 101 Cong., 2nd. Sess., March 14 and 15, 1990, p. 22.

16. U.S. House, Hearing, April 25, 1984, pp. 554-557.

17. Debbie Howell, "Defense Questions Sinclair," Garland, Texas, *News*, April 22, 1989.

18. U.S. House, Hearing, April 25, 1984, p. 401.

19. "Ex-Chief of Empire Savings Sued by FSLIC over Texas Land Deals," *American Banker*, August 30, 1984; U.S. House, House Report 98-953, pp. 14-15; U.S. House, Hearing, April 25, 1984, pp. 271, 357, 430, 553, 562.

20. *op. cit.,* Allen Pusey.

21. U.S. House Report, 98-953, p. 24.

22. U.S. House, Hearing, April 25, 1984, pp. 262, 430.

23. Robert Bork, Jr., "Never Give a Sucker an Even Break," *Forbes*, July 15, 1985, pp. 72, 77.

24. This section draws on the following sources: *Borrowed Money, Borrowed Time: The Fall of the House of Butcher*, a collection of 27 articles by *The Tennessean* and *The Knoxville Journal*, November 18, 1993; U.S. House, *Federal Supervision and Failure of United American Bank of Knoxville, Tenn., and Affiliated Banks*, 23rd Report by the Committee on Government Operations, House Report No. 98-573, 89th Cong., 1st. Sess., November 18, 1983; U.S. House, *Federal Supervision and Failure of United American Bank (Knoxville, Tenn.)*, Hearing before the Commerce, Consumer, and Monetary Affairs Subcommittee of the Committee on Government Operations, 98th Cong., 1st. Sess., March 15 and 16, 1983.

25. 12 CFR Part 2, Section 22.

26. U.S. House, Hearings, March 15 and 16, 1983, p. 571.

27. U.S. House, Hearings, March 15 and 16, 1983, pp. 572-573.

28. *Borrowed Time, Borrowed Money, ibid.,* pp. 9, 10.

29. Michael J. Stedman, "Doing Time: Advice from a Jailed Banker," *Bankers Monthly*, November 1988, p. 18.

30. *Borrowed Money, Borrowed Time, ibid.,* pp. 37-38.

31. U.S. House, Report No. 98-573, pp. 4, 36; U.S. House, Hearings, March 15 and 16, 1983, p. 39.

32. U.S. House, Hearings, March 15 and 16, 1983, p. 616.

33. U.S. House, Hearings, March 15 and 16, 1983, p. 569.

34. U.S. House, Hearings, March 15 and 16, 1983, pp. 21, 41, 170-172.

35. *Borrowed Money, Borrowed Time, ibid.,* pp. 23, 28.

36. U.S. House, Hearings, March 15 and 16, 1983, p. 606. Also see *Borrowed Money, Borrowed Time*, pp. 14-16.

37. U.S. House, Report No. 98-573, p. 11; Hearings, March 15 and 16, 1983, pp. 143, 592-593; Stedman, *ibid.,* p. 20; *Borrowed Money, Borrowed Time, ibid.,* pp. 10, 33.

38. *Borrowed Money, Borrowed Time, ibid.,* p. 29.

39. U.S. House, Report No. 98-573, p. 47.

40. U.S. House, Report No. 98-573, pp. 50-57.

41. Re Franklin National Bank Securities Litigation, 445 F.Supp. 723 (1978).

42. U.S. House, Report No. 98-593, p. 43; U.S. Hearing, March 15 and 16, 1983, pp. 120, 162-163, 258, 272-274, 287-288, 609.

43. For the terms of the Purchase and Assumption Agreement and the Indemnity Agreement, see U.S. House, Hearings, March 15 and 16, 1983, pp. 175-198.

11 THE ROLE OF DIRECTORS IN DETERRING FRAUD

The Office of the Comptroller of the Currency (OCC) found that deficiencies within boards of directors contributed to insider abuse and fraud, to bank failures, and to problem banks.[1] The boards of such banks were frequently weak (lacking oversight responsibilities and controls) overly aggressive, or some combination of the two. In contrast, none of the continuously healthy banks that the OCC examined had such deficiencies with their boards. The OCC concluded that one of the major differences between failed banks and healthy banks was the caliber of management that reflected the policies of an active and involved board of directors.

A study of 205 failed S&Ls came to a similar conclusion—the directors of virtually all of them failed to act prudently.[2] In another study of failed S&Ls, the boards were passive. One director said the thrift's board did not question business decisions of the former chairman because he owned the thrift. They thought that he could do as he pleased.[3] With that in mind, this chapter presents an overview of what bank boards should and should not do. By carrying out their duties correctly, bank directors can go a long way toward eliminating the conditions in which insider abuse and fraud can flourish.

Unfortunately, weak and ineffective boards of directors are not uncommon according to management expert Peter Drucker. He wrote, "But there is one thing all boards have in common, regardless of their legal position. *They do not function.* The decline of the board is a universal phenomenon of this century. Perhaps nothing shows it as clearly as [the fact that] the board, which, by law, is the governing organ of a corporation, was always the last group to hear [of] the trouble in the great business catastrophes of this century. Whenever a financial scandal breaks, the board's failure to act is blamed on stupidity, negligence, or on the failure of management to keep the board informed. But when such malfunction occurs with unfailing regularity, one must concede that it is the institution that fails to perform rather than individuals."[4] The massive failures of banks and S&Ls in recent years is strong evidence that there is a structural problem with our institutions. Drucker goes on to say that boards have become a legal fiction. While that may be so *de facto, de jure* they are charged with certain responsibilities for which they are held liable. Not only can banking regulators sue directors of failed institutions, but shareholders can institute class action suits too. In a class action suit pending in Los Angeles against certain officers and directors of the parent company of Lincoln Savings & Loan, the shareholders are charging securities frauds and racketeering arising from the sale of bonds that are virtually worthless that caused their stock to decline in value.[5]

The Responsibilities of a Bank's Board of Directors

The bank's stockholders elect a board of directors to oversee its affairs and to ensure competent management, thereby giving the board the ultimate responsibility for the success or failure of that bank. This applies whether the bank is independently owned or part of a holding company.

Statutes and regulations provide boards of directors with general guidelines with respect to their structure and duties. Federal banking regulations establish the minimum and maximum number of board members for national banks. They must have at least five, but no more than 25 board members. Similarly, S&Ls have requirements concerning the composition of their boards. For example, no more than two directors can be from the same family, nor more than two lawyers from the same law firm. Moreover, participation by independent directors is essential to provide perspective and objectivity to board decisions. The intent here is to eliminate conflicts of interest and promote independent judgment.

In addition to a regular board of directors, banks may have advisory directors who bring particular expertise to the board. Advisory directors usually play a limited role in board activities and may not be liable for board decisions.

The legal duties of directors are dictated by laws and regulations. Under common law, directors are expected to carry out their functions with "duty of care" and "duty of loyalty." These legal terms mean that directors are required to be diligent and honest in managing the affairs of the bank, and they authorize bank management to do only those things that the bank is permitted to do by law and regulations. The duty of care holds directors to a standard of care equal to that which a prudent man would use in similar circumstances.[6] In this regard, directors are expected to know what is going on at their banks. They have a "duty to investigate" existing problems or ones that may develop and to make sure that steps are taken to correct them. Failure to comply with the duty-of-care standard may be considered "negligence" in the eyes of the court that said: "Directors who willingly allow others to make major decisions affecting the future of the corporation wholly without supervision or oversight may not defend their lack of knowledge, for that ignorance itself is a breach of fiduciary duty."[7]

The duty-of-care standard does not expect directors to guarantee the conduct of a bank's officers or its profitability, or hold them accountable for errors in business judgment. It does, however, expect them to act in good faith and carry out their duties diligently.

The duty of loyalty prohibits directors from putting their personal or business interests, or those of others, above the interests of the bank. Directors may not take advantage of business opportunities that they learn of as a result of their position, without first offering them to the bank. Stated otherwise, directors cannot make inappropriate gains because of their connection with the bank. They can, however, do business with the bank provided that the relationships are fully disclosed to the board, which must determine the fairness of those transactions to the bank, and if there are conflicts of interest. For example, the president of a thrift formed a separate corporation to receive loan referral fees for identifying borrowers to that thrift. The FHLBB informed the thrift that its president was an affiliated person who could not properly accept such fees.[8] The board's guiding principle is that the bank comes first. In addition, directors cannot disclose confidential information about the bank or its customers that they acquired as a result of their position on the board.

National banks and other types of financial institutions are also subject to federal and state statutes. In determining liability under certain statutory provisions, Congress has required that directors may be liable for "knowing" violations of law. This means that the director knew, or should have known, the facts concerning the violations. Therefore, the courts presume that directors know the laws.

Finally, banks and their directors are subject to regulations from bank regulators and other government agencies. Bank regulators, such as the OCC, can take administrative actions against banks and directors who engage in unsafe or unsound practices. (These practices will be explained shortly.) The administrative actions include cease and desist orders, civil money penalties, and removal of individuals from office.

In summary, the board of directors is responsible for the welfare of a bank. The attitude of the directors towards ethics and internal controls is a major factor in preventing and detecting frauds. Laws and regulations set broad limits on what bank boards can or cannot do. However, the laws and regulations do not tell us much about how boards operate.

Typical Committees

The board of directors elects its own officers, which usually include a chairman, vice-chairman, and a secretary. Equally important, it elects the officers of the bank who are expected to carry out the plans, policies, and controls established by or approved by the board. Oversight then becomes the board's primary responsibility.

The oversight functions are carried out by various committees composed of board members. It is more efficient for large boards of directors to have a few committee members deal with specific areas of concern than to encumber the entire board. Moreover, certain committees are limited to particular members of the board. Committees can make decisions on the board's behalf, or they can report back to the full board for further consideration. In either case the full board of directors is responsible for all committee decisions.

To avoid misunderstandings, the purposes, responsibilities, authority, and duration of all committees should be set forth clearly in writing. In addition, these committees should be given the resources and authority to discharge their responsibilities. And last, but not least, they should be informed and vigilant.

The structure of committees varies from bank to bank, depending on the bank's size and needs. The typical committees found in banks and their general duties are presented here. In addition to their general duties, each committee must ensure that applicable laws and regulations are followed.

Executive committee. The executive committee is usually authorized to act on behalf of the full board of directors between its regular meetings. It may review and coordinate information from other committees as well as oversee bank operations.

Audit committee. This is a "watch dog" committee. Its primary responsibility is overseeing that the bank complies with applicable laws and regulations. This committee should be composed exclusively of independent directors, the minimum number should be no fewer than three independent directors, and the committee size should be small enough so that each member can be an active participant. The functions of the audit committee are (1) to select independent auditors and to work with internal auditors, (2) to review the auditor's and bank examiner's reports and to consider their recommendations, and (3) to report to the board the committee's recommendations for the issues raised by the auditors. The audit committee may also consider the bank's internal controls concerning fraud and other risks. In addition, it should follow up the changes that are recommended to ensure that they are carried out.[9]

This overview of the audit committee does not cover the details of their activities. However, they should meet at least quarterly with the internal and external auditors, they should evaluate the internal audit staff and programs, and they should review management actions to correct the weaknesses and problems outlined in internal and external audit reports and examinations. This listing is not complete, but it is sufficient to indicate the key roles played by this committee.

Asset/Liability committee. The mandate of this committee is to oversee the bank's entire balance sheet— capital, funding, and asset allocation. The major concerns of this committee include capital adequacy, interest rate sensitivity, and the quality of credits. Specific issues dealing with investments and lending are handled by other committees.

Investment committee. The scope of the investment committee is narrower than the asset/liability committee. The investment committee establishes investment strategies and objectives. To provide guidelines for management, the committee must approve an investment policy that takes into account liquidity, pledging requirements, size, risk, and diversification of the portfolio.

Loan committee. This committee establishes and revises lending policies to meet the changing needs of the bank. It must set standards for valid appraisals of real estate and other collateral. In some banks the loan committee participates in credit decisions. Therefore, the committee must have knowledge concerning the economy in the market area and have a clear understanding of financial statements. Above all, it should not be a "rubber stamp" for loan officers.

The committee may also be in charge of loan review, which may be external and internal, depending on the size and needs of the bank. Loan policies and loan review will be discussed shortly.

Trust committee. Banks with trust activities have special fiduciary responsibilities to safeguard the interest of the trust customers. An important part of this is the establishment of a so-called "Chinese wall" to separate trust activities from other activities of the bank and to avoid conflicts of interest between the trust department, the bank, and insiders. Like the other committees, it establishes policies and fees, and deals with other aspects of trust operations. A separate *trust audit committee* oversees an annual audit of trust activities. Banking regulations require that the trust audit committee consist of directors who are not bank officers. Moreover, the directors should not serve simultaneously on the trust audit committee and the trust committee.

Personnel committee. Quality personnel is the key to success. Thus, the board must establish policies to attract and maintain such persons. At the same time, personnel policies should be instituted that minimize the possibility of white-collar crime.[10] These should include periodic reviews of personnel policies and making sure that employees who handle money are adequately compensated so they do not embezzle funds to supplement their incomes. In addition, it should establish a written policy that adverse personal financial situations will not affect job security or promotion. This alerts the employer to potential problems and provides some measure of security to the employee. Along this line, employee education concerning white-collar crime and free and confidential financial counseling should be considered. All employees should be required to take regular vacations, which makes it difficult to cover up crimes on a continuing basis. Key financial personnel should be rotated for the same reason.

Lending Policies

The *Comptroller's Handbook for National Bank Examiners* describes what the OCC believes to be essential elements of a bank's formal written policy statements. The board writes the statements and management is expected to implement, administer, and amplify upon them. The focus is on lending to illustrate the OCC's elements of sound policies. Lending generates most of a bank's income and is where most, but not all, of the major frauds occurred.

Loans must be made with the following objectives in mind:

1. Loans must be made on a sound and collectible basis.

2. Funds must be invested profitably for the benefit of shareholders and the protection of depositors.

3. The bank should serve the legitimate credit needs of the community in which it is located.

The handbook gives the following overview of lending policies that apply to banks in general.[11]

> *The lending policy should contain a general outline of the scope and allocation of the bank's credit facilities and the manner in which loans are made, serviced, and collected. The policy should be broad in nature and not overly restrictive. The formulation and enforcement of inflexible rules not only stifles initiative, but also may, in fact, hamper profitability and prevent the bank from serving the community's changing needs. A good lending policy will provide for the presentation, to the board or a committee thereof, of loans that officers believe are worthy of consideration but which are not within the purview of written guidelines. Flexibility must exist to allow for fast reaction and early adaptation to changing conditions in the bank's earning asset mix and within its service area.*
>
> *In developing the lending policy, consideration must be given to the individual bank's available financial resources, personnel, facilities, and future growth potential. Such guidelines must be void of any dis-*

criminatory practices. A determination of who will receive credit, and of what type and at what price, must be made. Other internal factors to be considered include who will grant the credit, in what amount, and what organizational structure will be used to ensure compliance with the bank's guidelines and procedures. As authority is spread throughout the organization, the bank must have efficient systems for monitoring adherence to established guidelines. That can best be accomplished by an internal review and reporting system which adequately informs the directorate and senior management of how policies are carried out and provides them with information sufficient to evaluate the performance of lower echelon officers and the condition of the loan portfolio.

The *Handbook* also lists components that form the basis of sound lending policies for banks. (Not every component is applicable for every bank.)

Geographic limits. A bank should have geographic limits for its lending activities that reflect its trade area. The policy should state the restrictions and exceptions. New banks located in Iowa, for example, should not finance Texas real estate developments.

Distribution by category. Limitations should be placed on the aggregate distribution of total loans in various categories of loans such as commercial, real estate, consumer, agriculture, and so on. However, some flexibility is required to meet the changing needs of the bank and the community it serves.

Types of loans. Guidelines should be established in making specific types of loans (such as energy or out-of-area real estate development loans), depending on the expertise of the lending officers and other factors. Particular attention should be paid to loans secured by collateral that requires more than the normal policing and to types of loans where there have been abnormal losses.

Maximum maturities. Loans should be structured with realistic repayment plans taking into account the value of collateral. Making a 15-year loan on equipment that has an economic life of five years is asking for trouble.

Loan pricing. Loan pricing must reflect all relevant costs (cost of funds, overhead, compensating balances, fees, and so forth) and provide for a reasonable return. The rates established on loans should take risk into account, thereby attracting certain types of borrowers and discouraging others.

Maximum ratio of loan amount to appraised value and acquisition costs. Many bank fraud cases involve loans in excess of appraised values and appraised values in excess of real values. Guidelines must be established concerning appraisal procedures and the amounts that will be loaned relative to appraised values.

Maximum ratio of loan amount to market value and pledged securities. Banks can go beyond the restrictions on these loans imposed by Regulation U and establish additional policies for other types of marketable securities that are acceptable as collateral for loans.

Financial information. Current, complete, and accurate information concerning a borrower's credit standing is essential before credit is granted and during the term of the loan. The loan policy should explain the types of information required from businesses and individual borrowers, such as audited quarterly financial statements and so on.

Limits and guidelines on purchasing loans. Loan sales and participations are a common ingredient in bank fraud. Accordingly, policy should be established concerning the aggregate limits of such loans, contingent liabilities, and the manner in which they are evaluated, handled, and serviced.

Limitations on aggregate outstanding loans. Policy should limit the amount of loans outstanding relative to other balance sheet items.

Concentrations of credit. Diversification is considered an essential element of sound lending policy in order to balance out expected returns and risk. The problem with loan concentration is that when the repayment of those loans depends on one or more key factors that go bad, the entire concentrated part of the portfolio is affected.

Loan authority. Lending limits should be established and enforced for all loan officers, or groups of officers, based on their lending experience. The policy should also cover the loan approval process, especially for large loans.

Collections and charge-offs. The policy should define delinquent loans and explain how to deal with them, including appropriate reports to the board.

Two examples of loan policies containing these and other elements of sound lending are presented in Appendixes B and C at the end of the book. As a general rule, the length of a loan policy is directly related to the size of the bank where it is used. That is, small banks have short policy statements and large banks have large policy statements. Those shown at the end of the book are for medium-size banks. Keep in mind that most major frauds that have caused bank failures were at small- and medium-size banks.

Lending Authority

Policy statements vary from bank to bank. Nevertheless, it may be useful to examine differences in procedures for loan approval at a small-, medium-, and large-size bank. The procedures are presented only for purposes of illustration. They are not being endorsed as being appropriate for other banks.

First City Bank (FCB) has $29 million in assets, with the main office and two branches serving a city with a 70,000 population. As shown in Figure 11.1, FCB divides loans into four categories: secured, unsecured and overdrafts, loans to insiders, and loans to employees. FCB has four loan officers. Their lending authority ranges from $1,500 for unsecured loans, $7,500 for secured loans for the most inexperienced loan officer and $25,000 unsecured/$50,000 secured for the most experienced one. The president has the authority to approve unsecured and secured loans up to $100,000. Secured and unsecured loans above $100,000 must be approved by the officers' loan committee, which consists of the chairman, president, and vice-president of the bank. This committee can approve loans up to $200,000. Above that amount, loans must be approved by the executive committee. The executive committee and the board of directors must approve all loans to insiders. The executive committee must also approve all loans to employees.

Southwest Bank has $150 million in assets and is part of a holding company. Southwest places significant emphasis on commercial lending as opposed to loans to individuals. The bank has 10 loan officers. New officers' limits are $25,000 and are reviewed annually by the board of directors. With favorable reviews, lending limits might be raised to $100,000 within two years. Southwest's two most experienced officers have limits of $150,000. The president and chairman can approve secured and unsecured loans and loans to employees up to $250,000. Loans above that amount must be approved by the loan committee (bank's executive officers and loan officers) and must be reviewed by the board's loan committee (chairman, president, vice-president, and three rotating directors). Overdrafts must be approved by a designated employee with advice from a loan officer. The board's loan committee must approve all loans to insiders (see Figure 11.2).

Western Bankshares is a $4.8 billion holding company, with its banks divided into five regional areas. Each region has a regional loan committee that includes regional bank officers and directors. The lending authority in this bank is shown in Figure 11.3. Individual lending authorities range from zero for trainees to $500,000 secured/$400,000 unsecured for each of the regional presidents. The regional loan committee may approve loans up to $2 million. Loans between $2 million to $5 million require approval from the regional loan committee and two regional presidents. Loans above that amount require approval from the holding company loan committee.

Figure 11.1: First City Bank ($29 Million Assets)

	Secured	Unsecured & Overdrafts	Insiders	Employees
Legal Limit	Executive Committee	Executive Committee		
$200,000	Officers' Loan Committee	Officers' Loan Committee	Executive Committee and Board of Directors	Same as Secured/ Unsecured Plus Executive Committee
$100,000	President	President		
$50,000	Loan Officers			
$25,000		Loan Officers		

Figure 11.2: Southwest Bank ($150 Million Assets)

	Secured & Unsecured	Employees	Overdrafts	Insiders
Legal Limit	Loan Committee (Approval) and Board Loan Committee (Review)	Loan Committee (Approval) and Board Loan Committee (Review)		
$250,000			Designated Employee	Board Loan Committee
	President and Chairman	President and Chairman		
$150,000				
	Loan Officers	Loan Officers		

Figure 11.3:   Western Bankshares ($4.8 Billion Assets)

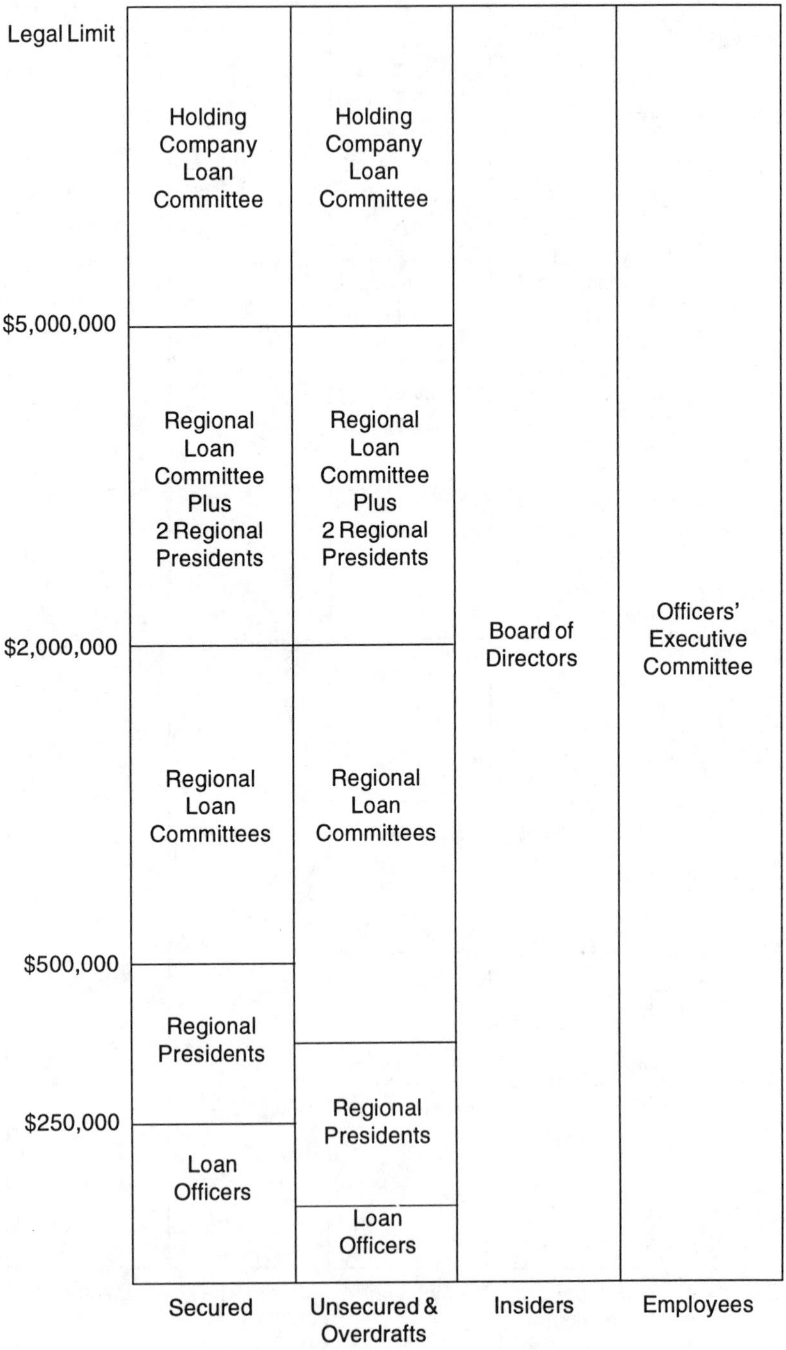

In Western Bank, a customer's total lending relationship is considered when a request for a new loan is made. If a customer has an outstanding loan for $100,000 and requests an additional $10,000, the request is considered a $110,000 loan in the approval process.

Loans to insiders must be approved by the board of directors, and employee loans by an officers' executive committee. This committee included a regional president and senior vice-presidents.

In reviewing the approval processes for the three banks, it is clear that large loans for all the banks are approved by higher authorities within the bank. Since most major fraud involve large loans, checks and balances must be established by the board. One check is the loan review process.

Loan Review

The primary purpose of loan review is to audit the lending function of the bank on a regular basis. Loan reviews should be used to determine if a bank's lending policies are being followed by its loan officers and credit analysts, and if there are potential loan losses or problem loans that have not been recognized. Early detection of potential problems permits the bank to take corrective actions before they become major problems.

The loan reviewers may be internal or external, depending on the size of the bank. Large banks are better able to afford an internal review system than small ones. Some of the factors that must be considered in establishing an internal review are:

1. *Structure of the loan review function.* Will loan review be centralized in the main bank or decentralized at the branches? Will each branch have its own loan review staff, or will there be only one loan review department?

2. *Reporting.* Who will be in charge of the loan review, and to whom does this person report? Are their potential conflicts of interest?

3. *Staffing.* How many employees will loan review need to support its function?

4. *Functions.* What will loan review do? Exactly what should the reviewer look for—documentation, credit analysis, external problems, or fraud?

5. *Scope.* Will all loans above or below a certain dollar amount be reviewed, or will a sample be taken?

Here is how a $3 billion bank holding company does its loan review. Its organization is based on functional lines where the main divisions are the corporate group, general banking, and investments. Loan review is operated at the holding company level, and it reports to the corporate group division manager, who reports to the vice-chairman of the board. It has a staff of 10 loan review officers and support personnel. The loan review officers are experienced in all areas of lending and knowledgeable in documentation.

The loan review department reviews, on an annual basis, all loans over $50,000 and they sample loans below that benchmark for consumer loans. Reports are written on each loan review stating whether it showed any signs of repayment problems or documentation problems. Problem loans are reviewed three or four times each year until the problems are resolved.

External reviews have certain advantages for small-size banks. According to a recent study, the costs of a permanent loan review staff may be too high for almost 60 percent of the banks—those with assets of $50 million or less.[12] Because of their small size, one advantage of an external review is an independent assessment of the loan review function. Another advantage is the ability to control the costs of the review. Finally, the directors of new banks may have little experience in the area of loan review. External reviews provide that experience. Along this line, it may be noted that there are a large number of failures among new *(de novo)* banks and savings and loan associations. The directors of *de novos* need all of the help they can get at a reasonable price.

Practices Deemed Unsafe or Unsound[13]

The board of directors of a bank is responsible for establishing the bank's operating practices. We have examined what banks are expected to do in the lending area to illustrate operating practices. Now let's look at the other side of the coin and learn what they should not do. According to the FDIC, certain practices are considered "unsafe or unsound." *Unsafe or unsound* refers to practices that are contrary to the generally accepted standards of prudent operation and, if continued, could result in the abnormal risk of loss to the bank, to its shareholders, or to the federal insurance fund. The following examples, based on the FDIC's *Manual of Examination Policies*, illustrate such practices. However, two caveats are in order. First, the examples do not cover every type of unsafe or unsound activity. Second, not every instance of these activities is unsafe or unsound. Each situation must considered on its own merits.

Lack of management actions deemed unsafe or unsound:

1. Failure to provide adequate supervision and direction over the bank's officers in order to prevent unsafe or unsound practices and the violation of laws and regulations.

2. Failure to make provision for sufficient reserves to cover possible loan losses.

3. Failure to make prompt postings to the general ledger.

4. Failure to account properly for transactions and to keep accurate books and records.

5. Failure to enforce loan repayment policies.

6. Failure to have proper documentation on the priority of liens on loans secured by real estate.

Management actions deemed unsafe or unsound:

1. Operating with inadequate capital to support the quality of assets held.

2. Engaging in hazardous lending and lax collection practices. Such practices include making loans with inadequate security, extending credit without first obtaining current and complete financial information about the borrower, extending credit in the form of overdrafts without proper controls, and inadequate diversification of loan portfolio.

3. Operating with inadequate liquidity or sources of funding.

4. Operating with inadequate internal controls on official checks and unissued CDs, failure to segregate duties of bank personnel, and the failure to reconcile differences in correspondent bank accounts.

5. Engaging in speculative investment policies.

6. Paying excessive dividends taking the bank's financial condition into account.

7. Paying excessive bonuses, salaries, fees, and commissions to insiders and their related interests.

Conditions of a bank deemed unsafe or unsound:

1. Maintaining very low net interest margins (interest income less interest expense divided by average earning assets).

2. Excessive overhead expenses.

3. Excessive volume of loans classified by the examiners.

4. Excessive net loan and lease losses.

5. Excessive volume of past-due loans.

6. Excessive volume of nonearning assets.

7. Excessive dependence on large-denomination liabilities.

The SERVE Principle

The activities of directors are summarized in the SERVE principle:[14]

- Select qualified management.

- Establish business goals, policies, standards, and procedures.

- Review business performance.

- Voice opinions and questions.

- Enforce compliance.

Ethical behavior is the final consideration. In this context, it refers to a director's choice for courses of action that benefit the bank, its stockholders and customers. The director's choices do not benefit his or her own interests and they do not harm others. If directors cannot comply with the SERVE principles, or if they have significant disagreements with other directors or management that cannot be resolved to their satisfaction, they should resign. The power of resignation is less costly for independent directors than for inside directors. Nevertheless, it is an option that should not be ignored.

Finally, but not least in importance, the directors should establish a code of ethics for all directors, officers, and employees of the organization. The code of ethics sends a strong message from the top of the organization down to all other levels as to how business is to be done.

Endnotes

1. *Bank Failure: An Evaluation of the Factors Contributing to the Failure of National Banks*, Washington: Comptroller of the Currency, June 1988, pp. 5-7, 15-16.

2. Philip F. Bartholomew, Financial Economist, Federal Home Loan Bank Board, Statement before the United States Sentencing Commission, April 7, 1989. Also see U.S. General Accounting Office, *Failed Thrifts: Internal Control Weaknesses Create an Environment Conducive to Fraud, Insider Abuse, and Related Unsafe Practices*, Statement of Frederick D. Wolf before the Subcommittee on Criminal Justice, Committee on the Judiciary, House of Representatives, GAO/T-AFMD-89-4, March 22, 1989, p. 13.

3. U.S. Government Accounting Office, *Thrift Failures: Costly Failures Resulted from Regulatory Violations and Unsafe Practices*, GAO/AFMD-89-62, June 1989, p. 18.

4. Peter F. Drucker, *Management: Tasks, Responsibilities, Practices*, New York: Harper & Row, 1974, p. 628.

5. "A Seat on the Board Is Getting Hotter," *Business Week*, July 3, 1989, p. 73.

6. *The Director's Book: The Role of a National Bank Director*, Washington, Comptroller of the Currency, August 1987, pp. 56-57; Alan E. Grunewald and Richard B. Foster, Jr., "Bank Directors' Liability for Negligence and the Business Judgment Rule," *Journal of the Midwest Finance Association*, Vol. 12, 1983, pp. 109-127; Michael Patriarca, "The Role and Responsibility of a Savings Institution Director," *Perspectives*, Federal Home Loan Bank of San Francisco, Fall 1988, pp. 2-6.

7. *Joy v. North*, 692 F. 2d 880, 896 (2nd Cir. 1982), cited in Federal Home Loan Bank Board Memoranda #R-62, "Directors' Responsibilities: FHLBB Guidelines; Procedures for Obtaining Information to Support Directors' Decisions," November 1988, 2689.

8. U.S. General Accounting Office, *Failed Thrifts*, March 22, 1989, *ibid.*, pp. 16-17.

9. See "Good Practice Guidelines for the Audit Committee," *Report of the National Commission on Fraudulent Financial Reporting*, National Commission on Fraudulent Financial Reporting, October 1987, pp. 179-182.

10. Joseph T. Wells, "White-Collar Crime: Myths and Strategies," *The Practical Accountant*, August 1985, pp. 43-45.

11. *Comptroller's Handbook for National Bank Examiners*, Washington: Comptroller of the Currency, Section 205.1, September 1977.

12. Fred H. Hays, Daniel L. Enterline, and Probir Roy, "Community Bank Directors: Should Your Bank Have an External Review?" *Journal of Commercial Bank Lending*, April 1989, pp. 21-29.

13. This section is based on the FDIC *Manual of Examination Policies*, parts of which appear in: U.S. House, *Federal Response to Criminal Misconduct by Bank Officers, Directors, and Insiders, Part 2*, Hearings before the Commerce, Consumer, and Monetary Affairs Subcommittee of the Committee on Government Operations, 98th Cong., 2nd Sess., May 2 and 3, 1984, pp. 1383-1384.

14. *The Director's Guide: The Role and Responsibilities of a Savings Institution Director*, Federal Home Loan Bank of San Francisco, 1988, p. 26.

12 INTERNAL CONTROLS, AUDITING, EXAMINATIONS, AND SECURITY

Having and using strong internal controls is one of the best deterrents against fraud and insider abuse at financial institutions. This chapter discusses internal controls, audits, examinations, and security officers in connection with detecting and deterring frauds and insider abuse.

What Are Internal Controls?

The term "internal controls" means different things to different people. In general it is defined as "a process, effected by an entity's board of directors, management and other personnel, designed to provide reasonable assurance regarding the achievement of the following categories:

- Effectiveness and efficiency of operations.
- Reliability of financial reporting.
- Compliance with applicable laws and regulations.[1]

The process of internal controls consists of five interrelated components:

1. The control environment—the corporate culture including integrity, ethical values, operating style, etc.

2. Risk assessment—the identification of external and internal risks relevant to the firm's objectives.

3. Control activities—policies and procedures that ensure the achievement of management's objectives.

4. Information and communications—internal and external communications necessary to control the business and provide external reporting.

5. Monitoring—the ongoing assessment of the quality of performance.

Reasons for Using Internal Controls

The General Accounting Office (GAO) found that "Pervasive internal control weaknesses are a major cause of bank failures."[2] Therefore, it follows that a substantial amount of fraud can be prevented using strong internal controls, as illustrated by the following case.[3] According to Bob Serino, deputy chief counsel of the operations section of the OCC, this situation was the best example of the worst controls that he knew of. The installment loan department of a community bank in Colorado was under the control of one individual. The loan officer's responsibilities included accepting applications, making credit decisions, and granting extensions and renewals. The bank's directors were pleased with the loan officer's performance. The installment loan portfolio increased in size and generated needed income. The portfolio had a low level of loan losses, and the volume of past due accounts was manageable. New customers were brought into the bank.

Over a three-year period, OCC examiners and external auditors criticized the bank for poor internal controls in all departments. Recognizing that smaller banks have limited personnel and have logistical problems in segregating duties, the importance of close supervision and review was continually stressed for areas where proper controls could not realistically be applied. Also, management reporting systems were weak and the board of directors was not receiving accurate information to fully exercise its duties and responsibilities. The reports that were reviewed by the board often were erroneous. Problems in the management information systems were repeatedly brought to the board's attention, but the problems continued.

As a result of the identified deficiencies, the scope of the examinations and audits was expanded. Subsequently, additional reporting errors were disclosed. Consistent reprimands for internal control deficiencies and reporting errors contributed to the dismissal of the installment loan officer.

The problem then multiplied. The quality of the installment loan portfolio deteriorated, and the volume of past-due loans increased. Loans were found to be undercollateralized, and the volume of extensions was extremely high. It was then discovered that the installment loan officer made fraudulent loans and embezzled the proceeds. Loans were made under fictitious names, either unsecured or secured, with the same collateral held for true loans. With complete control of the installment loan department, it was not difficult for the installment loan officer to extend payments on fraudulent loans, maintaining a current status. Consequently, new loans were created to pay maturing loans and a legal lending limit violation was concealed to prevent scrutiny of the loan portfolio. Management reports were generated manually and were easily manipulated to reflect a high-quality loan portfolio.

Research by external auditors and an enlightened board of directors disclosed that the defalcation amounted to more than $1 million. The bank's capital could not sustain a loss of that size, and shortly thereafter, the bank failed.

Devising and maintaining internal controls is management's responsibility. Internal controls can be defined as the plan of organization, methods, and measures used to safeguard assets, to ensure the accuracy and reliability of data, to ensure compliance with policies and applicable laws and regulations, and to promote management efficiency.[4] Stated otherwise, internal controls are procedures for prevention and detection within the context of accounting and administrative systems. They are intended to prevent individuals from taking unwanted actions, such as altering financial records, and they help detect errors and irregularities. *Errors* are unintentional mistakes or omissions. *Irregularities* are *intentional* mistakes or omissions and include fraudulent financial reporting. A loan that does not conform to an institution's loan policy may be an error. Making a fictitious loan is an irregularity. The mere knowledge of the existence of strong internal controls may be sufficient to deter some fraudulent acts. According to the Comptroller of the Currency, good internal controls exist when no one person is in a position to make significant errors or perpetrate significant irregularities without timely detection. Internal controls also allow managers and auditors to verify the accuracy of the accounting for transactions. Thus, internal controls are an essential element of good management. However, even the best control systems will not work if they are not used properly. Anyone who is intent on circumventing controls can probably do so.

There are additional reasons for using internal controls. First, the Foreign Corrupt Practices Act of 1977 has accounting provisions that apply to all publicly held companies having securities registered with the Securities and Exchange Commission.[5] The act requires such firms to keep reasonably detailed financial records reflecting their financial activities and disposition of assets. The act also requires firms to devise and maintain a system of internal controls sufficient to provide reasonable assurances that transactions are executed in accordance with management's authorization; that transactions are recorded to permit the preparation of financial statements in conformity with generally accepted accounting standards, and maintain accountability for assets; and that access to assets is permitted only with management's authorization.

Second, the board of directors of a financial institution has a fiduciary responsibility to its depositors and shareholders to provide an adequate internal control structure and to ensure that the controls are operating effectively.

The final reasons for using strong internal controls are that they serve as a buffer against adverse economic conditions and they can help deter insider abuse and fraud. A GAO study found that weaknesses in internal controls were a significant factor in bank failures.[6] The study covered external factors over which management had no control, such as adverse economic conditions and restrictions on branch banking. These factors affected all banks in Texas and other parts of the country. Controls must change to adapt to changing business environments and external factors. Some changes in the business environment that may weaken existing controls are the acquisition of new types of businesses where the existing accounting systems are left in place, the introduction of new products or technologies that may affect reserves for loan losses; and rapid growth, which causes problems because control procedures rely on individuals who become overloaded.[7] The GAO found that severe internal control weaknesses were pervasive in all of the banks that failed, while they were present to a lesser extent at healthy banks.

In a separate study of thrifts that failed, the GAO found that internal control deficiencies, violations of laws and regulations, and unsafe practices existed at all of the institutions that failed.[8] According to GAO director Frederick D. Wolf:

> *Some within the financial institutions industry have expressed the view that the unprecedented problems and resultant failures are largely due to economic downturns in certain regions. However, both of our reviews lead to a different conclusion. Well-managed institutions with strong internal controls appeared able to remain viable despite downturns in local economies. Conversely, existing problems at poorly run institutions were exacerbated by adverse economic conditions, often leading to failure.[9]*

The key points are that well-managed institutions survived; and strong internal controls are one aspect of good management. Conversely, lack of strong internal controls raises questions about the quality of management.

Establishing Internal Controls

In the past, accounting controls were considered separate from administrative controls. In April 1988, the American Institute of Certified Public Accountants (AICPA), considered the two together, describing them as the "internal control structure." The AICPA defines internal control structure as "The policies and procedures established to provide reasonable assurance that specific entity objectives will be achieved." The AICPA Statement on Auditing Standards Number 55, Consideration of the Internal Control Structure in a Financial Statement Audit, describes the three elements of an internal control structure: control environment, accounting system, and control procedures.

The first element—control environment—concerns the environment in which the controls are used. In short, the effectiveness of the controls depends on the collective effect of various factors, including management philosophy, organizational structure, the role of the board of directors and its committees, the communication of authority and responsibility, management control methods, the internal audit function, personnel policies and procedures, and environmental factors.

The second element—accounting system—deals with the methods and records used to report transactions and maintain accountability for assets and liabilities.

Control procedures is the final element. It deals with the policies and control procedures established to assure that management's objectives are carried out.

Auditing Standard Number 55 provides guidance for independent auditors who must evaluate the internal control structure of an organization and plan and perform an audit. Federal and state bank examiners have somewhat different but overlapping concerns in evaluating a bank's internal controls.

The *Comptroller's Handbook for National Bank Examiners* explains the Comptroller of the Currency's view of internal controls and provides detailed "Internal Control Questionnaires" for areas of concern to national bank examiners.[10] The OCC states that while procedures are an important element of internal controls, actual practices must be taken into account. In addition, the procedures must be performed by competent individuals. Equally important is independent performance. Independent performance refers to the effective segregation of duties or "positions," such as a cashier. For example, a cashier is the sole check signer and an assistant prepares the monthly reconcilement. Although both may be competent individuals, the assistant is under the direct supervision of the cashier. Therefore, the assistant's duties should be viewed as if they were performed by the cashier.

The Internal Control Questionnaires are a starting point for examiners to determine a bank's control procedures. The questionnaires are general in nature because the OCC recognizes that what applies to one bank may not apply to another. Accordingly, the questionnaires provide some insights into what the OCC considers good controls as well as problem areas that might undermine the controls. Figure 12.1 is the Internal Control Questionnaire for Commercial Loans, and it is used to illustrate a typical questionnaire. The asterisks by certain questions indicate that they are critical areas of concern that require substantiation by examiner observation or testing. Question number 3 is the first question so marked. It deals with the preparation and posting of subsidiary commercial loan records. The second critical question deals with the reconciliation of those records.

Figure 12.1: Commercial Loans Internal Control Questionnaire Section 206.4 (page 1 of 3)

Review the bank's internal controls, policies, practices and procedures for making and servicing commercial loans. The bank's system should be documented in a complete and concise manner and should include, where appropriate, narrative descriptions, flowcharts, copies of forms used and other pertinent information. Items marked with asterisks require substantiation by observation or testing.

Commercial Loan Policies

1. Has the board of directors, consistent with its duties and responsibilities, adopted written commercial loan policies that:
   a. Establish procedures for reviewing commercial loan applications?
   b. Define qualified borrowers?
   c. Establish minimum standards for documentation?
2. Are commercial loan policies reviewed at least annually to determine if they are compatible with changing market conditions?

Commercial Loan Records

*3. Is the preparation and posting of subsidiary commercial loan records performed or reviewed by persons who do not also:
   a. Issue official checks or drafts singly?
   b. Handle cash?
*4. Are the subsidiary commercial loan records reconciled daily with the appropriate general ledger accounts, and are reconciling items investigated by persons who do not handle cash?
5. Are delinquent account collection requests and past due notices checked to the trial balances that are used in reconciling commercial loan subsidiary records with general ledger accounts, and are they handled by persons who do not also handle cash?
6. Are inquiries about loan balances received and investigated by persons who do not also handle cash?
*7. Are documents supporting recorded credit adjustments checked or tested subsequently by persons who do not also handle cash (if so, explain briefly)?
8. Is a daily record maintained summarizing note transaction details, i.e., loans made, payments received and interest collected, to support applicable general ledger account entries?
9. Are frequent note and liability ledger trial balances prepared and reconciled with controlling accounts by employees who do not process or record loan transactions?
10. Is an overdue account report generated frequently (if so, how often _____)?
11. Are subsidiary payment records and files pertaining to serviced loans segregated and identifiable?

Loan Interest

*12. Is the preparation and posting of interest records performed or reviewed by persons who do not also:
   a. Issue official checks or drafts singly?
   b. Handle cash?
13. Are any independent interest computations made and compared or tested to initial interest records by persons who do not also:
   a. Issue official checks or drafts singly?
   b. Handle cash?

Figure 12.1:   Commercial Loans Internal Control Questionnaire
Section 206.4 (page 2 of 3)

Collateral
14. Are multicopy, prenumbered records maintained that:
    a. Detail the complete description of collateral pledged?
    b. Are typed or completed in ink?
    c. Are signed by the customer?
    d. Are designed so that a copy goes to the customer?
15. Are the functions of receiving and releasing collateral to borrowers and of making entries in the collateral register performed by different employees?
16. Is negotiable collateral held under joint custody?
17. Are receipts obtained and filed for released collateral?
18. Are securities and commodities valued and margin requirements reviewed at least monthly?
19. When the support rests on the cash surrender value of insurance policies, is a periodic accounting received from the insurance company and maintained with the policy?
20. Is a record maintained of entry to the collateral vault?
21. Are stock powers filed seperately to bar negotiability and to deter abstraction of both the security and the negotiating instrument?
22. Are securities out for transfer, exchange, etc., controlled by prenumbered temporary vault-out tickets?
23. Has the bank instituted a system which:
    a. Insures that security agreements are filed?
    b. Insures that collateral mortgages are properly recorded?
    c. Insures that title searches and property appraisals are performed in connection with collateral mortgages?
    d. Insures that insurance coverage (including loss payee clause) is in effect on property covered by collateral mortgages?
24. Are coupon tickler cards set up covering all coupon bonds held as collateral?
25. Are written instructions obtained and held on file covering the cutting of coupons?
26. Are coupon cards under the control of persons other than those assigned to coupon cutting?
27. Are pledged deposit accounts properly coded to negate unauthorized withdrawal of funds?
28. Are acknowledgements received for pledged deposits held at other banks?
29. Is an officer's approval necessary before collateral can be released or substituted?

Other
30. Are notes safeguarded during banking hours and locked in the vault overnight?
31. Are all loan rebates approved by an officer and made only by official check?
32. Does the bank have an internal review system that:
    a. Re-examines collateral items for negotiability and proper assignment?
    b. Test check values assigned to collateral when the loan is made and at frequent intervals thereafter?
    c. Determines that items out on temporary vault-out tickets are authorized and have not been outstanding for an unreasonable length of time?
    d. Determines that loan payments are promptly posted?
    e. Insures compliance with the requirements of governmental agencies insuring or guaranteeing loans?

Figure 12.1: Commercial Loans Internal Control Questionnaire Section 206.4 (page 3 of 3)

33. Are all notes recorded on a note register or similar record and assigned consecutive numbers?
34. Are collection notices handled by someone not connected with loan processing?
35. Are payment notices prepared and mailed by someone other than the loan teller?
36. Does the bank prohibit the holding of debtor's checks for payment of loans at maturity?
37. Concerning livestock loans:
    a. Are inspections made at the inception of credit?
    b. Are inspections properly dated and signed?
    c. Is there a breakdown by sex, breed, and number of animals in each category?
    d. Is the condition of the animals noted?
    e. Are inspections required at least annually?
38. Concerning crop loans:
    a. Are inspections of growing crops made as loans are advanced?
    b. Are disbursements closely monitored to assure that the proceeds are properly channeled into the farmer's operation?
    c. Is crop insurance encouraged?
39. In mortgage warehouse financing, does the bank hold the original mortgage note, trust deed or other critical document, releasing only against payment?
40. Concerning commodity lending:
    a. Is control for the collateral satisfactory, i.e., stored in the bank's vault, another bank, or a bonded warehouse?
    b. If collateral is not stored within the bank, are procedures in effect to ascertain the authenticity of the collateral?
    c. Does the bank have a documented security interest in the proceeds of the future sale or disposition of the commodity as well as the existing collateral position?
    d. Do credit files document that the financed positions are and remain fully hedged?
41. Concerning loans to commodity brokers and dealers:
    a. Does the bank maintain a list of the major customer accounts on the brokers or dealers to whom it lends? If so, is the list updated on a periodic basis?
    b. Is the bank aware of the broker's/dealer's policy on margin requirements and the basis for valuing contracts for margin purposes (i.e., pricing spot vs. future)?
    c. Does the bank attempt to ascertain whether the positions of the broker's/dealer's clients that are indirectly financed by bank loans remain fully hedged?

Conclusion
42. Is the foregoing information an adequate basis for evaluating internal control in that there are no significant, additional internal auditing procedures, accounting controls, administrative controls, or other circumstances that impair any controls or mitigate any weaknesses indicated above (explain negative answers briefly, and indicate conclusions as to their effect on specific examination or verification procedures)?
43. Based on a composite evaluation, as evidenced by answers to the foregoing questions, internal control is considered _____ (good, medium, or bad).

Source: Comptroller's Handbook for National Bank Examiners, August 1982.

Auditing: Closing the Expectation Gap

The Securities and Exchange Commission (SEC) is the principal federal agency involved in accounting and auditing standards for publicly traded companies. It establishes rules and regulations for public disclosure and independent audits. The SEC has accepted the Generally Accepted Accounting Principles (GAAP) promulgated by the Financial Accounting Standards Board and the Generally Accepted Auditing Standards (GAAS) promulgated by the AICPA as the standards for meeting its disclosure requirements. Federal banking regulators also impose reporting requirements for the institutions they regulate. Independent audits are an important part of the disclosure process.

> *Full, fair, and accurate disclosure of financial results is a cornerstone of our system of public securities markets ... The public accountant's audit is an important element in the financial reporting process because the audit subjects financial statements, which are management's responsibility, to scrutiny on behalf of shareholders and creditors to whom management is responsible.* [11]

Against this background, our primary concerns are with bank fraud and the ongoing operations of banks. We know that the existence and effective operation of internal controls reduces the chance for fraud and enhances the ability of a bank to survive. Nevertheless, fraud exists and banks fail for a variety of reasons. Therefore, the issues are: (1) to what extent can auditors detect fraud, (2) if they do discover fraud, what should they do about it?

How do we determine to what extent auditors detect and report financial difficulties that may affect the survival of bank? One difficulty in examining these issues involves the so-called "expectation gap," which is the difference between the public's and the accounting profession's expectations of auditors. The public expects auditors to be able to detect fraud or irregularities and to do something about it, such as reporting fraud to bank regulators or law enforcement officials. The public expects auditors to have some insight into the ability of firms to survive. The public confidence in auditors was shaken in the mid-1970s for reasons that will be explained shortly. This lack of confidence was expressed in the following accountant's report that appeared on the cover of *Forbes* (March 15, 1977).

> *To the directors and stockholders:*
> *We have examined the Consolidated Balance Sheet of the company and Consolidated subsidiaries as of December 31, 1976 and 1975. In our opinion, these financial statements present fairly the financial position of the companies, in conformity with generally accepted accounting principles consistently applied.*

> *On the other hand, there is a growing body of opinion that holds that our opinion is not worth a damn.*

As part of an effort to alter this opinion, Congress introduced legislation (House Bill 5439) in 1986 requiring auditors to detect and report material fraud directly to the SEC.

The accounting profession has a different set of expectations. What is an audit and the auditor's point of view?

> *According to the American Accounting Association: Auditing is a systematic process of objectively obtaining and evaluating evidence regarding assertions about economic actions and events to ascertain the degree of correspondence between those assertions and established criteria and communicating the results to interested users.*[12]

This comprehensive definition suggests that auditors should seek to determine if management's full and fair disclosures about their financial condition are represented fairly within the context of generally accepted accounting standards. To make this determination, auditors take into the account audit objectives for various components of the financial statements. Selected objectives for auditing a bank's assets are presented to illustrate one aspect of the audit process.[13] These audit objectives are:

1. *Existence or occurrence*—Determine if the assets presented in the balance sheet exist.

2. *Completeness*—Determine if the quantities of particular assets, such as securities, include all items on hand, held by others, or in transit. In addition, assure that all amounts that should be recorded are, in fact, recorded.

3. *Rights and obligations*—Determine if the bank has legal title to the assets, excluding collateral owned by others or pledged on loans.

4. *Valuation or allocations*—Determine that assets are properly valued at cost, market value, or fair value.

5. *Presentation and disclosure*—Determine that the assets are properly categorized in the balance sheet, and that their basis for valuation, pledging, or assignment is adequately disclosed in the financial statements.

All of this is done to determine if management is fair in its assertions about its assets. Different audit objectives are applied to other parts of the financial statements to determine "fairness." Unfortunately, by its very nature, fraud is covert and difficult for auditors and investigators to uncover.

This is especially true when a complex fraud involves numerous, seemingly unrelated banks and firms. Thus, the discovery of fraud is an infrequent by-product of the audit process. Therefore, it is not surprising that auditors' track records in discovering fraud are not good. Moreover, if fraud is discovered, it is often undisclosed to the public or regulatory authorities. There is a long history of controversy regarding auditors' reporting responsibilities.[14] They are guided by conflicting demands (the Code of Professional Ethics, SASs, laws, and so on), and are pulled by the interests of various stakeholder groups—shareholders, creditors, SEC, bank regulators, and others. Each of these groups expects the auditors to act for them, and consequently, auditors have compartmentalized their responsibilities. Their primary reporting responsibility is to the client for illegal acts, to the SEC for filings, to the IRS for tax returns, and to shareholders and creditors for their opinion on financial statements taken as a whole.

In the early 1970s, several large companies were exposed for making illegal or questionable payments to foreign officials as bribes to get contracts and for other purposes. In a 1976 program of voluntary disclosure to the SEC, some 250 companies admitted to such payments. In 1977, Congress enacted the Foreign Corrupt Practices Act requiring SEC registrants to maintain the accounting standards that were explained previously. The following year, the Commission on Auditor's Responsibilities (the Cohen Commission) recommended that auditors have a duty to search for fraud. In 1987, the National Commission on Fraudulent Financial Reporting (the Treadway Commission) made 49 recommendations to detect and deter fraudulent financial reporting.[15] Furthermore, the Treadway Commission examined 119 enforcement actions against public companies or individuals and 42 enforcement actions against public accountants or their firms brought by the SEC from 1981 to 1986. Their study revealed that fraudulent financial reporting was usually the result of environmental, institutional, or individual forces or opportunities. A frequent incentive for engaging in fraudulent reporting was to improve a company's financial appearance, or to postpone dealing with financial difficulties.

In 1988, the AICPA's Auditing Standards Board issued new Statements of Auditing Standards (SAS) that addressed some of these issues, but it did not resolve them to everyone's satisfaction. Traditionally, auditing standards have recognized the auditor-client relationship, and the auditor's primary responsibility for reporting illegal acts was to the client. This reporting relationship is changing, as is demonstrated in the following auditing standards. Although auditors report to their clients, the U.S. Supreme Court, in *United States v. Arthur Young & Co.*, emphasized that "The independent public accountant ... owes ultimate allegiance to the corporation's creditors and stockholders, as well as to the investing public."[16]

SAS No. 53, The Auditor's Responsibility to Detect and Report Errors and Irregularities

This standard states that auditors should exercise due care in auditing and the proper degree of professional skepticism to "achieve reasonable assurance that material errors or irregularities will be detected."[17] If irregularities are detected, the auditor must assess the risk that they will have a direct and material effect on the determination of financial statement amounts. If such a condition exists, the auditor should insist that the statements be revised; and if they are not, give a qualified or adverse opinion and disclose the reasons for doing so. The auditor should communicate the findings to the audit committee or the board of directors. Under certain conditions, a duty may exist to make disclosures to parties other than the client. Those conditions are:

- When the organization reports an auditor change to the SEC on Form 8-K.

- To a successor auditor when inquiries are made in accordance with SAS No. 7, *Communications Between Predecessor and Successor Auditors*.

- In response to a subpoena.

- To a funding agency or government agency requiring audits of organizations receiving their financial support.

SAS No. 53 goes on to say that because of ethical and legal considerations, the auditor may wish to get legal counsel before discussing the results with parties other than their client. It also states that the subsequent discovery of material misstatement in financial statements does not, in and of itself, mean that the audit was inadequate.

SAS No. 54, Illegal Acts by Clients

This standard defines illegal acts as violations of laws or government regulations. Illegal acts by clients are acts attributable to the entity whose financial statements are under audit, or acts by management or employees on behalf of the client. They do not include personal misconduct by the entity's personnel unrelated to their business activities.

The final determination of legality is normally beyond the scope of an auditor's professional competence. Keeping this in mind, auditors should consider laws and regulations from the perspective of their known relation to the audit objectives and report and/or disclose irregularities accordingly. The Financial Institutions Reform, Recovery and Enforcement Act of 1989 (Title XII) requires the FDIC (or other federal insurance corporations) to designate the applicable laws and regulations relating to safety and soundness that managements of financial institutions must consider. It also requires independent public accountants to review and report on management's assertions concerning their internal controls and compliance with applicable laws and regulations.

If the illegal act does not have a direct and material impact on the financial statements, and the audit was conducted in accordance with generally accepted auditing standards, there is no assurance that the illegal act will be detected or that any contingent liability that may result from that act will be disclosed. However, as in SAS No. 53, the auditor may have a duty to notify outside parties of the illegal acts.

SAS No. 58, Reports on Audited Financial Statements

This standard clarifies the auditor's role with new statements in the auditors' reports. The statements say that the financial reports are the responsibility of the entity's management, and the auditor's responsibility is to express an opinion on those statements. The auditor's report goes on to elaborate on the procedures performed and auditor assurance.

SAS No. 59, The Auditor's Consideration of an Entity's Ability to Continue as a Going Concern

This standard deals with the potential failure of a firm. The auditor has the responsibility in all audits to evaluate whether there is substantial doubt about the entity's ability to continue as a going concern for the next year. If there is substantial doubt, the auditor should consider the adequacy of disclosure and include an explanatory paragraph in the audit report to reflect that conclusion. If the firm's disclosures are not adequate in this regard, the auditor can give a qualified or adverse opinion. One member of the Auditing Standards Board dissented on voting on this SAS. He argued that without new auditing procedures to fulfill this new responsibility, the result widened, rather than narrowed, the expectation gap.

SAS No. 60, Communications of Internal Control Structure Related Matters Noted in an Audit

This standard concerns significant deficiencies or "reportable conditions" in the design or operation of the internal control structure. Auditors finding conditions that could adversely affect the organization's ability to produce reliable financial disclosures are required to report them to the audit committee or its equivalent.

SAS No. 61, Communications with Audit Committees

This standard requires auditors to ensure that the audit committee or its equivalent receive information regarding the audit that may assist them in overseeing the financial reporting and disclosure process for which management is responsible. The statement does not require such communications with management.

Auditor ability to detect and report the financial difficulties of banks in the recent past leaves a lot to be desired. By way of illustration, the GAO studied the most recent audit reports performed by certified public accountants (CPAs) on 11 failed S&Ls.[18] The study found that in six cases, the CPAs did not adequately audit and/or report the S&Ls financial or internal control problems in accordance with professional standards. The latest audit reports for the 11 S&Ls showed a combined net worth of about $44 million before failure. At the time the S&Ls failed, which ranged from 5 to 17 months after the audit reports, they had a combined *negative* net worth of about $1.5 billion. No doubt some of these failures occurred immediately after the audits were made. Nevertheless, that does not explain the following examples of CPA audits and disclosures:

- There was a lack of sufficient evidence in working papers that the CPA firm performed an analysis of the collectibility of acquisition, development, and construction (ADC) loans because the loans were new and the CPA firm assumed them to be collectible. In their defense, the *AICPA Audit and Accounting Guide for Savings and Loan Associations* contained little discussion of the risks associated with land and ADC loans.

- The audit lacked sufficient evidence in working papers that the CPA firm had identified and evaluated the effect of restructured loans. Federal examiners found that the S&L did not report that it had restructured about $625 million in loans during the period covered by the audit. In that same audit, the CPAs did not evaluate the collectibility of $30 million past-due loans guaranteed by two principal shareholders.

- A CPA firm did not properly disclose in its audit report that an S&L incorrectly reported $12 million in expected recoveries from lawsuits that were pending. The S&L used the expected recoveries to offset reported losses. Accounting principles prohibit the reporting of recoveries from lawsuits until the cases are resolved. Also, the CPA firm did not disclose its own findings that the S&Ls losses would probably be greater than reported.

- A CPA firm failed to disclose that an S&L had several hundred million dollars of loans secured by property in a limited geographic area. Most of the loans were made to principal shareholders of that association.

- Two CPA firms reported that their clients had no material weaknesses in internal controls despite the fact that the S&Ls were under formal regulatory enforcement actions for severe internal control weaknesses.

The expectation gap is narrower than it was before; but we still have a long way to go before it will be closed. High-profile cases and lawsuits against accounting firms keep the issue alive. For example, *Business Week* (September 27, 1992, p. 32) reported that following the collapse of Silverado Banking, the Colorado-based Savings and Loan, Washington-based Coopers & Lybrand was sued for not detecting its weak financial condition. In June 1991, Coopers agreed to pay the FDIC $20 million for its failure.

In August 1992, the lead article in *The Wall Street Journal* was about a $338 million judgment awarded against Price Waterhouse for allegedly failing to detect a weak loan portfolio in a Phoenix bank.[19]

In March 1994, Deloitte & Touche (D&T) agreed to pay $312 million to the government in settlement of claims based on alleged accounting and auditing failures at banks and S&Ls it audited.[20] Specifically, D&T failed to account for hedges in accordance with GAAP in its audit of Franklin Savings and Loan Association, Ottawa, Kansas; it failed to account for mark-to-market trading accounts in accordance with GAAP in its audit of Colombia Savings and Loan Association, Beverly Hills, California; and it was responsible for additional auditing failures at other thrifts in New Jersey and Colorado.

Some issues will never be resolved. For example, the author of a recent article stated that "… companies search for accounting methods that best suit the game plan. This results in a patchwork of accounting methodology that adheres to particular, and often conflicting, viewpoints while objectivity falls by the wayside."[21]

Another factor that inhibits the gap from closing is that auditors are not trained criminal investigators. Auditing methodology is directed toward objectivity and away from criminal investigation.[22] To illustrate one difference, consider the concepts of materiality and evidence. Auditors must determine if there is a "reasonable assurance" that important information about financial transactions is presented fairly. They set the desired level of assurance to fit the existing circumstance and acquire the information or evidence to achieve the desired level of assurance. Under the rules of law, matter offered in evidence in a case must be relevant to the issues and either tend to establish or disprove them. What is relevant and material, admissible and inadmissible is clearly delineated, and there is little room for "reasonable assurance."

Internal Auditors

The previous discussion centered on independent audits. However, the first line of defense against fraud is the internal auditors. The objective of the internal audit function is to assist the audit committee and management by providing them with an objective evaluation of the accuracy, adequacy, and effectiveness of various aspects of going operations. These include internal controls, audit trails, operational procedures, compliance, and so on.

A Bank Administration Institute report on *Bank Audit and Security* (1990) stated that today's internal auditors are less concerned with financial statement presentations. Their focus is on:

1. Identifying the bank's exposures.

2. Determining if systems are in place to protect the bank from losses.

3. Determining if systems are in place to provide real time to correct financial data.

The Institute of Internal Auditors (IIA) is a professional association that is dedicated to the professional development of internal auditors. The IIA conducts seminars and conferences on control, deterrence, and investigation of fraud, as well as publishing *Internal Auditor,* which contains articles dealing with fraud, internal controls, and other subjects.[23] The IIA Bookstore provides books, videos, software and other items.

The Role of Bank Examiners

Some readers may confuse bank examiners with auditors. Bank examiners are not auditors. Bank examiners perform two types of examinations: one for safety and soundness, and the other for compliance. Safety and soundness examinations are based on the CAMEL system. CAMEL is the Uniform Interagency Bank Rating System acronym for Capital adequacy, Asset quality, Management, Earnings, and Liquidity. In some states, such as Alabama, bank examiners review the adequacy of the audits. Compliance examinations determine whether banks are complying with existing laws and regulations, such as the Truth in Lending Act (Federal Reserve Regulation Z).

Bank examiners report their findings to the bank and can share their information with other regulatory and government agencies. When they find problems, they can take a series of actions in an attempt to correct the situation. The most extreme action is the closing of a bank.

Detection of fraud is an infrequent by-product of bank examinations. For example, a trainee examiner working in the First National Bank of Jacksonville, Alabama, discovered that three people who had loans with the bank used the same address. Further examination revealed more than 25 fictitious loans using the same address, and the bank failed.

One reason why detection of fraud is an infrequent by-product may be that bank examiners are not doing their jobs properly. A study by the GAO revealed that OCC examiners "did not comprehensively evaluate internal controls that were critical to the safe and sound operation of the banks they examined."[24] The study went on to say that insufficient work was performed to assess loan quality and reserves. The Office of Thrift

Supervision had similar problems. Another GAO study stated that the "OTS did not review enough loans to accurately assess the safety and soundness of individual thrifts."[25] Furthermore, the loans that were selected for examination were not representative of the thrift's portfolio. The OTS also failed to examine internal controls, and the conclusions of their exams were inconsistent. Finally, GAO studies of the Federal Reserve and the FDIC examinations were critical as well.[26] The Federal Reserve was also criticized because it did not assess the risks associated with bank loans to nonbank affiliates within holding companies. Finally, the GAO found that there were no formal programs to assess state examinations.[27] Don't count on examiners or the auditors to detect fraud or insider abuse!

Security Personnel

Security officers are responsible for developing and implementing systems intended to reduce robberies and other crimes. Their duties include:[28]

- Physical security
- Personnel security
- Investigations
- Computer security
- Communications security
- Crisis management

Experienced security personnel can help to deter and detect both large- and small-scale frauds. For example, communications between security officers of various banks resulted in tellers being alerted to Nigerian "flim-flam" operations being conducted in several southern states. The result of that communication was the arrest of the perpetrators.

Security personnel can also provide background information about selected borrowers as well as help verify other aspects of a loan request. This should be done before the loan is approved.

Endnotes

1. *Internal Control-Integrated Framework,* Executive Summary, Committee of Sponsoring Organizations of the Treadway Commission, September 1992, p. 1.

2. U.S. General Accounting Office, *Failed Banks,* GAO/AFMD-91-43, p. 7.

3. This case was written by Sara L. Strait, National Bank Examiner.

4. This discussion drew on the following sources: Committee on Auditing Procedure, American Institute of Certified Public Accountants, *Internal Control,* New York, AICPA, 1949, p. 6; U.S. General Accounting Office, *Bank Failures, Independent Audits Needed to Strengthen Internal Control and Bank*

Management, GAO/AFMD-89-25, May 1989, p. 15; Jack C. Robertson and Frederick G. Davis, *Auditing*, 3rd ed. (Plano, Texas: Business Publications, Inc., 1982), pp. 204-206; American Institute of Certified Public Accountants' Statement on Auditing Standards Number 55, "Consideration of the Internal Control Structure in a Financial Statement Audit"; *Comptroller's Handbook for National Bank Examiners*, Comptroller of the Currency, Section 001.1.

5. The Foreign Corrupt Practices Act amends the Securities Exchange Act of 1934, 15 U.S.C. 78q(b1). The affected companies must have $3 million or more in assets and have 500 or more shareholders.

6. U.S. General Accounting Office, *Bank Failures, ibid.*, pp. 3, 25, 39.

7. Kenneth A. Merchant, *Fraudulent and Questionable Financial Reporting: A Corporate Perspective* (Morristown, N.J.: Financial Executives Research Foundation, 1987), p. 14.

8. U.S. General Accounting Office, *Thrift Failures: Costly Failures Resulted from Regulatory Violations and Unsafe Practices*, GAO/AFMD-89-62, June 1989, p. 62.

9. U.S. General Accounting Office, *Failed Financial Institutions: Reasons, Costs, Remedies and Unresolved Issues*, Statement of Frederick D. Wolf before the Committee on Banking, Finance, and Urban Affairs, House of Representatives, GAO/T-AFMD-89-1, January 13, 1989, p. 11.

10. The *Comptroller's Handbook for National Bank Examiners* is distributed to national banks. The publication is loose-leaf and is updated periodically.

11. U.S. General Accounting Office, *CPA Audit Quality: Status of Actions Taken to Improve Auditing and Financial Reporting of Public Companies*, GAO/AFMD-89-38, March 1989, pp. 8-9.

12. Robertson and Davis, *Auditing, ibid.*, p. 4. The text also presents other, but narrower definitions of auditing.

13. *Audits of Banks* (New York: American Institute of Certified Public Accountants, 1983), pp. 35-36.

14. R. K. Mautz and Hussein A. Sharaf, *The Philosophy of Auditing* (Sarasota, Florida: American Accounting Association, Monograph No. 6, 1961).

15. *Report of the National Commission on Fraudulent Financial Reporting*, National Commission on Fraudulent Financial Reporting, October 1987; U.S. General Accounting Office, *CPA Audit Quality: Status of Actions, ibid.*, pp. 11, 13.

16. *U.S. v. Arthur Young & Co.*, 465 U.S. 805, 8-7-818 (1984).

17. Statement on Auditing Standards No. 53, *The Auditor's Responsibility to Detect and Report Errors and Irregularities*, AICPA, April 1988, p. 3.

18. U.S. Government Accounting Office, *CPA Audit Quality: Failures of CPA Audits to Identify and Report Significant Savings and Loan Problems*, GAO/AFMD-89-45, February 1989; U.S. General Accounting Office, *The Need to Improve Auditing in the Savings and Loan Industry*, Statement of

Frederick D. Wolf before the Committee on Banking, Finance and Urban Affairs, House of Representatives, GAO/T-AFMD-89-2, February 21, 1989.

19. Lee Berton and Stephen J. Adler, "How Audit of a Bank Cost Price Waterhouse $338 Million Judgment," *The Wall Street Journal,* August 14, 1992, p. A1.

20. "Deloitte & Touche Settles with OTS, RTC & FDIC," Joint Release, FDIC, RTC, OTS, March 14, 1994.

21. James R. Davis, "Ambiguity, Ethics, and the Bottom Line," *Business Horizons*, May-June 1989, p. 67.

22. David L. Nich and Robert D. Miller, "White-Collar Crime," *The Internal Auditor*, December 1984., pp. 24-27.

23. The Institute of Internal Auditors, 249 Maitland Ave., Altamonte Springs, FL 32701, phone 407-830-7600.

24. U.S. General Accounting Office, *Bank Examination Quality*, (OCC), GAO/AFMD-93-14, February 1993, p. 2.

25. U.S. General Accounting Office, *Thrift Examination Quality*, (OTS), GAO/AFMD-93-11, February 1993, p. 3.

26. U.S. General Accounting Office, *Bank Examination Quality*, (FDIC), GAO/AFMD-93-12, February 1993; U.S. General Accounting Office, *Bank Examination Quality*, (FRB), GAO/AFMD-93-13, February 1993.

27. U.S. General Accounting Office, *Bank and Thrift Regulation*, (FRB), GAO/AFMD-93-15, February 1993.

28. *Security in Financial Institutions: The Role of the Security Officer*, Bank Administration Institute, 1990.

Appendix A HOW TO DETECT POTENTIAL FRAUD AND INSIDER ABUSE

This appendix contains the warning signs or red flags published in the FDIC's *Manual of Examination Policies*. The manual is used by bank examiners to detect potential fraud and insider abuse. The subject areas for which red flags are presented here include:

- Corporate culture/ethics
- Insider transactions
- Loan participations
- Real estate lending
- Secured lending
- Third-party obligations
- Lending to buy tax shelter investments
- Linked financing/brokered deposits
- Credit cards and ATM transactions
- Advance fee schemes
- Offshore transactions
- Wire transfers
- Money laundering
- Securities trading activities
- Miscellaneous

A caveat is in order. The presence of one or more red flags does not mean that insider abuse is occurring or that there is fraud being committed. It does mean that further investigation is required. It also suggests that the institution's policies may require changes, and/or exceptions to their policies must be well documented.

Corporate Culture

1. Absence of code of ethics.

2. Absence of a clear policy restricting or requiring disclosure of conflicts of interest.

3. Absence of a policy restricting gifts and gratuities.

4. Lack of oversight by the institution's board of directors, particularly outside directors.

5. Absence of planning, training, hiring and organizational policies.

6. Absence of clearly defined authorities and lack of definition of the responsibilities that go along with the authorities.

7. Lack of independence of management in acting on recommended corrections.

8. CEO controls internal and outside auditors.

9. Lax control and review of expense accounts.

Insider Transactions

1. Insider lending personal funds to customers or borrowing from customers.

2. Insider involvement in silent trusts or partnerships and/or shell corporations.

3. Insider appears to receive special favors from institution customers or shows unusual favoritism toward certain institution customers.

4. Insider purchases assets from the institution, directly or indirectly, and there is no evidence of independent appraisal of the assets.

5. Insider has apparent reciprocal lending arrangements with insiders of other institutions and his/her institution has correspondent relationship with those institutions.

6. Insider is involved in a business that arranges its financing through the institution.

7. Insider "perks" include use of expensive, institution-owned automobiles, boats, airplanes, housing, etc., where the institution's earnings do not appear to support such extravagance.

8. Insider heavily indebted and debt service appears to require most, if not all, of the insider's salary.

9. Insider financial statements show large or unusual fluctuations. Net worth cannot be reconciled from disclosed sources of income.

10. Insider is financing large purchases (home, auto, etc.) through private, nonbanking sources that may have a business relationship with the institution.

11. Insider financial statements reflect heavy concentration of high-risk investments and speculative ventures.

12. Insider sells personal assets to third party and the institution provides financing without the benefit of independent appraisal.

13. Insiders and their interests frequently appear on transactions suspense items listings or on computer-generated past-due loan lists, but do not appear on the "updated" version presented to the board of directors or to examiners.

14. Insider "unofficially" guarantees loans and/or loan participations.

15. Insider is responsible for clearing up audit exceptions on loan balance confirmations.

16. Insider "forgets" to process credit entry for official bank checks causing the account to be out-of-balance because checks are sometimes paid (debited) before the credit is posted, sometimes several days later.

17. Insider conducts a cash turnover over $10,000 but "forgets" to have the institution file a Currency Transaction Report or asks an employee to "structure" the transaction to avoid filing the report.

18. Insider's stock in the institution is pledged to secure loans obtained from sources other than financial institutions. If true, what is the purpose of the loan and are the payments current?

19. Insider conducts personal business from institution using equipment, supplies, employees, etc., and/or spends most of the time out of the institution on business unrelated to the institution.

20. Insider has substance abuse problems or is known to associate with people who have these problems.

21. Insider is known to associate with "high rollers."

22. Insider suggests that institution change servicers or vendors even though there appears to be no problem with the current servicers or vendors.

23. Insider abruptly suggests changes in outsider auditors or legal counsel.

24. Insider loans increase dramatically at about the same time as the institution is recapitalized.

25. Insider's major assets are parcels of real estate that appear to increase in value at a rate that is not consistent with market conditions.

26. Insider sells his stock to an Employee Stock Option Plan, sometimes arranging for the ESOP to obtain a loan to purchase the stock.

27. Insider's interests have a direct business relationship with the institution and compensation for services is not commensurate with the level of services provided.

28. Insider agrees to buy fixed assets from the institution with the understanding that the institution will repurchase them at some future date.

29. Insider receives incentive pay or "bonuses" based on volume of loans generated.

30. Insider buys a home from a builder whose development project is financed by the institution.

31. Insider is involved in "churning" the institution's securities portfolio.

32. Insider arranges sale of EDP equipment at book value in connection with the conversion to a new data processing servicer. Also check "side" deals.

33. Insider authorizes ORE related expenses such as landscaping, remodeling, etc., when such expenses do not appear justified (may be making improvements or repairs to personal residence).

34. Insider makes frequent trips at the institution's expense to areas where the institution has no business relationships.

35. Insider will not allow employees to talk to examiners.

36. Insider keeps an unusual number of customer files in his/her desk.

37. Insider is making payments on other borrowers' loans.

38. Insider's loan is being paid by someone else.

39. Insider receives commissions on credit life insurance premiums and those commissions are not properly adjusted in cases where the insurance company gives rebates for borrower's prepayment of the loan or gives refunds to borrowers for premium overcharges.

40. Insider sells some of his/her personal stock of the institution to borrowers (as a condition for approving loan) and buys more stock from the institution at about the same time that the institution is under pressure to increase capital.

41. Insider purchases investment securities for his personal portfolio through the institution but "forgets" to reimburse the institution until a few days or weeks later, and then only if the investment has increased in value. In spite of the increase in value, the insider only pays the original purchase price to the institution.

42. Insider's accounts at the institution are frequently overdrawn. Deposits to cover overdrafts come from loans or some undisclosed source.

43. Insider maintains total control over the institution and does not allow other officers and employees to make independent decisions.

44. Insider has past-due loans at other financial institutions.

45. Insider maintains signed, blank notes in personal or customer loan files.

46. Insider is rumored to have financial problems due to divorce, business failure, gambling losses, etc.

47. Insider maintains several personal accounts outside of his/her own institution.

48. Insider frequently takes loan papers out of the institution for customer signatures; personally handles the disbursement of the loan proceeds; routinely cashes checks for customer loan proceeds; and insists on personally handling certain past-due accounts as a "special favor" to certain customers.

49. Insider insists that different audit firms audit different divisions or departments. (Hopes there will be no comparison of findings between firms.)

50. Insider insists that different departments be audited at different times. (Makes it easier to hide fraudulent interdepartmental transactions.)

Loan Participations

1. Excessive participations of loans between closely related institutions, correspondent institutions, and branches or departments of the lending institution.

2. Absence of any formal participation agreement.

3. Poor or incomplete loan documentation.

4. Investing in out-of-territory participations.

5. Reliance on third-party guaranties.

6. Large paydown or payoff of previously classified loans.

7. Some indication that there may be informal repurchase agreements on some participations.

8. Lack of independent credit analysis.

9. Volume of loan participations sold is high in relation to the size of the institution's own loan portfolio.

10. Evidence of lapping of loan participations. For example, the sale of a loan participation equal or greater than, and at or about the same times as, participation that has matured or is about to mature.

11. Disputes between participating institutions over documentation, payments, or any other aspect of the loan participation transaction.

12. Formal participation agreements are missing; therefore, responsibilities and rights of all participating institutions may be unclear.

13. Participations between affiliated institutions may be "placed" without the purchasing institution having the benefit of reviewing normal credit information, particularly where there is dominant ownership and a "rubber stamp" board of directors.

14. Payments that are not distributed to each participant according to the participation agreement may indicate preferential treatment; or where the participants are affiliated, it may indicate an attempt to disguise the delinquent status of the loans in the weaker institution.

15. Informal guaranties by insiders may be one method of disguising insider transactions.

16. There is some indication that the credit information contained in the selling institution's files is not the same as the credit information in the purchasing institution's files.

17. Be aware of reciprocal arrangements in the sale/purchase of participations. For example, Institution A sells a 100% participation in a loan to an insider of the selling institution to institution B, which in turn sells a 100% participation in a loan to one of their insiders to institution A.

18. There are a number of outstanding items in correspondent accounts just prior to or during an examination or audit which relate to participations purchased or sold.

19. There is some indication that payments on participations purchased are being made by the selling institution without reimbursement from the borrower.

Real Estate Lending

1. An unusually large number of loans in the same development are exactly equal to the institution's loan-to-value (LTV) ratio for real estate mortgages.

2. The institution has an unusually high percentage of "No Doc" loans. (A "No Doc" loan is one in which extensive documentation of income, credit history, deposits, etc., is not required because of the size of the downpayment, usually 25% or more. Theoretically, the value of the collateral is to protect the lender.)

3. Borrower has never owned a home before and does not appear to have the financial ability to support the size of the downpayment made.

4. Property securing a loan has changed ownership frequently in a short period of time. Related entities may be involved.

5. Insured value of improvements is considerably less than appraised value.

6. Appraiser is a heavy borrower at the institution.

7. Appraisal fee is based on a percentage of the appraised value.

8. Borrower furnishes his/her own appraisal which is a photocopy of an appraisal signed by a reputable appraiser.

9. Use of "comparables" which are not comparable.

10. Appraisal is based on an estimated future value.

11. All comparables are new houses in the same development that were built by the same builder and appraised by the same appraiser.

12. An unusual number of "purchases" are from out of the area or out of state.

13. Credit history, employment, etc., are not independently verified by the lender.

14. Large number of applicants have income from sources that cannot be verified, such as self-employment income.

15. Applicant makes $90,000 per year and only wants to purchase a $90,000 home.

16. Applicant is 45 years old but the credit history only dates back five years.

17. The institution's normal procedure is to accept photocopies of important documents rather then to make their own copies of the originals.

18. If copies of income tax returns are provided, columns are uneven and/or do not balance.

19. Appraiser is from out of the area and is not likely to be familiar with local property values.

20. Close relationship exists between builder, broker, appraiser and lender.

21. Construction draws are made without visual inspections.

22. All "comparables" are from properties appraised by the same appraiser.

23. Generally, housing sales are slow, but this development seems unusually active in sales.

24. There seems to be an unusual number of foreclosures on 90% to 95% loans with Private Mortgage Insurance on homes in the same development built by the same builder. (Sometimes it is cheaper for the builder to arrange for a straw buyer to get the 95% loan and default then it is to market the home if the market is sluggish.)

25. Applications received through the same broker have numerous similarities.

26. Sales contracts have numerous crossed out and changed figures for sales price and downpayment.

27. Appraiser for project owns property in the same project.

28. Lending officer buys a home in a project financed by the institution.

29. Assessed value for tax purposes is not in line with appraised value.

30. The project is reportedly fully occupied, but the parking lot always appears to be nearly empty.

31. The parking lot is full, but the project appears empty. Nobody is around in the parking lot, pool, etc.

32. After a long period of inactivity, sales suddenly become brisk.

33. Sales contract is drawn up to fit the lender's LTV requirements. Buyer wants an $80,000 home but has no down payment. The lender only lends 80% of appraised value or selling price. Contract is drawn up to show a selling price of $100,000 instead of the actual selling price of $80,000.

34. Builder claims a large number of presold units not yet under construction, while many finished units remain unsold.

35. Employment of prospective borrower/purchaser is 100 miles from location of property while comparable housing is readily available within 10 miles of employment.

36. Applicant's stated income is not commensurate with his/her stated employment and/or years of experience.

37. Applicant's financial statement shows numerous assets that are self-evaluated and cannot be readily verified through independent sources.

38. Applicant claims to own partial interest in many assets but not 100% of any asset, making verification difficult.

39. Appraised value of property is contingent upon the curing of some property defect such as drainage problems.

40. Applicant's financial statement reflects expensive jewelry and artwork but no insurance coverage is carried.

41. Applicant's tax return shows substantial interest deductions, but financial statement shows little debt. For example, the borrower's tax return shows substantial mortgage interest deductions, but the self-prepared financial statement shows no mortgage or a very small mortgage.

42. Appraised value of a condominium complex is arrived at by using the asking price for one of the more desirable units and multiplying that by the total number of units.

43. Loans are unusual considering the size of the institution and the level of expertise of its lending officers.

44. There is a heavy concentration of loans to a single project or to individuals related to the project.

45. There is a heavy concentration of loans to local borrowers with the same or similar real estate collateral which is located outside the institution's trade area.

46. There are many loans in the names of trustees, holding companies, and/or offshore companies, but the names of the individuals involved are not disclosed in the institution's files.

47. A loan is approved contingent upon an appraised value of at least a certain amount and the appraised value is exactly that amount.

48. Independent reviews of outside appraisals are never conducted.

49. The institution routinely accepts mortgages of other loans through broker but makes no attempt to determine the financial condition of the broker or to obtain any references or other background information.

50. Borrower claims substantial income but his/her only credit experience has been with finance companies.

51. Borrower claims to own substantial assets, reportedly has an excellent credit history and above average income, but is being charged many points and a higher than average interest rate, which is indicative of high-risk loans.

52. The institution allows borrowers to assign mortgages as collateral without routinely performing the same analysis of the mortgage and mortgagor as they would perform if the institution were the mortgagee.

53. Asset Swaps—sale of real estate or other distressed assets to a broker at an inflated price in return for favorable terms and conditions on a new loan to a borrower introduced to the institution by the broker. The new loan is usually secured by property of questionable value and the borrower is in weak financial condition. Borrower and collateral are often outside the institution's trade area.

Secured Lending

1. Lack of independent appraisals of collateral.

2. Significant out-of-territory lending.

3. Loans with unusual terms or conditions.

4. Poor or incomplete documentation used to intentionally conceal material facts.

5. Loans that are unusual considering the size of the institution and the level of expertise of its lending officers.

6. Heavy concentration of loans secured by same or similar types of collateral.

7. Financing of 100% of the value of any collateral that is subject to rapid depreciation or wide fluctuation in market value.

8. Appraisals which appear to be made to cover the borrower's loan request rather than to reflect the true value of the collateral.

9. Appraisal fee based on amount of loan or on appraised value of collateral may encourage inflated appraisals.

10. Review of records indicates numerous related-party purchases and sales of the collateral which could be used to inflate the collateral price far beyond actual market value.

11. Loans in the names of trustees, holding companies, and offshore companies may disguise the identity of actual owners.

12. Assigned notes and mortgages are accepted as collateral without verifying all underlying documentation and conducting normal credit analysis on the obligor.

Third-Party Obligations

1. Documentation on guaranties is incomplete.

2. Loans are secured by obligations of off-shore institutions.

3. Lack of credit information on third-party guaranty.

4. Financial statements reflect concentrations of closely held companies or businesses that lack audited financial statements to support their value.

5. A guaranty signed in blank may be used indiscriminately by some dishonest individuals to cover weak loans. Guaranties signed in blank may also be legally unenforceable if contested.

6. Guaranties that are separate from the notes may contain restrictions that could render them worthless unless the restrictions are closely followed.

7. Third-party obligor is not informed of assignment of obligation to institution which may allow payments to be diverted to some use other than payment of the loan.

8. Guaranties or letters of credit to guarantee payment from insurance companies are accepted without evaluation of the financial

soundness of the guarantor and its ability to honor the guaranties or letters of credit if necessary.

9. Guaranties or letters of credit from insurance companies are not directly verified with the issuer.

10. The institution's audit procedures do not include a request for acknowledgment of guaranties by guarantors.

11. Corporate guaranties are used, but there is no information in the institution's files to support the authority of the corporation to make the guaranties or to indicate that they are still in force.

12. The institution purchases substandard consumer contracts from a third party relying on recourse to the seller without doing proper analysis of seller's financial condition.

13. The institution purchases substandard consumer contracts for automobiles, home improvement loans, etc., while relying on some type of insurance for delinquencies, skips, etc., without verifying the financial condition of the insurer.

Lending to Buy Tax Shelter Investments

1. Block loans to individuals to buy tax shelters arranged by a tax shelter promoter.

2. Shelters which promise tax deductions that would not appear to withstand the scrutiny of the IRS.

3. Specific use of invested funds cannot be ascertained.

4. Loan payments are to be made by a servicing company.

5. Investments reflect no economic purpose except to generate tax write-offs.

6. Financial "no cash" deals where transactions are structured to avoid any actual cash flow. For example, a long-term CD is matched against a loan payable for the proceeds of the CD at its maturity. Interest accumulates on the CD in an amount equal to or greater than the compound interest owed on the corresponding loan. The depositor/borrower never provides or receives any cash but still gets the tax write-off.

Linked Financing/Brokered Deposits

1. Short-term, volatile deposits are used to fund long-term loans of questionable credit quality.

2. A generous point spread exists between the loan interest rate and the interest rate on the deposits, which are usually below prevailing market rates.

3. Out-of-territory lending to previously unknown borrowers.

4. Large dollar deposits are offered in consideration for favorable treatment on loan requests, but deposits are not pledged as collateral for the loans.

5. Brokered deposit transactions where the broker's fees are paid from the proceeds of related loans.

6. Institution is presented with a large loan request that cannot be funded without the use of brokered deposits.

7. An unsolicited offer to purchase the institution comes at about the same time as brokered deposits and related loans are processed.

8. Long-term, discounted CDs are pledged or matched at face value (not actual book value) and are used to repay the loan automatically.

Credit Cards and ATM Transactions

1. Lack of separation of duties between the card issuing function and the issuance of personal identification number (PIN).

2. Poor control of unissued cards and PINs.

3. Poor control of returned mail.

4. Customer complaints.

5. Poor control of credit limit increases.

6. Poor control of name and address changes.

7. Frequent malfunction of payment authorization.

8. Unusual delays in receipt of cards and PINs by the customers.

9. The institution does not limit the amount of cash that a customer can extract from an ATM in a given day.

10. Evidence that customer credit card purchases have been intentionally structured by a merchant to keep individual amounts below the "floor limit" to avoid the need for transaction approval.

11. Credit card merchant accounts are opened without obtaining any background information on the merchant.

12. Credit card merchant account activity reflects an increase in the number and size of chargebacks.

13. The institution's credit card merchant is depositing sales drafts made payable to a business or businesses other than the business named on the account.

14. Credit card merchant frequently requests the wire transfer of funds from the merchant account to other institutions in other parts of the country or to offshore institutions almost immediately after deposits are made.

15. Merchant is engaged in telemarketing activities and is subject to frequent consumer complaints.

16. The institution contracts with third-party servicer to process credit card customer and merchant transactions without verifying the financial stability and reputation of the servicer.

17. The institution contracts with a third party to establish and market a secured credit card program without verifying the financial stability and reputation of the third party and without determining the institution's potential liability for participation in the program.

18. Credit card merchant account deposits appear to exceed the level of customer activity observed at the merchant's place of business.

19. Merchant has access to EDC (electronic data capture) equipment but frequently inputs credit card account numbers manually. Be especially alert if manually keyed transactions exceed 10% of total transactions.

20. Merchant has a sudden or unexplained increase in the level of authorization requests from a particular merchant location.

Advance Fee Schemes

1. A person having no previous relationship with the institution suddenly appears and offers fantastic opportunities for the institution and/or its customers.

2. Broker claims to be part of a major financial organization, but this claim cannot be verified.

3. Broker claims to have access to huge sums of money from a secret, undiscoverable, or unverifiable source.

4. Broker becomes irritated if the institution suggests that references be checked.

5. Broker makes frequent references to such terms as "ICC for 254, 290, or 322" and frequently uses the terms "emission rate, prime

bank notes, tranches, letters of commitment, bank acceptances, arbitrage, hedge contracts, or escrow agreements."

6. Broker initially requests an advance for his services but often "reluctantly" agrees to defer the fee until settlement of the transaction.

7. As the deadline for settlement nears, the broker urgently requests an advance on his fee to cover expenses such as travel, documentation, communication, costs, etc.

8. Broker states that funds will be forthcoming from some offshore bank in the Caribbean or South Pacific.

9. Attempts to verify the broker's references are unsuccessful.

10. Broker's references include telephone numbers which are answered by machines and addresses which are mail drops, hotel rooms, etc.

11. Broker proposes a self-liquidating loan where earnings from a deposit or other investment will be such that they will pay the principal and interest on the loan with no additional funds needed from the borrower.

12. Broker conducts most of the negotiations by telephone or telex and appears to resist any meeting with the institution's counsel.

13. Broker repeatedly delays the settlement of the deal citing numerous "technical" problems.

14. The deal frequently falls through at the last minute while the broker searches for another source of funds.

15. Broker asks institution to serve as a transfer bank, middleman, or agent in the transfer of funds between a sending institution and a receiving institution.

16. Broker who originally presents the deal may be known to the institution but other persons involved may be unknown to the institution and have questionable backgrounds.

17. Broker asks for the institution's telex numbers and frequently, long, instructional telexes from the lender's agent are received by the institution.

18. The receiving institution may be asked to send a number of letters, contracts, or telex messages to the lender's agent or the lender's institution.

19. Broker expresses a great deal of urgency in completing the transaction so that the loan will not be lost.

20. Broker offers funds that the borrower can invest in U.S. Treasury Notes or similar investments at a 4 or 5 point spread which will help the borrower to cover part of the fees, but only offers flimsy excuses as to why the lender does not directly invest in these instruments.

21. Broker does not allow borrower or institution any direct contact with the proposed lender, often citing confidentiality requirements by the lender or some sensitive political situation in the lender's home country.

22. Broker often requests that the borrower's institution issue a standby letter of credit to the foreign lender to guarantee payment.

23. Broker is often a name dropper, but the people named are either deceased or impossible to contact for reference because of political reasons.

Offshore Transactions

1. Loans made on the strength of a borrower's financial statement when the statement reflects major investments in and income from businesses incorporated in bank secrecy haven countries such as Panama, Cayman Islands, Netherlands, Antilles, Montserrat and others.

2. Loans to companies domiciled in bank secrecy haven countries.

3. Loans secured by obligations of offshore institutions.

4. Transactions involving an offshore "shell" institution whose name may be very similar to the name of a major, legitimate institution.

5. Frequent wire transfers of funds to and from bank secrecy haven countries.

6. Offers of multi-million dollar deposits at below market rates from a confidential source to be sent from an offshore institution or somehow guaranteed by an offshore institution through a letter, telex, or other "official" communication.

7. Offshore companies are used to disguise the true identity of borrowers or guarantors.

8. No independent verification of the financial strength of the offshore institution is available from any source.

9. In order to make an offshore bank transaction appear legitimate, innocent third parties are brought into the scheme, unaware of its fraudulent nature.

Wire Transfers

1. Lack of separation between authority to initiate a wire transfer and authority to approve a wire transfer.

2. Indications of frequent overrides of established approval authority and other internal controls.

3. Intentional circumvention of approval authority by splitting transactions.

4. Wire transfers to and from bank secrecy haven countries.

5. Frequent or large transfers for persons who have no account relationship with the institution.

6. Large or frequent wire transfers against uncollected funds.

7. Frequent requests for immediate wire transfer of funds from a credit card merchant account to institutions in other parts of the United States, offshore institutions, or foreign institutions.

8. Frequent wire transfers from accounts with numerous cash deposits of just under $10,000 each.

9. Frequent errors in payment by authorized system officials.

10. Lack of secure wire transfer system safeguards such as the password and other details of wire transfer transactions.

11. Unconfirmed wire transfer request initiated by telephone.

12. Incoming wire transfers in which the account name and account number do not match.

13. Wire transfer or payment request that does not conform to established procedures.

14. Absence of written funds transfer agreements between the institution and its customers.

15. Large international funds transfers to or from the accounts of domestic customers in amounts and of a frequency that are not consistent with the nature of the customer's known business activities.

16. Receipt of funds of multiple cashier's checks, money orders, traveler's checks, bank checks, or personal checks that are drawn on or issued by U.S. financial institutions and made payable to the same individual or business in U.S. dollar amounts that are below the $10,000 Bank Secrecy Act reporting threshold and which are then wire transferred to a financial institution outside the United States.

17. The deposit of funds into several accounts and then aggregated into one account followed by the wire transfer of those funds from that account outside of the United States when such action is not consistent with the known business of the customer.

18. Any other unusual international funds transfer requests wherein the arrangements requested appear to be inconsistent with normal funds transfer practices, e.g., where the customer directs the institution to wire transfer funds to a foreign country and advises the institution to expect same-day return of funds from sources different from the beneficiaries initially named, thereby changing the source of the funds.

19. A pattern of wire transfers of similar amounts both in and out of the customer's account on the same day or next day.

20. Wire transfers by customers operating a cash business, i.e., customers depositing large amounts of currency.

21. Wire transfer volume is extremely large in proportion to asset size of institution.

22. The institution's business strategy and financial statements are inconsistent with large volumes of wire transfers, particularly out of the United States.

Money Laundering

1. Increase in cash shipments that is not accompanied by a corresponding increase in number of accounts.

2. Cash on hand frequently exceeds limits established in security program and/or blanket bond coverage.

3. Large volume of cashier's checks, money orders, traveler's checks, etc., sold for cash to noncustomers in amounts ranging from several hundred dollars to just under $10,000.

4. Large volume of wire transfers to and from offshore institutions.

5. Large volume of wire transfers for noncustomers.

6. Accounts which have a large number of small deposits and a small number of large checks with balances of the accounts remaining relatively low and constant. The accounts have many of the same characteristics as accounts used for check kiting.

7. A large volume of deposits to several different accounts with frequent transfer of major portions of the balances to a single account at the same institution or at another institution.

8. Loans to offshore companies and loans secured by obligations of offshore institutions.

9. Large volume of cashier's checks, money orders, and/or wire transfers deposited to an account where the nature of the account holder's business would not appear to justify such activity.

10. Large volume of cash deposits from a business that is not normally cash intensive, such as a wholesaler.

11. Cash deposits to a correspondent account by any means other than through an armored carrier.

12. Large turnover in large bills that would appear uncharacteristic for the institution's location.

13. Cash shipments which appear large in comparison to the dollar volume of Currency Transaction Reports filed.

14. Dollar limits on the list of customers exempt from currency transaction reporting requirements which appear unreasonably high considering the type and location of the businesses. No information is in the institution's file to support the limits.

15. Currency Transaction Reports, when filed, are often incorrect or lack important information.

16. List of exempted customers appears unusually long.

17. Customer expresses some urgent need to be included on the institution's list of customers exempted from currency transaction reporting requirements.

18. Customer requests information on how to avoid filing of Currency Transaction Reports on cash transactions involving amounts over $10,000.

19. Upon being informed of the currency transaction reporting requirements, customer withdraws all or part of the transaction to avoid filing the CTR.

20. Customer frequently conducts cash transactions in amounts just under $10,000 each.

21. Customer refuses to provide information required to complete CTR.

22. Corporate customer makes frequent, large, cash deposits and maintain high balances but does not avail itself of other services such as loans, letters of credit, payroll services, etc.

23. Customer almost never comes to the institution but has numerous couriers making deposits to the account.

24. A large increase in small-denomination bills and a corresponding decrease in large-denomination bills with no corresponding CTR filings.

25. Customers who open accounts providing minimal or fictitious information or information which is difficult or expensive for the institution to verify.

26. Customers who decline to provide information that normal customers would provide to make them eligible for credit or other banking services that normal customers would regard as valuable.

27. Customers who appear to have accounts with several institutions within the same locality, especially when there is a regular consolidation of balances in the accounts and transfer of funds out of the accounts by wire transfer, or other means, to offshore institutions or to large domestic institutions.

28. Customers whose deposits frequently contain counterfeit bills or bills which appear musty or extremely dirty.

29. Customers who have deposit accounts at the institution but frequently purchase cashier's checks, money orders, etc., with large amounts of cash.

30. Retail customer who deposits a large volume of checks but seldom, if ever, requests currency for its daily operations.

31. Retail business has dramatically different patterns of cash deposits than similar businesses in the same general location.

32. Exempted customer frequently requests increases in exemption limits.

33. Substantial increase in cash deposits in any business without any apparent cause.

34. Substantial increase in cash deposits by professional customers using client accounts or in-house company accounts such as trust accounts, escrow accounts, etc.

35. Customers who make or receive large transfers to or from countries associated with production, processing, and marketing of narcotics.

36. Size and frequency of cash deposits increases rapidly without any corresponding increase in non-cash deposits.

37. Size and frequency of cash deposits is not consistent with observed activity at the customer's place of business.

38. Customer makes large, frequent cash deposits but checks or other debits against the account are not consistent with the customer's stated line of business. For example, customer claims to be in the retail jewelry business, but checks are mostly to individuals and/or firms not normally associated with the jewelry business.

39. Customer frequently deposits large amounts of currency that is wrapped in currency straps that have been stamped by other financial institutions.

40. Customer frequently deposits strapped currency or currency wrapped in rubber bands that is disorganized and does not balance when counted.

41. Customer is often observed entering the safety deposit box area just prior to making cash deposits of just under $10,000.

Securities Trading Activities

1. Management lacks the expertise needed to fully understand the ramifications of proposals made by brokers, and/or they perceive an unrealistic opportunity to enhance income.

2. Investments bear no reasonable relationship to the institution's size or its capital accounts.

3. Overreliance is placed on the purported safety of the securities since they involve U.S. Government issues.

4. Little or no attention is given to "interest rate risk" prior to the transaction taking place.

5. Delayed settlements over unreasonable time periods sometimes allow management to make imprudent purchases and avoid booking the transaction on a timely basis.

6. The institution engages in reverse repurchase agreements with brokers, which allows the institution to erroneously deter recognition of losses.

7. Securities held for short-term trading are not appropriately identified and segregated from those that are held primarily as a source of investment income.

8. Trading account securities are not revalued periodically and are not reported consistently at market value or lower of cost or market value.

Miscellaneous

1. Lack of supervision of lending activities by officers of the institution.

2. Lack of lending policies or failure to enforce existing policies.

3. Lack of code of conduct or failure to enforce existing code.

4. Dominant figure allowed to exert influence without restraint.

5. Lack of separation of duties.

6. Lack of accountability.

7. Lack of written policies and/or internal controls.

8. Circumvention of established policies and/or controls.

9. Lack of independent members of management and/or board.

10. Entering into transactions where the institution lacks expertise.

11. Excessive growth through low-quality loans.

12. Unwarranted concentrations.

13. Volatile sources of funding such as short-term deposits from out-of-area brokers.

14. Too much emphasis on earnings at the expense of safety and soundness.

15. Compromising credit policies.

16. High-rate/high-risk investments.

17. Underwriting criteria allows high-risk loans.

18. Lack of documentation or poor documentation.

19. Lack of adequate credit analysis.

20. Failure to properly obtain and evaluate credit data, collateral, etc.

21. Failure to properly analyze and verify financial statement data.

22. Too much emphasis on character and collateral and not enough emphasis on credit.

23. Lack of balance in loan portfolio.

24. Poor loan administration after credit is granted.

25. Unresolved exceptions or frequently recurring exceptions on exception report.

26. Out-of-balance conditions.

27. Purpose of loan is not recorded.

28. Proceeds of loan are used for a purpose other than the purpose recorded.

29. Lax policies on payment of checks against uncollected funds.

30. The institution is defendant in a number of lawsuits alleging improper handling of transactions.

Source: FDIC's *Manual of Examination Policies*, Division of Bank Supervision, "Bank Fraud and Insider Abuse" (1-90), pp. 8.3-1–8.3-23.

Appendix B   Lakeside Bank—Loan Policy

Note: Chapter 11 addressed the issue of loan policies. Appendixes B and C examine the loan policies of two banks. They are presented to illustrate different approaches to loan policies. They are not being held out as the "ideal" loan policies because each bank's needs are different.

* * *

Lakeside Bank shall have a standing executive committee elected by the board that will also serve as the directors' loan committee. It shall consist of the chairman of the board, president, and senior loan officer as permanent members, and not less than two other directors to serve at the pleasure of the board.

The executive committee shall review and approve all loans $15,000 and over, and approve all loans over $500,000 prior to the loan being made. In case of emergency, loans over $500,000 may be approved by the president, executive vice-president, and one member of the executive committee. These emergency loans must be ratified by the entire committee at their next meeting. The committee shall keep minutes of its meetings and report its actions in writing at each regular meeting of the board. Non-salaried directors shall be paid a fee as set by the board.

There shall be an officers' loan committee which shall consist of the president and vice-presidents in charge of commercial and installment loans. This committee shall meet daily to review all loans made the preceding day and approve or disapprove all applications requiring their approval as set out in the loan policy.

I. GENERAL POLICY

It is the general policy of the board that all loans should have a plan of liquidation at the time they are granted. This is considered to be the keystone of sound credit administration and all loan and discount committees and lending officers are requested to observe this basic principle when approving loans. It is recognized that there will be exceptions to this policy on rare occasions. The board believes these exceptions should be held to conditions where loans are fully collateralized by cash surrender value of life insurance policies, savings accounts, certificates of deposit, and government bonds with adequate margin. The lending officer should state the plan of liquidation in writing on the note or make it a part of the credit file. This is a requirement on all loans made, whether submitted to the committee for approval or not.

All new loans to customers having a total indebtedness in excess of $15,000 must be supported by a completed loan memorandum. This memorandum should contain the name, date, amount, and rate of the loan. Also, it should tell the purpose, repayment plan, and source of those funds. If there is no arrangement made other than a set maturity, it is assumed that the loan will be paid off on that date. This memorandum should be made a part of the credit file and any subsequent changes to the original terms should be reflected as a change in the original memo.

II. TRADE AREA

This board believes that sound local loans are one of the most satisfactory and profitable means of employing the bank's funds. Therefore, it is the intent of the board that with few exceptions the bank's lending area be limited to Lake County and the adjoining counties covering the northern part of the state. It is recognized that there will be occasions when exceptions to this policy are desirable. These exceptions should be rare. Also, reasons for exception to the policy should be clearly set forth in the minutes of the appropriate committee meeting. This policy does not prohibit participation with other banks of substantial and recognized standing when we have funds available for lending that cannot be readily invested in our local trade area.

III. DESIRED LOANS

It will be the policy of the board of directors of this bank not to be content with accepting and consummating all sound loans *offered* to the bank. The bank will be aggressive in seeking desirable loans of the type described hereinafter.

Loans of the following types will be considered desirable provided each loan meets the test of a sound, prudent loan:

   a. Loans to business concerns on a short-term basis, against a satisfactory balance sheet and earnings statement, usually for not more than 180 days.

   b. Loans to business concerns secured by a chattel mortgage on marketable business equipment, such loans to be amortized over a period of not more than 60 months, or 72 months, when approved by the officers' loan and discount committee. The amortization terms are to be such that the residual value of the business equipment will at all times be equal to or greater than the unpaid balance of the loan. Proof of insurance and a UCC-1 filed with the Secretary of State are required.

c. Loans to business concerns secured by accounts receivable and inventory. Because accounts receivable may be proceeds of inventory, a security interest in both is necessary and should be perfected by filing a UCC-1. It is also recommended that regular aging reports be requested and verified periodically.

It is recognized that there will be exceptions where it is not practical for our customer to make an assignment of his accounts receivable on a notification basis. It is accepted by the board that such loans will be limited to a few of the bank's best customers. Also, the loan will have additional proper collateral, as herein provided, or a satisfactory balance sheet and earnings statement, in which case the loan should be approved additionally by the officers' loan and discount committee. The board regards accounts receivable financing as somewhat more hazardous than the normal type of lending conducted by the bank. All committees and lending officers are required to give such loans careful scrutiny and greater than average surveillance at all times, with strict requirements as to liquidation or substitution of additional collateral of other accounts receivable at any time the accounts receivable are not liquidated in accordance with terms.

In addition, proper precautions and due diligence are to be exercised to avoid the commingling of funds on such accounts. In no instance shall accounts receivable be accepted when they are more than 60 days beyond date of invoice.

d. 1. Loans secured by negotiable U.S. Government bonds or state, county, or municipal bonds properly supported by credit information. Such loans to be not more than 90% of the market value of the bonds.

2. Loans secured by securities listed on a recognized exchange or over-the-counter market; such loans to be not more than 80 percent of the market value of the collateral and to comply in all respects with Regulation U of the Federal Reserve System. The banks will *not* make loans to carry securities where Regulation U margin requirements apply. All stock certificates or registered bonds must have the proper stock power attached.

3. Although loans secured by the listed market securities depend on the collateral, it also is prudent to obtain a personal financial statement of the borrower and to know his credit background. This information should be part of the credit file on the loan and be presented to the appropriate committee at the time of loan approval.

4. Loans with securities as collateral should be checked at each renewal as to value and marginal requirements and each officer notified when the margin becomes lower than previously stated on a loan for which he is responsible.

5. The customer should be notified at the time of borrowing of his responsibility to provide additional collateral and that the occasion might arise when the bank would be required to sell collateral to protect its loan.

6. All security loans should have a definite repayment program agreed to by the customer. Such repayment should be from sources other than the sale of securities to eliminate tax problems and to avoid misunderstandings with the customers.

NOTE: It is recognized by the board that there will be situations where individual circumstances may vary. It is our desire to consider each customer's particular problem and to serve the needs of the customer. However, such variations from the foregoing securities policy must be approved by the officers' loan and discount committee and a memorandum clearly stating the reasons for deviating from the policy and the conditions under which the loan is being made must be submitted.

e. Loans against the cash surrender value of life insurance policies should not exceed the cash surrender value if the loan is to be considered a fully secured loan and must be accompanied by the proper assignment form and questionnaire to the insurance company.

f. Loans secured by the assignment of savings accounts and certificates of deposit in this bank must have an interest rate 1 percent greater than that paid on the security. We recommend that the loan officer try to charge 3 percent more than the rate on the security.

g. Loans secured by the assignment of savings accounts and certificates of deposit in other lending institutions must be acknowledged in writing by the issuing institution. Knowledge of the financial strength and abilities of the issuing institution is essential.

h. Real estate loans, secured by first liens on improved real estate, including improved farm land, and improved business and residential properties, shall be in the form of an obligation or obligations secured by mortgages. The amount of such loan shall not exceed 66 2/3 percent of the appraised value of the real estate offered as security when made on a non-amortized basis. No such loan shall be made for a term longer than one year, except that ...

1. Any such loan may be made in an amount not to exceed 80 percent of the appraised value of the real estate offered as security, and for a term of not longer than 10 years, if the loan is secured by an installment amortized mortgage. The amortized term may be for a period up to 15 years with the prior approval of the officers' loan and discount committee. Real estate mortgages taken as additional collateral do not have to meet the percent of appraised value requirement.

2. Real estate appraisals on which mortgage loans are based shall be made by appraisers approved by the officers' loan and discount committee. Appraisals up to $150,000 in value may be made by two loan officers of this bank. Exceptions to this must be initialed by the president or executive vice-president.

3. Hazard insurance is required in amounts and with companies acceptable to the bank on all real estate. This also includes flood insurance where necessary.

4. Title insurance is required on all real estate loans in excess of $15,000. For loans less than $15,000 we can accept a title opinion at the option of the loan officer.

5. Regardless of the value of the security, real estate mortgage loans shall not be made to borrowers who do not have a satisfactory credit record, nor in cases where it appears likely that the property may have to be liquidated to satisfy the debt.

i. Unsecured consumer installment personal loans and loans secured by appliances to persons of good character with an assured income and satisfactory credit records, when the purpose of the loan will be of ultimate benefit to the borrower; such loans to be payable in monthly installments not to exceed 36 months or in a single payment of 90 days or less, and perfected by the proper UCC-1 recording.

j. Personal loans secured by new or used automobiles, pick-up trucks, boats, motors, trailers. Terms should not exceed the following:

- Current year new cars/60 months
- Previous year new cars/42 months
- One- and two-year models/36 months
- Three-year models/30 months
- Four- and five-year models/24 months

- Older models/12 months

    1. All such loans must have current titles showing Lakeside Bank as lienholder, inspection report or bill of sale, and proof of insurance coverage showing Lakeside Bank as lienholder.

k. Loans secured by a chattel mortgage on livestock. The herd securing any such loan shall be registered livestock and be approved by the officers' loan and discount committee. Such loans shall not exceed 70 percent of the appraised value of the livestock securing the loan, and shall be for a term of not more than 12 months.

l. Personal loans secured by second mortgages on personal homes. Such loans to be repayable in monthly installments not to exceed 120 months. These loans must have the same documentation required for first mortgages in (h) above. In addition, there should be notification to and acknowledgment by the first mortgagee of our second mortgage.

m. Personal loans secured by new mobile homes, with adequate down payment, shall be repayable within 120 months. All mobile homes must be properly insured and our lien perfected by title or UCC-1 recording as appropriate.

n. Loans to business concerns and/or individuals for the purpose of financing insurance premiums, policy to be assigned to bank with insurance company's acknowledgment of assignment and agreement to rebate premium directly to bank in case of cancellation. Each such loan will have a recourse endorsement by the agent guaranteeing payment. Two months' premium must be paid down so that rebate amount always exceeds amount of loan and repayment to be made in equal monthly installments of no more than 10 months.

o. Construction mortgage loans, where the amount advanced does not exceed the permanent loan commitment and where the loan matures prior to the expiration of the permanent loan commitment. A checklist of needed items is available in the collateral department.

p. Officers are encouraged to put as many loans as possible on variable interest rates.

IV. UNDESIRABLE LOANS

Loans of the following type are considered undesirable loans for this bank and ordinarily will be declined unless specifically approved by the officers' loan and discount committee for reasons that appear to justify an exception to the bank's general policy:

    a.   Accommodation loans will not be made to poor credit risks on the strength of a good endorser. If the loan will not "stand on its own feet," the loans should be made to the endorser and the endorser should make a loan to the person whom he wishes to accommodate.

    b.   Capital loans to a business enterprise where the loan cannot be repaid within a reasonable period, except by borrowing elsewhere or by liquidating the business.

    c.   Loans to a new enterprise if the repayment of the loan is solely dependent upon the profitable operation of the enterprise.

    d.   Loans to persons whose integrity or honesty is questionable.

    e.   Real estate mortgage loans secured by property located outside the bank's recognized trade area.

    f.   Loans secured by an assignment against undistributed estate.

    g.   Loans secured by stock in a closed corporation that has no ready market. This type of stock may be taken as additional collateral for loans.

    h.   Loans for the purpose of enabling the borrower to speculate on the futures market of securities or commodities, unless the loan is properly collateralized and liquidation is not dependent on a rise in the market.

    i.   Loans for the purpose of financing speculative transactions.

V. LOANS TO EMPLOYEES, DIRECTORS, OFFICERS, AND RELATIVES OF LENDING OFFICER

    a.   Lending officers will not make loans to their personal relatives, but should refer them to another lending officer to avoid any conflict of interest.

    b.   All loans to directors, whose total debt exceeds $25,000, must have prior approval of the entire board of directors.

    c.   Officers' indebtedness to any bank or other financial institution will be reported to the president in writing within 10 days of the indebtedness. The president shall report this to the board at its next regular meeting. Each officer shall submit a financial statement and a list of his indebtedness by February 20th of each calendar year to the president, who, in turn, shall submit this information to the executive committee.

d. Officer and employee loan policy attached hereto as Addendum "A." (*Note*: The addendum is not included in this Appendix.)

VI. FINANCIAL INFORMATION

a. A financial statement not over 15 months old is required for the following.

1. All unsecured loans over $2,500.

2. All secured loans over $15,000 unless fully secured by cash surrender value of life insurance, savings accounts, certificates of deposit, or listed marketable stocks with a 20 percent margin.

b. Prior year operating statements are required on all business loans requiring a financial statement. In some cases the tax return is acceptable.

c. Business financial statement submitted by CPA's should be a review or audit report.

d. Unsecured loans to business firms involving $100,000 or more should have a certified public accountant's unqualified audit report as to the financial condition of the company within the current 12-month period. Where individuals are involved and if required the loan officer shall verify assets and liabilities and submit a written summary of action taken with respect to his recommendations.

e. A current credit application is required for any loan to an individual when a personal financial statement is not required. A report from a consumer reporting agency is required for the following:

1. Individual debtors and co-signers;

2. Endorsers and guarantors;

3. Principal officers of a closely held corporate borrower;

4. Owners or partners of an unincorporated business.

f. A current trade report should be obtained on loans to businesses. In addition, loans to contractors should also be supported by direct checks of suppliers on a periodic basis.

VII. INTEREST RATES

a. It is the policy of the board of directors that a loan should be turned down rather than made at an unprofitable interest rate.

b. We wish to compete for all good loans; but do not believe that unprofitable interest rate loans should be made, regardless of competition.

c. It is the desire of the board of directors that there should be a uniformity of interest rates based on the quality of credit risk, and it is the belief of the board that where the risk is greater, the interest rate should be commensurate with the risk. In addition, consideration should be given to deposit relations and other factors contributing to total yield.

VIII. PAST-DUE POLICY

Officers will receive a list of all past-due installment loans and all past-due commercial loans every seven days. All lending officers will meet periodically to review past-due loans. A list of all commercial loans with appropriate comments which have been past due since the 25th of the preceding month will be presented to the board of directors and all lending officers monthly.

IX. COLLECTION POLICY

The basic policy of the board of directors is that bank officers use all means available to them for the collection of indebtedness properly due the bank, including all legal action available by law. It is recognized that on some past-due loans, there will be mitigating circumstances which require careful consideration as to collection tactics that will be employed. In some cases, the president is charged with the responsibility of reviewing all facts with the bank's general counsel, and a course of action determined. Should the circumstances indicate the need for further consideration, a special meeting of the executive committee shall be called and a decision made as to proper action. The controlling action should, in all cases, be to take every step open to us to collect money due or to protect the bank from any loss.

X. CHARGE-OFF POLICY

The board recognizes that the lending of money is a business and necessarily includes some risks. The management is willing to undertake such reasonable risks. Some losses are to be expected, and it is the intention of the board that adequate reserves for losses be maintained at all times. It will be a policy of this bank to charge off known losses at the end of each calendar quarter. These charge-offs shall be approved by the executive committee and reported to the board at its next regular meeting. Also it is the firm intention of the board to administrate the lending operations so that it will not be necessary for the examining authorities to recommend actions for charge-offs.

XI. OVERDRAFT POLICY

    a.   It is the policy of the board of directors that employees' over-drafts will not be tolerated. (See separate overdraft policy in personnel manual.)

    b.   Overdrafts by bank customers will be honored where an associated account exists which covers the overdraft, and on which the bank has the legal right of offset. (See FIRA of 1978 for over-drafts on directors.)

    c.   Overdrafts where there are no associated accounts on which the bank has the legal right of offset will not be honored except in specific circumstances where officers feel it is important to do so. Customer's accounts that repeatedly have overdrafts and returned checks will be reviewed for the purpose of closing the account.

XII. LOAN AUTHORITY

Loan Limits - The executive committee may approve loans up to the limits authorized by Lakeside Holding Company Loan Administration Policy. Loan limits will be delegated to the various lending officers based on the officer's lending experience. A loan limit will be set up for each of the following types of loans:

    a.   Fully secured by one of the following:

        1. Savings accounts.

        2. Certificates of deposit.

        3. Cash surrender value of life insurance.

    b.   Fully secured by marketable collateral such as: chattel mortgages, various types of assignment, etc.

    c.   Unsecured.

XIII. LAKESIDE HOLDING COMPANY LOAN POLICY

The loan policy adopted by the Holding Company board and amended from time to time is considered an additional loan policy for the bank. The policies set out by the Holding Company board are hereby considered as a part of this loan policy.

XIV. COMPLIANCE

The board insists that all laws and regulations of all governmental authorities be strictly adhered to by all officers and employees. Compliance with the following is a must requirement:

a. Regulation Z - Truth in Lending and Fair Credit Billing Act.

b. Regulation B - Equal Credit Opportunity Act.

c. Regulation C - Home Mortgage Disclosure Act.

d. Regulation U.

e. Regulation X - Real Estate Settlement Procedures Act.

f. All Usury laws.

g. The Community Reinvestment Act.

h. Financial Institutions Regulatory and Interest Rate Control Act of 1978.

XV. LOANS TO FEDERAL, STATE, COUNTY AND MUNICIPAL OFFICE HOLDERS

All lending officers should be sensitive to any loans that are made to federal, state, county and municipal office holders. At the same time, it is understood that there is a need in most cases to make such loans, and we want to accommodate all reasonable requests that fall within our normal loan policy from these officeholders. All lending officers, being aware of the present climate in which we operate, should submit to the officer's executive committee on an annual basis a report of all loans made and then outstanding to any federal, state, county and municipal office holders. In addition, it will be the responsibility of each lending officer to make certain that all such loans are completely documented and include memoranda detailing amounts, interest rates, repayment schedules, purpose, financial data, and credit reports.

XVI. CONCENTRATIONS OF CREDIT

a. The board requires that all excess funds be invested daily through the sale of federal funds to other banks. Sales should only be made to holding companies and approved banks and sales to any *one* bank should not exceed 25 percent of our stockholder's equity.

b. The executive committee is charged with the responsibility of preventing excessive concentrations of credit to any industry or related group of individuals.

XVII. LOAN REVIEW

A continuing loan review program is essential. The program should emphasize the following:

1. Credit evaluation and rating.

2. Loan officer evaluation and training.

3. Documentation.

4. Compliance with loan policy.

5. Compliance with all federal and state laws.

XVIII. TAX-FREE LOANS

A request for tax-exempt financing should be considered on the following basis:

a. The borrower should meet all the lending criteria required in the granting of commercial loans.

b. The granting of the request should provide an economic benefit for the community (jobs) and the bank (deposits and related banking business).

c. The terms are not to exceed 15 years.

d. Rates shall float with holding company base rate.

e. The senior corporate loan officer or senior corporate investment officer should be consulted before committing to any tax-exempt funding over $100,000 and quoting a rate.

f. In the event that the holding company is required to restrict tax-free income, the letter of credit guaranty may be used to facilitate financing. For a fee our bank would issue a letter of credit to back the bonds and they would be sold to someone else. All other requirements of tax-exempt loans would also apply to these guarantees.

XIX. RELEASING COLLATERAL

The release of collateral from any active loan requires the signature of two loan officers and a documenting memorandum in the credit and collateral file. The exception to this policy is where a specific lot release was negotiated at the inception of the loan.

XX. EXTENSIONS POLICY

Extensions - It is the policy of the bank to grant an extension of an installment loan payment(s) only in special or unusual situations, where it can be clearly exhibited by the customer that his or her problems are of a short-term nature. Below is a more definitive description of the bank policy.

  a. No free extension will be granted.

  b. No more than one extension in a 12-month period without prior approval from the head of the installment loan department.

  c. A customer with a note two or more installments past due will not be granted a 30-day extension unless the other delinquent payments are collected.

Renewals - It will be the policy to allow a customer to renew a loan that is past due when it can be documented that such renewal will help the customer and the bank is in a stronger position as a result of the renewal.

Before approving the renewal of a past-due loan, the lending officer should develop full information as to the reason for the request. The documentation in the file will be:

  a. Memorandum giving reasons for the renewal, what it did for customer and the bank.

XXI. CHARGE-OFF POLICY

All loans (accounts) will be charged off when it is determined they are uncollectible but not later than when the loan is 90 days past due. Delinquencies are to be determined on a contractual basis and not on a recency of payment basis. For example, payment due on 4-20-94 is 30 days delinquent 5-20-94 and would be 90 days delinquent 7-20-94, at which time the loan is to be charged off. If the 3-20-94 payment was made on 7-20-94, the account is still 90 days past due and subject to immediate charge off, unless it can be ascertained recovery will be received within the next 45 days from:

  a. Collection of a physical damage insurance policy.

  b. Collection on sale of marketable collateral.

  c. Other collateral such as cash value life insurance or savings accounts.

  d. Unspecified reasons that are approved by the head of the installment loan department.

A list of all loans not charged off after 90 days by reasons of the above exceptions or for any other reason should be reported to the president at the end of each quarter.

XXII. STUDENT LOANS

The board encourages participation in the guaranteed student loan program. It shall be the duty of the officers' executive committee to set the requirements and limits for this program.

XXIII. LETTERS OF CREDIT

All letters of credit issued by this bank must be signed by the president or executive vice-president. The loan officer should submit all credit information, collateral documentation, and final draft of the letter to obtain approval. Collateral documentation required is the same as for a loan made under the same conditions.

All letters of credit involving international companies or anything other than simple domestic letters will be issued through the bank's International Department.

Check guarantee letters to the Alcohol Beverage Control Board of the State are not considered letters of credit for requirements of this section. However, they can only be signed by the president or executive vice-president.

XXIV. MASTERCARD AND VISA

We encourage the issuance of these cards to build the base of receivables for this bank. The president is authorized to enter into an agreement with the holding company to issue cards and service these accounts for this bank.

Appendix C Metropolitan Bank—
Loan Policy

This document contains the official loan policy of Metropolitan Bank. Its purpose is to set forth in writing the concepts by which the loan function shall be governed within the bank.

In keeping with the general requirements of the loan policy, all loan personnel are required to apply the appropriate, existing banking regulations to carry out the loan program in a manner consistent with the directives of the board of directors and the bank's executive management. This policy is supported by the bank's interest rate and Maturity Manual which contains significant information used in the lending process. Adherence to the general guidelines contained in this policy is required at all times, significant variations shall be deemed unacceptable. This policy shall apply to all members of the bank's staff who exercise loan authority and shall remain in effect until it is amended or rescinded.

General Statement

The lending policy of Metropolitan Bank shall at all times be flexible enough to meet the needs of our trade area. In addition, strong emphasis is given to providing good service and prompt decisions; and all loan personnel are required to apply their knowledge and skills in lending a competent and efficient manner. It is the intent of senior management to place sufficient authority in the hands of loan officers and loan committees to serve our present customer base effectively and to assist in the securing of loan relationships from the bank's prospective customers. Loan decisions made independently within the assigned loan limits are encouraged.

In all cases the loan portfolio with recognition of the mix and the loan to deposit ratio required by senior management should:

1. Satisfy demand.

2. Provide a reasonable diversification.

3. Obtain a reasonable balance of maturity distribution.

4. Acknowledge the requirements of the bank's high credit standards and indicate the generally conservative nature of its lending posture.

5. Carry proper and profitable interest rate differentials.

When considering a loan request of any nature, proper consideration shall always be given to the applicant's overall banking relationship. This approach to credit will provide assistance in pricing the loan, as well as providing the opportunity to develop additional bank business.

As a commercial bank, we are entrusted with the ability to create money through the extension of credit. We should all be aware of the fact that acceptable growth and profitability depend, to a large degree, upon a consistent and workable loan policy.

Geographical Lending Area

It is the opinion of executive management that the primary lending area for the bank is constituted within the corporate boundaries of Sierra, Highland, and Boulder Counties. The majority of our loans are generated within these counties and the immediate surrounding area. Loans extended outside our immediate trade area should be restricted to national line accounts and purchased loan participations.

Types of Loan Sought

- *Wholesale*—Primarily lines of credit issued to national concerns that are not necessarily located within the bank's immediate trade area.

- *Commercial*—Loans made to business interest that may be secured or unsecured. The loans are balance related and extended to provide the credit requirements of the business community.

- *Real Estate*—Loans which are made on a basis consistent with the bank's policy, which may be amended from time to time. The loans may be secured by residential or commercial real estate and may or may not be balance related.

- *Consumer*—Personal and consumer loans made for various purposes secured and unsecured and not necessarily balance related.

Broadly, the make-up of our loan portfolio on a percentage basis shall be:

Wholesale	5%
Commercial	40%
Real Estate	20%
Consumer	35%

Concentration in any one area of service or industry should not exceed 10 percent of the total loan portfolio. Wholesale loans shall be generally limited to "prime rate" accounts. The installment loan portfolio shall not contain a concentration in any one consumer category that would exceed 25 percent of the total installment loan portfolio, except for motor vehicles. It should be noted that outstandings on VISA are considered an installment credit within the loan policy.

Our basic maturities shall be as follows:

- *Single Payment Loans*—Naturally mature within 90 days. Extended maturities on single payment loans can adversely affect the bank's average lending rate.

- *Term*—Term loans made to businesses shall normally mature in no more than five years and be payable monthly. All term loans extended shall be repaid on at least a quarterly basis and be fully secured.

- *Real Estate Loans*—Residential and commercial mortgage loans may be made with maturity and repayment schedules which will vary with the marketplace as determined by executive management. This category includes construction loans for residential or commercial purposes.

- *Installment*—Certain types of loans are exempted such as second mortgage or real estate, 10 years, and loans on new mobile homes, 10 years.

- *Repayment Provision*—An understanding of the repayment provision shall be reached with the borrower at the inception of the loans. If the note itself does not specify the terms of repayment then the repayment provision should be incorporated into an appropriate credit file memorandum. Rolling stock of any type, machinery, or other forms of depreciable equipment that is in use shall have a specific repayment plan. Preferably repayment will be in the form of monthly or quarterly payments which will retire the debit within the useful life of the collateral. It is highly desirable that a plan of repayment be an integral part of all loans made by the bank's lending officers.

Percentage of Loans to Appropriate Balance Sheet Items

It is the policy of Metropolitan Bank to meet the credit demands generated within its trade area. A-loan-to-deposit ratio of 65 percent to 75 percent is desirable and appears to be sufficient to meet the needs of our borrowers. Other factors that will have significant bearing upon an acceptable loan-to-deposit ratio are liquidity, types of loans, concentration and general economic conditions that directly relate to the bank's performance. The upper limits of a desirable loan-to-deposit ratio may be changed from time to time at the discretion of executive management.

Interest Rate Structures

Interest on loans is the single source of bank income and traditionally represents the major portion of total earnings. The basis of this important source of income is directly influenced by the factors of supply and demand in the money market. The effects of economic conditions that weigh heavily on the strength or weakness of loan demand usually dictate the general level of interest rates throughout the country and in our immediate trade area. Therefore, the setting of loan interest rates for the various types of credit extended will reflect the existing market conditions and will bear a relationship to the prime lending rate. The setting of interest rates shall be within the legal contract rate structures provided for by federal and state regulatory agencies.

The following factors should be considered when setting an interest rate on a given loan.

1.   Supply and demand in the money market.

2.   The cost of money within the bank.

3.   The prevailing market levels of rates for the type of loan being considered.

4.   Borrower's overall relationship with the bank.

Taking into consideration the fundamentals contained above, interest rates on loans should always represent a fair value both to the bank and to the borrower.

General Policies on Collateral and Documentation

- *Stocks and Bonds*—On closely held stocks we should not normally accept the shares for collateral unless there is a known market usually represented by a repurchase letter from a responsible, prospective buyer. Normal advance should not exceed 33 1/3 percent of book value. Over-the-counter stocks with known markets should be held in the range of 60 percent to 65 percent. Listed stocks may be taken up to 75 percent of value depending on the market and the stocks' recent trading history. Corporate and municipal bonds may be taken with advance equal to 80 percent of the current market value. Recent developments have indicated a severe deterioration in this category of collateral. United States Government bonds may be taken as collateral with advances up to 90% of the current market value. Consideration should be given to maturity, interest rates, and current prices in the government bond market.

- *Savings Accounts or Certificates of Deposit*—100 percent of available balance may be advanced, with the passbook or instrument in hand with the proper assignment and acknowledgement.

- *Cash Value Life Insurance*—Loans may be made up to the net cash value indicated for the year prior to the loan request. Close attention should be given to the possibility of automatic premium loan provisions in lending against cash value of life insurance.

- *Real Estate*—Advances may be made on improved residential property up to 90 percent of appraised value or cost, whichever is less. Improved commercial real estate loans may be made up to 80 percent of appraised value or cost, whichever is less. "Cost" may be waived due to the circumstances of the loan request. Accurate appraisals are desirable in all types of real estate lending.

- *Automotive*—Loans may be advanced to 80 percent of cost for new and to the average loan value for used autos and small trucks with a physical appraisal of the vehicle. The Black Book shall be used as a source to determine the average loan values for used vehicles. Large trucks, buses, and specialty type vehicles shall be financed on the basis of 66 2/3 percent of cost for new purchases and 50 percent for used. The advance can be adjusted upwards to consider the strong type commercial borrower and type of dealer recourse.

- *Construction, Farm, and Other Special Types of Machinery and Equipment*—Loans may be made equal to 66 2/3 percent of cost. Special emphasis should be given to U.C.C. filing on untitled equipment.

- *Inventory and Accounts Receivable*—Loans made purely against inventory should not exceed 50 percent of stated value with consideration being given to salability and perishability. Loans secured by accounts receivable should not exceed 80 percent of the accounts acknowledged as current within 60 days. Based upon the strength of the borrower, receivables financing may be made with or without notification of the assignment and with or without direct payment being made to the bank through the use of a collateral account. Approval of the senior loan committee is required.

- *Other Forms*—Other forms of collateral may be taken at the option of the bank. When dealing with collateral other than the normal types of bank collateral, use your common sense and, if you are in doubt, discuss it with your department head or senior loan officer.

All loan personnel shall be expected to be familiar with the various forms of documentation used in the bank in order to establish the debt and to secure proper lien positions in collateral taken. Loan personnel shall be expected to maintain at their desk or have immediate access to the *Comptrollers' Manual for National Banks, the Federal Reserve Bank Regulations, and Departmental Operating Procedures*. It is the bank's intention to comply with all laws, regulations, and interpretations issued by regulatory authorities pertaining to the extension of credit.

In cases where written commitments are desirable, the commitment letter shall be carefully reviewed to be certain the bank is fully protected in the matters of commitment. All written commitments must have an expiration date which normally should not exceed one (1) year. It is desirable for the senior loan officer or the members of the senior loan committee to review all letters of commitment before they are mailed from the bank. Formal lines of credit may only be granted with the concurrence of one (1) executive officer. It shall be the bank's policy to require audited statements when total loans of a business interest exceed $250,000, regardless of the basis of the credit. This requirement may be exempted based upon the type of collateral pledged and the basis of repayment. Waivers shall be granted by action of the bank's senior loan committee. When in doubt concerning documentation or matters of commitment, advice of bank counsel should be sought.

The requirements contained in this section of the loan policy represent normal and desirable conditions. It should be recognized by all persons exercising loan authority that *reasonable* variations will be allowed based upon the unique circumstances of a loan request. Exceptions or variations, which in the loan officer's judgment are justified, shall be detailed in an appropriate memorandum directed to the credit file of the borrower.

Authorized Appraisers

All collateral pledged to the bank to secure loans shall be properly appraised in order to determine the appropriate percentage of advance against value. The bank recognizes the sources of appraisal for commodities, stocks and bonds, and automobiles, et cetera as provided for by various financial media and publishing houses. Items of collateral which do not have a readily available and dependable source of valuation shall be appraised by at least two (2) bank lending officers. When possible, those officers making the appraisal should not be involved in the process of the loan applications. A statement of value signed by those persons making the appraisal shall be placed in the appropriate collateral file.

Real estate appraisals shall be made by a qualified, certified real estate appraiser prior to the granting of commitment. Following the determination of a fair market value, the maximum loan amount will be calculated within the bank's current policy. All real estate loans made by the bank shall comply without exception to the appropriate federal and state statutes and meet the requirements of RESPA Revised, Federal Flood Insurance, and the disclosure of real estate loan location as required by Census Tract Coding.

Annual appraisals are required on all real estate loans when the principal balance exceeds $250,000. This requirement specifically addresses commercial real estate loans which may, in part, be secured by machinery and equipment in addition to real estate.

The executive vice-president or the senior loan officer of the bank shall from time to time designate those loan officers who are authorized to provide the appraisals as required above.

Loans to Directors and Their Interests

Metropolitan Bank recognizes its responsibility to provide for the normal borrowing requirements of the members of its board of directors and their various interests. In the extension of credit to directors and their interests, all lending personnel shall be expected to apply the requirements placed on all other credit applicants. Compromises such as low rates, high advance, and extended maturities shall be deemed unacceptable in every case. We should normally require the submission of any information necessary to render good credit judgment on all loans granted to directors and their interests. Loans to directors, or influenced by a director, which may be classed as accommodations, are discouraged.

All loans within this category shall be made on an "arm's length" basis. Situations in the loan officer's opinion that deserve special consideration should be deferred to the president, executive vice-president, or senior loan officer.

Inappropriate Credit Practices

It is the intention of the bank to meet the credit requirements of its customers with a full range of loan services; however, our loans should be for constructive purposes. It is in this light that the following types of credit would be deemed inappropriate:

1. Loan requests that represent high-risk speculative ventures should be avoided.

2. We should not necessarily encourage unwarranted expenditures through the extension of credit that might appropriately be deferred.

3. Loans to businesses only for the purpose of acquiring their own capital stock should be avoided.

4. Unsecured "front side" or "down payment" loans should be avoided at all times. Unsecured equity financing usually represents an extremely weak credit.

5. Loan requests should always be handled at "arm's length." All persons with loan authority shall refrain from taking applications for credit in which they have a personal interest in the transaction. Loans of this type shall be referred to a disinterested loan officer for processing.

6. Loans for purely speculative purposes with respect to the various commodity and stock markets.

7. Loans for obvious land speculation transactions in which there is not a well-defined plan of development with a source of permanent financing.

Undesirable loans, such as those mentioned above, can easily be avoided through the application of good lending techniques, compliance with regulations and, of equal importance, the use of common sense.

Recommended Loan Authority Structure

All loans shall be extended on a secured or unsecured basis with specific limits assigned in each lending category to officers who have been granted loan authority. Loan authorities are assigned on the basis of the borrower's total debt relationship, including all names in which he may borrow, and should not be applied on the basis of single transactions. No officer shall commit to any loan, or combination of loans, that would create a total liability in excess of his secured limit. The loan officer may request another with greater lending authority to join in the making of loans which exceed his limits. In this regard, the officers shall be required to initial all loan documentation.

Within the context of loan authority, secured loans are usually those collateralized by liquid, self-evident, and fully negotiable collateral. This type of preferred collateral is, in most cases, held by the bank with proper assignments, which allows the collateral to be sold and the loan balance liquidated without action on the part of the borrower. Loans may be secured by other types of collateral as described earlier in this loan policy. These loans are subject to proper documentation and should be made within the limits of recommended advances and maturities. All other loans will be considered unsecured for loan authority purposes. Formal lines of credit and letters of commitment that exceed a loan officer's authority may only be granted and issued by the senior loan committee, the executive committee or an executive officer. Lending limits for individual loan officers and the various committees shall be established or amended from time to time by executive management.

Specific Lending Procedures

In order to proceed in a specific manner, procedures of the bank for certain types of loans and operating procedures have been established by the loan departments. Necessary additions or deletions will be made based upon recommendations of executive management.

Nondiscriminatory Practices

The lending division will make credit available to all creditworthy persons without regard to race, color, religion, national origin, sex, marital status, age; because all or part of the applicant's income derives from any public assistance program; or because the applicant has in good faith exercised any right under the Consumer Credit Protection Act.

It will continue to be the policy of the lending division to extend credit to present and future customers that qualify under our standards. It will also be the continued policy of the lending division to extend credit to our customers without discriminating against them on a prohibited basis with respect to any aspect of a credit transaction.

The lending division does not deny mortgage or home improvement loans to anyone for reasons of race, color, religion, sex, or national origin. The division does not discriminate in the fixing of the amount, interest rate, duration, or other terms, such as application and collection procedures.

Synopsis

While this loan policy is not all inclusive, it does give a clear indication as to the bank's position in the lending process. It is the opinion of bank management that if you are adhering to the guidelines contained in the loan policy, you will be performing your duties within acceptable parameters.

The loan policy is subject to annual review by the bank's executive officers, and interim additions or deletions may be made as deemed necessary.

Index

About the Author

Dr. Benton E. Gup received his undergraduate and graduate degrees from the University of Cincinnati. At present, he holds the Robert Hunt Cochrane/Alabama Bankers Association Chair of Banking at the University of Alabama (Tuscaloosa, Alabama) He also held banking chairs at the University of Virginia and the University of Tulsa. Dr. Gup is the author of 13 books, including *Interest Rate Risk Management* (with Brooks), *Bank Fraud: Exposing the Hidden Threat to Financial Institutions*, *Commercial Bank Management* (with Fraser and Kolari), *Cases in Bank Management* (with Meiburg), and other titles. His articles on financial subjects have appeared in *The Journal of Finance*, *Journal of Money, Banking, and Credit*, *Journal of Banking and Finance*, *Bankers Magazine*, and elsewhere. Dr. Gup is an internationally known lecturer. He has lectured on financial topics in Australia, Japan, South Africa, and New Zealand. He serves as a consultant to both industry and government.